Numerical Analysis

with

Algorithms and Computer Programs in C++

AJAY WADHWA
Associate Professor of Physics
Sri Guru Tegh Bahadur Khalsa College
University of Delhi

PHI Learning Private Limited
New Delhi-110001
2012

₹ 195.00

NUMERICAL ANALYSIS WITH ALGORITHMS AND COMPUTER PROGRAMS IN C++
Ajay Wadhwa

ISBN-978-81-203-4545-4

The export rights of this book are vested solely with the publisher.

Published by Asoke K. Ghosh, PHI Learning Private Limited, M-97, Connaught Circus, New Delhi-110001 and Printed by Raj Press, New Delhi-110012.

To my beloved children

SOMIN and TARUSHI

To my beloved children

SOMIN and TARUSHI

Contents

Preface

The study of *numerical methods* is an essential part of the courses prescribed for the undergraduate students in physical sciences, mathematics, and engineering.

This textbook is an outgrowth of my several years of teaching the subject at the University of Delhi during my academic career of last 20 years. It is an ideal text for the undergraduate science courses in physics, electronics, mathematics, computer science as well as for the undergraduate courses in engineering of all disciplines. It is a balanced presentation between theory and practicals of numerical methods. In preparing this text, special care has also been taken to keep the presentation simple and lucid.

The book contains nine chapters. In order to compile and run C++ programs, a compiler of C++ language is required to be installed on the computer. Hence, one chapter, that is, Chapter 0 has been especially written to provide an introduction to C++ compilers. Chapter 1 describes the different types of numerical errors that occur while using numerical methods. Chapters 2 and 3 provide numerical methods for solving nonlinear and transcendental equations, and simultaneous linear equations. Chapter 4 deals with numerical techniques for interpolating a polynomial function. Chapters 5 and 6 discuss numerical methods used for differentiating and integrating functions. Chapter 7 presents numerical methods for finding solutions to differential equations. The book concludes with Chapter 8 that deals with numerical methods for curve fitting.

The book follows a simple style of building the student's understanding of the subject matter. Numerous examples have been solved to illustrate the concepts of numerical methods. Each method is accompanied by an algorithm and a corresponding computer program written in C++. Since different types of C++ compilers are in use, instructions have been given with each computer program to 'run' it on any kind of compiler. All computer programs have been test run on 'Linux Ubuntu C++' as well as Windows-based 'Dev C++', 'Visual C++' and 'Turbo C++' compiler systems. A large number of laboratory-tested programming examples and exercises are given in each chapter. Previous years' questions have been included for the benefit of the students.

This book is suitable for a one-semester course in Numerical Analysis. It endeavours to provide students with a clear understanding of the theory and problem-solving approaches. It is hoped that the students will have productive time with this text and enjoy its programming aspects. It would be my pleasure to receive suggestions from students and teachers alike, aimed at making this book more comprehensive and useful.

Finally, I take this opportunity to thank many hard-working people of my publisher PHI Learning, who fully deserve my gratitude for their efforts in publishing this book.

AJAY WADHWA
ajayw3@gmail.com

0

A Note on C++ Compilers

In order to compile and run C++ programs, a compiler of C++ language is required to be installed on the computer. A compiler is a set of programs that creates the object/machine code of the program which is written in a high-level language such as C++. The object code file is processed in the CPU of the computer to produce the desired output on the computer screen. As we know, computers have different types of operating systems (O/S) such as DOS-based Windows, Linux-based Ubuntu, Redhat and Knoppix. Each of these O/S has specific C++ compilers. While the C++ compilers in Linux-based O/S such as Ubuntu, etc. are inbuilt, for other O/S the C++ compiler has to be loaded by external means. For example, in the case of Windows we need to install a Turbo C++, DEV C++ or Visual C++ compiler from an optical device or a pen drive. Obviously, there are many advantages when the C++ compiler is inbuilt in the O/S.

Although the C++ program code is independent of the compiler used for it in the O/S but still there are small changes that are required to be made in the header files at the beginning of the program. We will introduce the setup of C++ compilers of the Linux-based Ubuntu/Redhat/Knoppix O/S and then briefly discuss the C++ compilers of the Windows O/S, as they are quite well known.

0.1 Ubuntu/Redhat/Knoppix O/S

In these operating systems the C++ programs are written in the **gedit text editor window** which is an inbuilt application. In Figure 0.1 we show a C++ program **p11.cpp** written in the gedit window. The C++ programs are given suitable name with extension **.cpp**. The gedit text editor is a very versatile editing application of these systems which themselves are the counterpart of the more popular Windows O/S. For example, the Ubuntu system has an inbuilt office software corresponding to Windows compatible MS Word,

MS Excel, MS Powerpoint, etc. Whereas we need to load Turbo C++ software in Windows O/S to edit C++ programs, in Ubuntu we have an inbuilt text editor to edit C++ programs. The main advantage of Linux-based O/S is that there are almost no security issues to worry about.

There also exists another freeware text editor called ***Emacs*** in these O/S which can be downloaded from the Ubuntu/Knoppix/Redhat software centre easily.

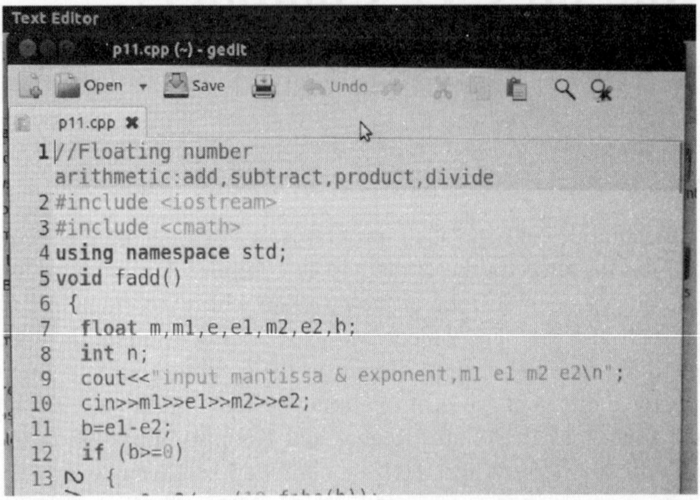

Figure 0.1 'gedit' text editor window showing C++ program p11.cpp.

For compiling and running C++ programs in these O/S we need to open an application window called '**Terminal**'. In this window the **$** prompt appears on the screen. In order to compile a C++ program we have to write the following command.

$ c++ *filename*.cpp –o *filename*out

'press enter'

If a $ prompt appears, that implies the successful compilation of the program. Otherwise error messages are printed on the screen.

To 'run' the program after successful compilation, we need to write the following command against the $ prompt.

$ ./*filename*out

'press enter'

In Figure 0.2 we show the commands for compiling and running the C++ program **p11.cpp** (shown in Figure (0.1)).

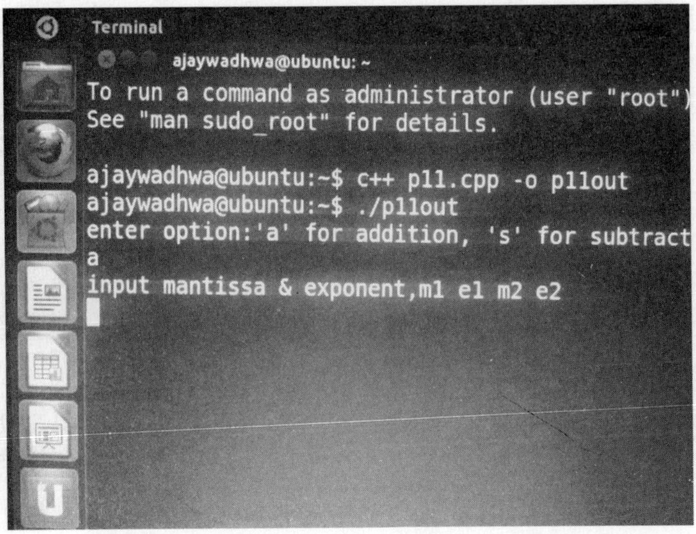

Figure 0.2 'Terminal' window in Ubuntu O/S for compiling C++ programs.

0.2 Windows O/S

For compiling and running programs in Windows O/S we can use three types of compilers—the Dev C++ compiler, Turbo C++ compiler and the Visual C++ compiler. All these are menu-driven interactive window compilers in which a command menu appears on the screen as shown in Figures 0.3, 0.4 and 0.5 respectively. The programs are directly written in the **edit window** of the screen. For compiling and running the programs, suitable commands from the menu can be chosen. The most serious drawback of using Windows-based C++ compiler is the security issues and susceptibility to virus attacks.

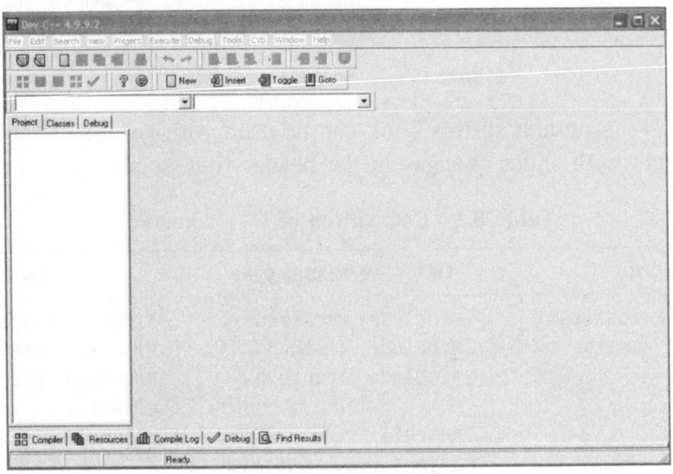

Figure 0.3 Dev C++ compiler.

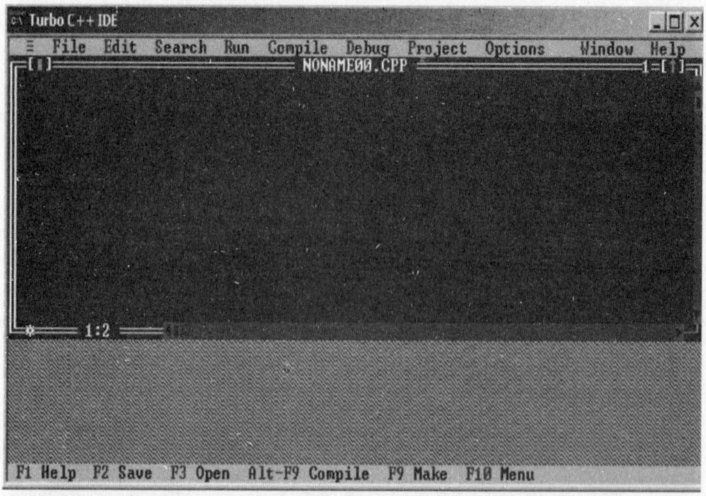

Figure 0.4 Turbo C++ compiler.

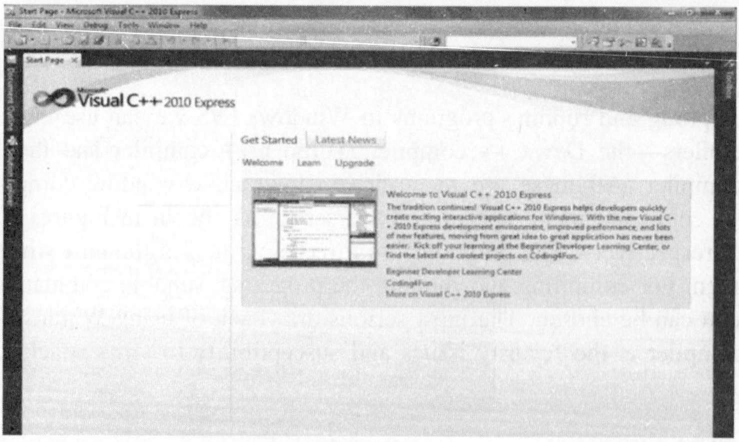

Figure 0.5 Visual C++ compiler.

The C++ programs in this book can be used with any of the above types of compilers with slight changes in the header files as shown in Table 0.1.

Table 0.1 Comparison of C++ compilers

Ubuntu	Dev C++/Visual C++	Turbo C++
`#include <iostream>`	`#include <iostream>`	`#include <iostream.h>`
`#include <cmath>`	`#include <math.h>`	`#include <math.h>`
–	`#include <conio.h>`	`#include <conio.h>`
–	–	`clrscr()`
–	`getch()`	`getch()`
`using namespace std`	`using namespace std`	–

From this table we infer that the following header files and functions should be used:

- `#include <iostream.h>` (for Turbo C++)
- `#include <conio.h>` (not required in Ubuntu)
- `#include <math.h>` (for Dev and Turbo)
- use `getch()` before closing the bracket '}' of the `main()` function in Dev and Turbo C++ only. Not required in Ubuntu.
- use `clrscr()` after the opening bracket '{' of the `main()` function in Turbo C++ only. Not required in Ubuntu and Dev/Visual.
- `using namespace std` is not required in Turbo C++

We now give an example of program **p22.cpp** taken from Chapter 2 of the book to illustrate the differences to be made in using it with different compilers.

In Ubuntu O/S the program p22.cpp requires no changes and should be written as given in Chapter 2.

The program p22.cpp with **Turbo C++** compiler will be as follows:

```
//FIXED-point iteration method
#include <iostream.h>
#include <math.h>
#include <conio.h>
#define eps 0.0001
inline float f(float x)
 {
 return 1/(9-x*x);
 }
void fpt()
 {
 float a,c;
 int count,maxit;
 char option;
 cout<<"For default input values enter 'y' else 'n'\n";
 cin>>option;
 if (option=='y')
 a=0;
 else
 {
 cout<<"input initial root value\n";
 cin>>a;
 }
 maxit=50;
 for (count=1;count<=maxit;count++)
 {
   c=f(a);
```

```
   if (fabs((c-a)/c)>eps)
   a=c;
   else
   break;
  }
 cout<<"root= "<<c<<endl;
 cout<<"f(root)= "<<f(c)<<endl;
 cout<<"iterations= "<<count<<endl;
 }
main()
{
 clrscr();
 fpt();
 getch();
 }
```

The program p22.cpp with Dev/Visual C++ will be as follows:

```
//FIXED-point iteration method
#include <iostream>
#include <math.h>
#include <conio.h>
#define eps 0.0001
using namespace std;
inline float f(float x)
 {
  return 1/(9-x*x);
  }
void fpt()
 {
    float a,c;
    int count,maxit;
    char option;
    cout<<"For default input values enter 'y' else 'n'\n";
    cin>>option;
    if (option=='y')
    a=0;
    else
    {
    cout<<"input initial root value\n";
    cin>>a;
    }
    maxit=50;
    for (count=1;count<=maxit;count++)
```

```
    {
        c=f(a);
        if  (fabs((c-a)/c)>eps)
           a=c;
           else
           break;
      }
  cout<<"root=  "<<c<<endl;
  cout<<"f(root)=  "<<f(c)<<endl;
  cout<<"iterations=  "<<count<<endl;
  }
main()
{
  fpt();
  getch();
  }
```

1

Estimation of Errors in Computation

1.1 Introduction

Numerical analysis is concerned with the study of numerical methods to solve complex scientific and engineering problems through computers by means of basic arithmetic operations like addition, subtraction, multiplication and division. The most useful aspect of numerical analysis is that a numerical solution can be obtained for a problem which may or may not have an analytical solution. Numerical methods exist for the following applications:

1. To find the roots of nonlinear equations.
2. To find the solution of a system of equations (linear and nonlinear).
3. To find the value of a function at some point using interpolation techniques.
4. To perform differentiation and find the derivatives of a function at a point.
5. To perform integration and find the integral value of a function over an interval.
6. To perform multiple integrations in n-dimensions.
7. To solve ordinary and partial differential equations.
8. To find the best curve-fit for a set of data points.

In each of these numerical methods a common procedure is to repetitively perform a set of steps in order to converge to the solution. The numerical solution is always an approximation to the actual solution and the difference between these two solutions is called the *error* in computation. A numerical method should be able to give a solution as close to the actual solution as possible in order to minimize the computational error.

1.2 Significant Digits and Floating-Point Representation

A computer is capable of performing only the basic arithmetic operations of addition, subtraction, multiplication and division and, therefore, the result of these operations is either an integer or a real number containing a fixed number of digits.

The accuracy of a numerical result can be judged by the number of **significant digits** that are used to represent its value. For example, the approximate value of π can be computed as 3.14 or 3.14159 or 3.1415926 with increasing accuracy. As the number of significant digits increases, the accuracy of the result improves. The number of significant digits in a number can be determined by applying the following rules.

1. All nonzero digits in a number are significant.
2. All zeros between the two nonzero digits are significant.
3. All zeros to the left of the leftmost nonzero digit are not significant.
4. All zeros to the right of the rightmost nonzero digit are significant.
5. Digits in the exponent part of a floating number are not significant.
6. In the case of an integer value, the trailing zeros are not significant if the value can be rewritten in exponent form. For example, the numerical value 5500 can be rewritten as 55×10^2 and so the significant digits are only two.

The significant digits in a number also define the **precision** of the numerical result. Precision means the number of decimal positions in a floating-number value. For example, the number 25.3694 has six significant digits and a precision of 10^4; the number 0.007472 has four significant digits but a precision of 10^{-6}. In other words, it means that the number 25.3694 is correct up to 1 part in 10,000 and the number 0.007472 is correct up to 1 part in a million.

The numerical values obtained through numerical methods are generally real numbers which can be written in two ways:

1. Fixed-point representation (without exponent)
2. Floating-point representation (with exponent)

For example, the real number 3.25×10^8 is rewritten as 3.25e8 in floating-point representation. The real numbers are stored in computer memory in the **normalized floating-point form** in which the decimal point of the real number is shifted to the left of the leftmost significant digit. For example, the floating-point number 0.01e–3 can be written in the normalized form as 0.1e–4; 3.25e8 can be written in the normalized-floating form as 0.325e9. Moving the decimal point to the left of the most significant digit of a number is called **normalization**. The fractional part of this value is called **mantissa** and the remainder part is known as **exponent**. The absolute value of mantissa must lie in the interval {0.1, 1.0} for positive numbers and in the interval {–1.0, –0.1} for negative numbers. The value of the exponent is machine dependent but its value should preferably lie in the interval {e99, e–99}. All arithmetic operations like addition, subtraction, multiplication and division must be performed on the normalized floating-point numbers. The reason for using the normalized floating-point numbers is that the computer memory stores all numbers in the normalized binary floating-point format. One such standard format is the IEEE 32-bit format which is commonly known as **single-precision** ('float' data type in C language) mode. In this single-precision mode, 32-bits (4 bytes) are reserved for a real number for storing a 24-bit mantissa, a 7-bit exponent, and a 1-bit sign. In contrast to this, there also exist computers that can use **double-precision** arithmetic ('double' data type in C language) in which a normalized floating number will have 64-bits reserved for it in the computer memory. The extra bits in double-precision increase the range of magnitudes and help to minimize the accumulation of round-off errors. For simplicity, in converting a floating number to its normalized form we will retain *four digits in mantissa.*

We now consider a few examples of arithmetic operations on floating-point numbers while restricting the size of mantissa to four digits.

For example, if we have to add 0.6578e5 to 0.8363e3, first we must make their exponents equal (normalization) and then add the resulting numbers. That is,

$$0.6578e5 + 0.0083e5 = 0.6661e5$$

The final result of any arithmetic operation must be expressed in the normalized form by appropriate shifting of the decimal. For example, if we add 0.72e10 to 0.32e10, we get 1.04e10, which is not in the normalized form. By shifting the decimal, we obtain the normalized form as 0.1040e11.

In the subtraction of floating-point numbers, we need to be careful in making the mantissa ≥ 0.1. For example, consider

$$0.5452e3 - 0.5424e3 = 0.0028e3$$

Since the most significant bit (MSB) of the mantissa is zero, the leftmost nonzero digit of mantissa is shifted left to finally obtain 0.2800e1 as the correct result.

In multiplication, the mantissa of two numbers are multiplied and their exponents are added to obtain the product. For example,

$$0.1110e10 \times 0.1230e12 = 0.0137e22$$

This result in normalized form is written as 0.1370e21.

In the division of two floating numbers the mantissa of the numerator is divided by the mantissa of the denominator and the exponent of the denominator is subtracted from the exponent of the numerator. The quotient of the mantissa is normalized. For example,

$$0.2200e1 \div 0.1100e - 19 = (0.22/0.11)e20 = 0.2000e21$$

An error condition called **overflow** occurs in computation when the result of an arithmetic operation causes the exponent to become greater than e99.

The condition of overflow often occurs during multiplication. For example,

$$0.1100e61 \times 0.4400e49 = 0.0490e110 = 0.4900e109$$

The above computation results in an overflow error due to limitation of computer memory.

Similarly, an error condition called **underflow** occurs when the value of the exponent in the result becomes less than e–99. For example, if the result of an arithmetic operation is 0.175e–100, the computer will show an underflow error.

1.3 Algorithm for Performing Arithmetic Operations on Floating-Point Numbers and Conversion to Normalized Forms

We now give a step-by-step procedure called *algorithm* for performing arithmetic operations like addition, subtraction, multiplication and division on floating numbers and converting the result so obtained to a normalized form. This algorithm is transformed to a computer program written in C++ language and is presented at the end of this chapter (see **p11.cpp**).

1. Declare/define functions/subprograms to add **(fadd)**, subtract **(fsub)**, multiply **(fprod)** and divide **(fdiv)**.
2. Start the (main) function.
3. Define the main function which calls for the appropriate subprogram/ function according to the given choice.
4. Stop (main).

Details of function/subprogram **fadd**:

1. Start
2. Input mantissa (m1, m2) and exponents (e1, e2) of the two numbers
3. Define b = e1 – e2
4. If b > 0
    - m2 = m2/10^k
    - e = e1

   else
    - m1 = m1/10^k
    - e = e2

   endif
5. m = m1 + m2

   if m > 1
    - m = m/10
    - e = e + 1

   endif
6. Output m, e
7. Return

Details of function/subprogram **fsub**:

```
1. Start
2. Input mantissa (m1, m2) and exponents (e1, e2) of two numbers
3. Define b = e1 – e2
4. If b > 0
      m2 = m2/10^k
      e = e1
   else
      m1 = m1/10^k
      e = e2
   endif
5. m = m1 – m2
6. Repeat
      m = m*10
      e = e – 1
   until | m | < 0.1
7. Output m, e
8. Return
```

Details of function/subprogram **fprod**:

```
1. Start
2. Input mantissa (m1, m2) and exponents (e1, e2) of two numbers
3. m = m1*m2
4. e = e1 + e2
5. While |m| < 0.1
      m = m*10
      e = e – 1
   endwhile
6. While |m| ≥ 1
      m = m/10
      e = e + 1
   endwhile
7. If e > 99 output "overflow"
   else
      if e < –99 output "underflow"
         else output m, e
8. Return
```

Details of function/subprogram **fdiv**:

```
1. Start
2. Input mantissa (m1, m2) and exponents (e1, e2) of two numbers
3. m = m1/m2
4. e = e1 – e2
```

```
5. While |m| < 0.1
      m = m*10
      e = e − 1
   endwhile
6. While |m| ≥ 1
      m = m/10
      e = e + 1
   endwhile
7. If e > 99 output "overflow"
   else
      if e < –99 output "underflow"
         else output m, e
8. Return
```

1.4 Errors in Computation

The existence of errors in numerical computations cannot be ignored. An error is defined as a quantity by which the actual or exact value differs from the computed value. Errors can be classified, according to the sources of their origin, into the following types:

1. *According to the experimental method:* An erroneous collection of data in an experiment or survey gives rise to the errors that are commonly called **empirical errors** or **instrumental errors**. Such errors are generally unavoidable, but can be minimized by better techniques and higher precision instrumentation. For example, a stop watch of least count (L.C.) (1/100)th of a second will give more accurate computations than the one with a L.C. of 0.1 second.

2. *Due to the computing device:* Errors arising from limitations of a computing device such as the computer, are called **conversion/computational errors**. Such errors occur due to the inability of the computer to accept and process the exact value of input data. For instance, the round-off error arises because a certain number of digits cannot be retained by the computer for calculation due to its own limitation. For example, let us perform the addition of two numbers 0.1 and 0.4 by a computer. The computer will convert these numbers to binary forms as follows:

$$0.1 = 0.0001\ 1001; \qquad 0.4 = 0.0110\ 0110$$

On addition, sum = 0.0111 1111

$$= 0.25 + 0.125 + 0.0625 + 0.03125 + 0.015625 + 0.0078125 + 0.00390625$$

$$= 0.49609375$$

This computed result differs from the actual result 0.5 by 0.00390625 due to conversion of the decimal numbers to their binary form and then due to rounding off the binary numbers by the computer.

The above two types of errors are unavoidable and hence are also collectively termed **inherent errors**.

3. *Due to the chosen numerical technique/method:* Errors arising from this method are called **numerical/procedural errors**. Such types of errors can creep into the calculations by two ways—*rounding-off* and *truncation.*

The error which is produced by removing digits to a given decimal place is called the **round-off error**. If a number is to be rounded off to the *n*th decimal place, digit 1 is added to the *n*th decimal digit if the $(n + 1)$th decimal digit is greater than or equal to 5, otherwise the *n*th decimal digit is kept unchanged. For example, if the number 8.8851 is to be rounded off to the second decimal place, we will rewrite it as 8.89.

Truncation errors are caused when a certain process is terminated by rejecting a finite number of terms of the mathematical expression. For example, consider the following exponential function series

$$e^x = 1 + x + \frac{x^2}{2!} + \frac{x^3}{3!} + \frac{x^4}{4!} + \frac{x^5}{5!} + \frac{x^6}{6!}$$

In the above series if we neglect the last four terms, a truncation error will be introduced for a given value of x. The value of this truncation error will be the difference between the value calculated by taking all the seven terms and the value calculated by taking three terms.

1.5 Absolute and Relative Errors

Let us assume that a set of data items is given in a tabulated form and we are required to find the average value of the given numbers by some numerical method. This will give us an approximate value of the mean which will be different from the actual/true value of the mean.

In general, we can say that a quantity x can have an actual/true value x_t and an approximate value x_a. The absolute value of the difference between the actual/true value and the approximate value of this quantity is called *absolute error* which is denoted by

$$E_a = | x_t - x_a | \tag{1.1}$$

A more relevant type of error which takes into account the relative magnitude of the quantity under study is called the *relative error*. The relative error is defined as the ratio of absolute error to the absolute actual value (or true value) of the quantity and is denoted by

$$E_r = \frac{| x_t - x_a |}{| x_t |} \tag{1.2}$$

The percentage relative error is defined as the relative error multiplied by 100, that is

$$\%E_r = E_r \times 100 \tag{1.3}$$

As a general rule, an accuracy up to n-significant digits can be obtained when the relative error is less than 10^{-n}.

1.6 Calculation of Absolute and Relative Errors due to Truncation and Rounding Off

Suppose the value of a quantity x is given in normalized form as

$$x = 0.d_1d_2d_3 \ldots d_kd_{k+1} \ldots \times 10^n$$

where $d_1d_2d_3 \ldots$ are the decimal digits and n is the exponent.

If the computer truncates this value of x up to k digits, the absolute error in x due to truncation is given by

$$E_a = g \times 10^{n-k}$$

where g represents the truncated part of the number f in normalized form which lies in the range $\{0, 1\}$. So, the maximum absolute error in x is obtained by using $g_{\max} = 1$ in the above relation. Hence

$$\left.\begin{aligned} (E_a)_{\max} &= 10^{n-k} \\ \text{As a special case when } n = 0, & \\ (E_a)_{\max} &= 10^{-k} \end{aligned}\right\} \tag{1.4}$$

The relative error due to truncation up to k digits is given by

$$E_r = \frac{|g \times 10^{n-k}|}{|f \times 10^n|} \tag{1.5}$$

The maximum relative error is obtained by using $f_{\min} = 0.1$ and $g_{\max} = 1.0$ in Eq. (1.5) as

$$(E_r)_{\max} = 10^{-k+1} \tag{1.6}$$

The maximum relative error is also known as **machine epsilon** because the quantity k, which represents the length of the mantissa in the number, is a machine-dependent quantity.

Similarly, the maximum absolute error due to rounding off to k digits of a number is given by

$$(E_a)_{\max} = 0.5 \times 10^{n-k} \tag{1.7}$$

As a special case when $n = 0$,

$$(E_a)_{\max} = 0.5 \times 10^{-k} \tag{1.8}$$

The maximum relative error due to rounding off is given by

$$(E_r)_{\max} = 0.5 \times 10^{-k+1} \tag{1.9}$$

EXAMPLE 1.1 Given $x = 0.004998$. Calculate the maximum relative error if the value of x is truncated to three decimal digits by the computer.

Solution

Let $x = 0.004998$

$$= 0.4998 \times 10^{-2}$$

After truncation to three decimal digits, we get

$$x = 0.499 \times 10^{-2}$$

The relative error in x is obtained from Eq. (1.5) as

$$E_r = \frac{|0.4998 - 0.499| \times 10^{-2}}{|0.4998| \times 10^{-2}}$$

$$= 0.00160064$$

or $$E_r = 0.160 \times 10^{-2}$$

Therefore, $$(E_r)_{\max} = 10^{-2}$$

We can also directly use Eq. (1.6) for $(E_r)_{\max}$ with $k = 3$, which gives

$$(E_r)_{\max} = 10^{-k+1} = 10^{-2}$$

1.7 Error Propagation due to Arithmetic Operations

In the process of numerical computations, arithmetic operations of addition, subtraction, multiplication and division are repeatedly carried out on data. The error produced at one point of the calculation propagates to the next step of calculation by itself.

Suppose there are two numbers x and y, which are truncated by the computer and E_x and E_y are the absolute errors in them. The total maximum absolute error produced when x and y are added or subtracted is given by the sum of the absolute errors in x and y as

$$(E_{a,\text{total}})_{\max} = |E_{a,x}| + |E_{a,y}| \tag{1.10}$$

While summing up various numbers of different absolute errors, the following rules are followed in computing the total error:

1. The number with the largest absolute error is identified.
2. All the other numbers are rounded off with one more decimal digit than the identified number having the largest absolute error.
3. All the numbers are now summed up.
4. The final sum is rounded off by discarding one decimal digit.

When the numbers x and y are multiplied or divided, the total maximum relative error is given by the sum of the relative errors in x and y as

$$(E_{r,\text{total}})_{\max} = |E_{r,x}| + |E_{r,y}| \tag{1.11}$$

When a functional relation of the following form is given

$$y = f(x_1, x_2, x_3, \ldots, x_n)$$

the total relative error in y is given by

$$E_r = \frac{\Delta y}{y} = \left(\frac{\partial y}{\partial x_1}\right)\left(\frac{\Delta x_1}{y}\right) + \left(\frac{\partial y}{\partial x_2}\right)\left(\frac{\Delta x_2}{y}\right) + \cdots + \left(\frac{\partial y}{\partial x_n}\right)\left(\frac{\Delta x_n}{y}\right) \tag{1.12}$$

1.8 Iterative Processes and Rate of Convergence

In most numerical methods, a set of steps is repeatedly performed for the calculation of the result. This is termed an **iterative process** and it is continued till the difference between the consecutive values of the result becomes negligible or comes within a prescribed limit. The rate of convergence of an iterative process is determined by the number of iterations taken to converge to the result. The iterative process is said to converge to the result x (say) if there exists a constant c called the **convergence factor** and another constant p called the **order of convergence** such that the ratio of the magnitude of absolute error in the $(i + 1)$th iteration to the magnitude of the pth power of absolute error in the ith iteration is a constant c in the limit of infinite number of iterations, that is,

$$\frac{|E_{i+1}|}{(|E_i|)^p} = c \quad \text{(a constant)} \tag{1.13}$$

where E_i is the absolute error in the ith iteration and E_{i+1} is the absolute error in the $(i + 1)$th iteration.

The above formula means that the error in the $(i + 1)$th iteration is proportional to the pth power of the error in the ith iteration and so the rate of convergence of the numerical method is of order p. The higher the value of p, the faster will be the rate of convergence. The rate of convergence is a measure of how fast the truncation error decreases in a numerical method.

1.9 Numerical Examples

EXAMPLE 1.2 What is the truncated approximate value of $\pi/4$ up to four significant digits? Calculate the absolute and relative errors due to truncation.

Solution

As $\pi/4 \approx 0.7854$ up to four significant digits, therefore, the absolute error due to truncation is given by

$$E_a = \left| \left(\frac{22}{28} \right) - (0.7854) \right| = 0.00031$$

And the relative error is $E_r = \frac{E_a}{22/28} = \frac{0.00031}{22/28} = 0.00039$

The maximum absolute error can be found directly by using Eq. (1.4) with $k = 4$ as $(E_a)_{max} = 10^{-4}$.

EXAMPLE 1.3 If $y = 4x^6 - 5x$, and the absolute error in x is 0.04, determine the absolute error in y at $x = 1$.

Solution

From Eq. (1.12), we have the absolute error in y at $x = 1$ as

$$\Delta y = \left(\frac{\partial y}{\partial x} \right) (\Delta x) = (24x^5 - 5)0.04 = 0.76$$

EXAMPLE 1.4 Add the following nine numbers and calculate the total absolute error in the final sum: 15.45, 0.647, 0.000358, 0.0215, 305.2, 243.2, 0.1532, 0.1734, and 8.12.

Solution

Using Eq. (1.8), with $k = 1$ the numbers with the largest absolute error of 0.5×10^{-1} (= 0.05) are 305.2 and 243.2, being rounded off to one decimal digit each.

Therefore, according to the rules given in Section 1.7, we round off the other numbers to two decimal digits (see rule 2) to find the total sum as

$$\begin{aligned} R &= 15.45 + 0.64 + 0.00 + 0.02 + 305.2 + 243.2 + 0.15 + 0.17 + 8.12 \\ &= 572.59 \end{aligned}$$

Now we round off the final sum to one decimal digit to obtain $R = 572.6$.

In the above sum, the absolute error in each of the numbers 305.2 and 243.2 is 0.05 and in each of the remaining seven numbers it is 0.005. The total error due to the addition of the given nine numbers is, therefore, given by

$$E_a = 2(0.05) + 7(0.005) = 0.14$$

after rounding off by discarding one decimal digit.

EXAMPLE 1.5 Find the sum of the square roots of numbers 3, 5 and 7 correct up to three significant digits and evaluate the absolute error in the sum.

Solution

The sum after rounding off the given numbers to three significant digits is given by

$$\sqrt{3} + \sqrt{5} + \sqrt{7} = 1.73 + 2.24 + 2.65 = 6.62$$

The maximum absolute error according to Eq. (1.8) in the above sum due to rounding off to two decimal digits is given as

$$E_a = 0.005 + 0.005 + 0.005 = 0.02$$

EXAMPLE 1.6 Determine the significant digits in the following numbers with their given absolute errors and relative errors:

(a) 11.2461 with $E_a = 0.25 \times 10^{-2}$
(b) 1.5923 with $E_r = 0.1 \times 10^{-3}$
(c) 0.3941 with $E_a = 0.25 \times 10^{-2}$

Solution

In (a), $E_a = (1/4) \times 10^{-2} < (1/2) \times 10^{-2}$ with $k = 2$ according to Eq. (1.8). Therefore, the given number is correct up to two decimal digits. Therefore, the total number of significant digits in it is 4. Hence the given number 11.2461 should be written as 11.25 after rounding off.

In (b), $E_r = 0.1 \times 10^{-3}$, therefore, the absolute error is

$$E_a = E_r \times 1.5923 = 0.15923 \times 10^{-3} < 0.5 \times 10^{-3}$$

Hence according to Eq. (1.8), we have $k = 3$. Therefore, the number 0.15923 is correct up to three decimal digits. Therefore, the total number of significant digits in it is three. It should therefore be written as 0.159 after rounding off.

In (c), $E_a = (1/4) \times 10^{-2} < (1/2) \times 10^{-2}$ with $k = 2$ according to Eq. (1.8). Therefore, the number 0.3941 is correct up to two decimal digits. Hence the total number of significant digits in it is two. It should therefore be written as 0.39.

EXAMPLE 1.7 Using the floating-point representation, determine the roots of the quadratic equation:

$$x^2 - 10^3x + 25 = 0$$

Solution

$$x = \frac{10^3 \pm \sqrt{10^6 - 10^2}}{2}$$

Now, $$10^6 = 0.1 \times 10^7$$

and $$10^2 = 0.1 \times 10^3$$

$\therefore$ $$10^6 - 10^2 = 0.1 \times 10^7 - 0.1 \times 10^3 = 0.1 \times 10^7$$

and $$\sqrt{0.1 \times 10^7} = 0.1 \times 10^4$$

The roots are, therefore, $\dfrac{0.2 \times 10^4}{2}$ and 0.

The above computation will be performed by the computer and due to its limited precision, one root will be calculated as zero.

EXAMPLE 1.8 Using the floating-point representation, calculate $(a + b)/c$, if $a = 0.1000\text{e}1$, $b = 0.3000\text{e}1$ and $c = 0.2000\text{e}{-3}$.

Solution

$$a + b = 0.4000\text{e}1 \text{ and therefore } (a + b)/c = 0.2000\text{e}5$$

Exercises

1. Round off the following numbers up to four significant digits:
   (a) 2456.782 (b) 0.000243468
   (c) 8.0002 (d) 0.34026
   (e) 2.5555

   [**Ans.** (a) 2457 (b) 0.0002435 (c) 8.000 (d) 0.3403 (e) 2.556]
2. Find the sum of the following numbers:
   5.2146, 20.12, 11.2356, 1.8948 [**Ans.** 38.46]
3. Find the relative percentage error if 4/3 is approximated to 1.33.
   [**Ans.** 0.25%]
4. Find the number of significant digits in the number 1.8921, if the relative error is 0.1×10^{-2}. [**Ans.** 3]
5. Determine the number of terms of the exponential function e^x required in such a way that their sum is correct up to five decimal digits at $x = 1$.
   $$e^x = 1 + x + \frac{x^2}{2!} + \frac{x^3}{3!} + \cdots + \frac{x^n}{n!}$$ [**Ans.** $n = 9$]
6. If $a = 0.5555\text{e}1$, $b = 0.4545\text{e}1$, $c = 0.4535\text{e}1$, calculate $b - c$, $a*b$, $a*c$. (*means the product). [**Ans.** 0.1e–1, 0.2524e2, 0.2519e2]
7. Find 0.1e5 ÷ 0.9999e3. [**Ans.** 0.1e2]
8. Find the roots of the equation $x^2 + 2x - 2 = 0$ using the floating-point arithmetic. [**Ans.** 0.7320e0 and –0.2732e1]

   Also, show that the roots do not satisfy this equation.
9. If $a = 0.5665\text{e}1$, $b = 0.5556\text{e}{-1}$, $c = 0.5644\text{e}1$, calculate $a + b - c$.
   [**Ans.** 0.7600e–1]
10. In Exercise 9, calculate $a - c + b$ and show that $a + b - c$ is not the same as $a - c + b$. [**Ans.** 0.7656e–1]

C++ Programs

The C++ programs can be implemented on any O/S, namely

1. Windows O/S using Turbo C++, Dev C++ and Visual C++ compilers.
2. Linux-based Ubuntu/Knoppix/Redhat O/S using GNU C++ compiler.

These compilers have been discussed in Chapter 0. No change is required if Ubuntu is used.

While using Turbo C++, Dev C++ and Visual C++ compilers, note the following points for every program.

- Use header file `#include <iostream.h>` (for Turbo C++ only)
- Use header file `#include <math.h>`
- Use header file `#include <conio.h>`
- Use `getch()` function before the closing bracket '}' of the `main()` function.

Program: p11.cpp

```
//Floating number arithmetic:add,subtract,product,divide
#include <iostream>
#include <cmath>
using namespace std;
void fadd()
   {
     float m,m1,e,e1,m2,e2,b;
     int n;
     cout<<"input mantissa & exponent,m1 e1 m2 e2\n";
     cin>>m1>>e1>>m2>>e2;
     b=e1-e2;
     if (b>=0)
       {
         m2=m2/pow(10,fabs(b));
         e=e1;
       }
     else
       {
         m1=m1/pow(10,fabs(b));
         e=e2;
       }
   //addition
     m=m1+m2;
     if (m>1)
       {
         m=m/10;
```

```
            e=e+1;
          }
          cout<<"sum is "<<m<<"e"<<e<<endl;
      }
void fsub()
      {
        float m,m1,e,e1,m2,e2,b;
        int n;
        cout<<"input mantissa & exponent,m1 e1 m2 e2\n";
        cin>>m1>>e1>>m2>>e2;
        b=e1-e2;
        if (b>=0)
          {
            m2=m2/pow(10,fabs(b));
            e=e1;
          }
      else
        {
          m1=m1/pow(10,fabs(b));
          e=e2;
        }
      //subtraction
        m=m1-m2;
        do
          {
            m=m*10;
            e=e-1;
          }
      while (fabs(m)<0.1);
        cout<<"difference is "<<m<<"e"<<e<<endl;
      }
void fprod()
      {
        float m,m1,e,e1,m2,e2,b;
        int n;
        cout<<"input mantissa & exponent,m1 e1 m2 e2\n";
        cin>>m1>>e1>>m2>>e2;
      //multiplication
        m=m1*m2;
        e=e1+e2;
        while (fabs(m)<0.1)
          {
            m=m*10;
```

```
            e=e-1;
          }
        while (fabs(m)>=1)
          {
            m=m/10;
            e=e+1;
          }
        if (e>99)
          cout<<"overflow\n";
        else
            if (e<-99)
              cout<<"underflow\n";
            else
              cout<<"product is" <<m<<"e"<<e<<endl;
      }
  void fdiv()
      {
        float m,m1,e,e1,m2,e2,b;
        cout<<"input mantissa & exponent,m1 e1 m2 e2\n";
        cin>>m1>>e1>>m2>>e2;
      //division
        m=m1/m2;
        e=e1-e2;
      while (fabs(m)<0.1)
          {
            m=m*10;
            e=e-1;
          }
      while (fabs(m)>=1)
          {
            m=m/10;
            e=e+1;
          }
      if (e>99)
        cout<<"overflow\n";
      else
            if (e<-99)
              cout<<"underflow\n";
            else
              cout<<"quotient is "<<m<<"e"<<e<<endl;
      }
  main()
```

```
{
   char  option;
   cout<<"enter option:'a' for addition, 's' for subtraction,
   'p' for product, 'd' for division\n";
   cin>>option;
     if  (option=='a')
     fadd();
     if  (option=='s')
     fsub();
     if  (option=='p')
     fprod();
     if  (option=='d')
     fdiv();
}
```

2

Numerical Methods for Nonlinear and Transcendental Equations

2.1 Introduction

A general form of the nonlinear equation can be written as $f(x) = 0$, in which the function $f(x)$, which should be continuous, can be expressed in two ways:

1. Polynomial algebraic function $f(x) = a_n x^n + a_{n-1} x^{n-1} + \cdots + a_0 x^0$ with $a_n \neq 0$.
2. Transcendental function, for example, $f(x) = \sin(x) + (1/x) - \tan(x)$.

To look for a numerical solution of the above equations—algebraic or transcendental—means to find the roots $x = \alpha_i$ $(i = 1, 2, 3, \ldots, n)$ of the equation for which $f(x) = f(\alpha_i) = 0$.

In science and engineering applications, numerical methods are used for solving these kinds of equations because the conventional direct methods as studied by us in algebra do not exist (for example, the case of transcendental equations) or they fail to give solution (for example, algebraic equations of order greater than 4). Numerical methods are based on iterative techniques in which the first step is the estimation of an initial approximate value of a root of the given equation and the second step involves refining this value of the estimated root through repeated iterations in order to finally obtain the value of the root of the equation to a desired degree of accuracy. There are various iterative numerical methods in which the initial approximation is taken by either using the graphical method or using the tabulation method.

2.2 Graphical Method

When the function $f(x)$ is a simple function of the variable x, a plot of $f(x)$ vs x is drawn as shown in Figure 2.1(a), and the point at which this curve meets the x-axis is taken as the initial approximation to the actual root of the given equation.

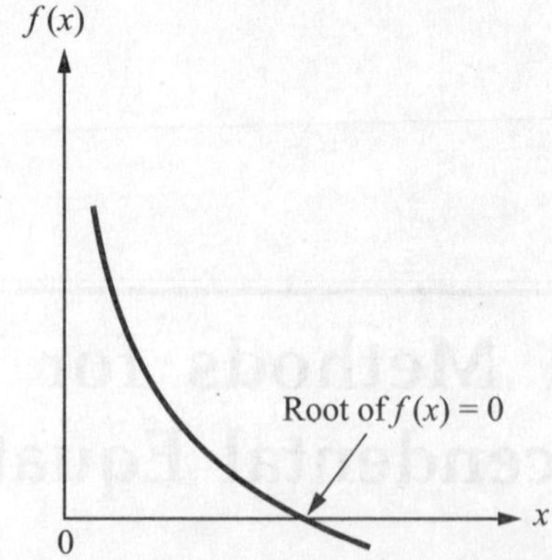

Figure 2.1(a) Graphical method for simple functions.

If the function $f(x)$ is some complicated function containing logarithmic or transcendental functions, then the given equation is rewritten in the form $\phi_1(x) = \phi_2(x)$, where ϕ_1 and ϕ_2 are simple functions of x. By plotting ϕ_1 and ϕ_2 vs x, we can find the intersection points which represent the roots of the given equation. For example, let us consider the transcendental equation given by $f(x) = e^{-x} - 2x - 1 = 0$. This equation can be rewritten as $e^{-x} = 2x + 1$. Identifying $\phi_1(x) = e^{-x}$ and $\phi_2(x) = 2x + 1$ and plotting them as shown in Figure 2.1(b), we can find the point of intersection of the two curves at $x = x_1$ which gives the initial approximate value of the root of the given equation.

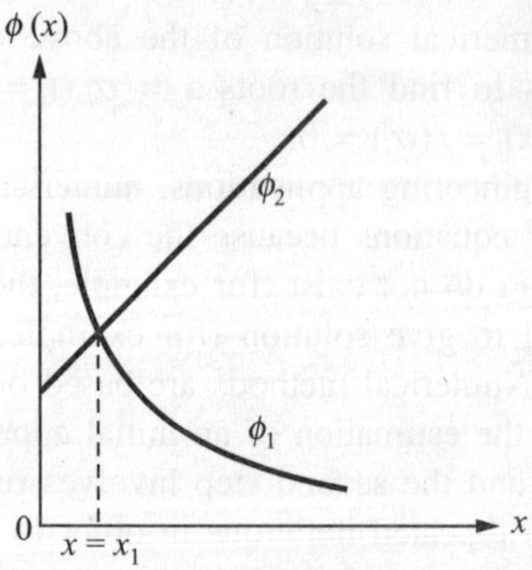

Figure 2.1(b) Graphical method for complex functions.

2.3 Tabulation Method

In the tabulation method, the Rolle's theorem from differential calculus is used. According to this theorem, "if the function $f(x)$ is real valued and continuous in the interval $x = a$ to $x = b$ and the product $f(a) \cdot f(b) < 0$, then there exists at least one real root of the equation $f(x) = 0$ which lies in the interval $[a, b]$". For example, let us consider the equation

$$f(x) = x^3 - 3x^2 + x + 1 = 0$$

Now, taking different values of x, Table 2.1 is constructed for $f(x)$ as shown below.

Table 2.1 Tabulation method

x	−1	0	2	3	4
$f(x)$	−4	1	−1	4	21

Applying the Rolle's theorem, we observe that there are three intervals, [−1, 0], [0, 2] and [2, 3], in which the condition $f(a)\cdot f(b) < 0$ is satisfied corresponding to the three roots. We give below an algorithm that can be used to write a computer program for the implementation of the tabulation method.

For a polynomial equation the largest possible root is given by

$$x_{\max} = \frac{-a_{n-1}}{a_n}$$

This value can be taken as the initial approximation to find the root of the equation. Also, a search interval $[-x_{\max}, x_{\max}]$ can be defined through the following value of $x_{\max}$.

$$x_{\max} = \left[\left(\frac{a_{n-1}}{a_n}\right)^2 - 2\left(\frac{a_{n-2}}{a_n}\right)\right]^{1/2}$$

2.4 Algorithm (AL21) for Search Interval Using the Tabulation Method

This algorithm is transformed to a computer program written in C++ language and presented at the end of this chapter (see **p21.cpp**).

Let x_i and x_f be the initial and final values of the interval over which $y = f(x)$ is to be tabulated. Let Δx be the increment in the value of x.

1. Define the inline function $f(x) = x^3 - 4x - 9$.
2. Declare/define the function/subprogram **sit** to find the search interval.
3. Start the (main) function.
4. Define the main function which calls the appropriate subprogram/function according to the given choice.
5. Stop (main).

Details of function/subprogram **sit**:

1. Start
2. Input the initial value x_i, the final value x_f and the increment Δx.
3. Let $x = x_i$
4. While $x \leq x_f$
   $y = f(x)$
   output x, y
   $x = x + \Delta x$
   endwhile
5. Return

2.5 Iteration Methods

After obtaining an initial approximation to the value of the root using the search interval, a suitable iterative method is required to evaluate the actual root of the equation. Iterative methods can be classified into two types:

1. Methods which bracket the root in the search interval.
2. Methods which do not bracket the root in the search interval.

In Category 1, we will study three methods:

(a) Fixed-point iteration method or successive approximation method
(b) Bisection method
(c) False-position (Regula Falsi) method.

In Category 2, we will study four methods:

(a) Newton–Raphson method
(b) Generalized Newton's method
(c) Secant method
(d) Muller's method

In each of these iteration methods we first take an initial approximation to the value of the root, and then an iterative process begins in which small increments to the successive values of the independent variable x are given in order to satisfy the equation $f(x) = 0$. The value of the function $f(x)$ may not be exactly zero but can be made closer to zero to a desired degree of accuracy. We can set different conditions to choose the value of the degree of accuracy.

Suppose

x_i = current approximate value of the root
x_{i+1} = next approximate value of the root
ε = a very small number ($\varepsilon << 1$) representing the degree of accuracy.

Condition 1: $|f(x_{i+1})| \leq \varepsilon$, the iterative process should terminate with x_{i+1} as the root.

Condition 2: If $|x_{i+1} - x_i| \le \varepsilon$, the iterative process should terminate with x_{i+1} as the root.

Condition 3: If $\dfrac{|x_{i+1} - x_i|}{|x_{i+1}|} \le \varepsilon$, the iterative process should terminate with x_{i+1} as the root.

2.6 Fixed-Point Iteration Method or Successive Approximation Method

Consider an equation $f(x) = 0$, for which we have to find a root that satisfies the equation. We can rewrite the above equation as

$$x = \psi(x)$$

Let us assume that α is the desired root of the equation. Now by using the tabulation technique, we find the search interval $[a, b]$ in which the initial approximation x_0 to the root α lies. The first approximation x_1 to the root is then given by

$$x_1 = \psi(x_0)$$

Using this value as the new approximation to the root, we get the second approximation to the root as

$$x_2 = \psi(x_1)$$

Similarly, the successive approximations to the root can be written as

$$x_3 = \psi(x_2);\quad x_4 = \psi(x_3);\quad x_5 = \psi(x_4);\ \ldots;\ x_{n+1} = \psi(x_n)$$

Hence the value of the root in the $(i + 1)$th iteration is given by

$$x_{i+1} = \psi(x_i) \tag{2.1}$$

The formula (2.1) is called the *fixed-point iteration formula.*

The sequence of approximations $(x_0, x_1, \ldots, x_n)$ may or may not converge to the actual root of the equation because convergence depends upon the nature of the chosen function $\psi(x)$ as well as on the choice of the initial approximation x_0. In this respect the following conditions of convergence must be satisfied:

1. The condition of convergence is

$$|\psi'(x)| < 1 \tag{2.2}$$

Therefore, before computation, the function $\psi(x)$ should be so chosen that its first derivative lies in the range $-1 < \psi'(x) < 1$ for values of x belonging to the search interval in which the root lies. The convergence is fast when $\psi'(x)$ is small.

For example, consider the equation $x^3 - x - 0.1 = 0$. The search interval in which the root lies is $[1, 2]$. We can express this equation in the following ways:

(i) $x = (x + 0.1)^{1/3} = \psi_1(x)$
(ii) $x = x^3 - 0.1 = \psi_2(x)$
(iii) $x = 0.1/(x^2 - 1) = \psi_3(x)$

In order to make a right choice out of the above three forms of $\psi(x)$, we make use of Condition (2.2) of convergence and obtain the following results:

$\psi_1'(x) = (1/3)(x + 0.1)^{-2/3}$; therefore, $|\psi_1'(x)| < 1$ in the interval [1, 2].
$\psi_2'(x) = 3x^2$; therefore, $|\psi_2'(x)| > 1$ in the interval [1, 2].
$\psi_3'(x) = -0.2x/(x^2 - 1)^2$; therefore, $|\psi_3'(x)| > 1$ in the interval [1, 1.2] and $|\psi_3'(x)| < 1$ in the interval [1.2, 2].

Thus, we see that the best choice for the function is $\psi_1(x)$ because it satisfies the condition of convergence.

2. The second condition for convergence is related to the choice of the initial approximation to the root. The number of iterations will be less and convergence will be fast if the initial approximation is close to the value of the actual root.

EXAMPLE 2.1 Find a root of the equation $x^3 - 9x + 1 = 0$ correct up to three significant digits using the fixed-point iteration method.

Solution

Rewriting the above equation as

$$x = \frac{1}{9 - x^2}$$

We choose,
$$\psi(x) = \frac{1}{9 - x^2}$$

The search interval for this function is [0, 1] because the equation $f(x) = 0$ gives

$$f(0) = 1, f(1) = -7 \quad \text{and so} \quad f(0) \cdot f(1) < 0$$

$$\psi'(x) = \frac{2x}{(9 - x^2)^2} \quad \text{and so} \quad \psi'(0) = 0,\ \psi'(1) = 0.03$$

implying that the condition of convergence $|\psi'(x)| < 1$ is satisfied for the interval [0, 1].

To compute the root, we take $x = 0$ as the initial value of the root and evaluate the LHS and RHS of the expression $x = \dfrac{1}{9 - x^2} = \psi(x)$.

For iteration $i = 0$, $x_0 = 0$, $\psi(x_0) = 0.11$
For iteration $i = 1$, $x_1 = 0.11$, $\psi(x_1) = 0.1113$

Continuing like this, we can construct Table 2.2 of iterations as follows:

Table 2.2 Table of iterations—Example 2.1

i	x_i	$\psi(x_i)$
0	0	0.11
1	0.11	0.1113
2	0.1113	0.11126
3	0.11126	0.111264
4	0.111264	0.1112641

Thus, correct up to three significant digits, the root is 0.111.

2.7 Algorithm (AL22) for Fixed-Point Iteration Method

This algorithm is transformed to a computer program written in C++ language and presented at the end of this chapter (see **p22.cpp**).

Let a be the initial value of the root.

1. Define the inline function $f(x) = x^3 - 4x - 9$.
2. Define eps = 0.0001.
3. Declare/define the function/subprogram **fpt** to find the search interval.
4. Start the (main) function.
5. Define the main function which calls the subprogram/function according to given choice.
6. Stop (main).

Details of function/subprogram **fpt**:

```
1. Start
2. Input the initial value of root a
3. Input maximum number of iterations, maxit
4. For count = 1 to maxit in steps of 1
   c = f(a)
   if |(c – a)/c| > eps
   a = c
   else
      exit for loop
   endfor
5. Output root, count, f(root)
6. Return
```

2.8 Bisection Method

The first step in this method is the determination of the bisecting interval in which the root of the equation $f(x) = 0$ lies. This can be done by using either the graphical method or the tabulation method. The second step is bisecting the interval in successive iterations using the point of bisection on the x-axis and converging to the root.

Suppose $f(x) = f(a)$ be the value of the function at $x = a$ and $f(x) = f(b)$ be the value of the function at $x = b$ such that

$$f(a) \cdot f(b) < 0 \tag{2.3}$$

where $[a, b]$ is the search interval obtained by using the graphical/tabulation method containing the root of the given equation.

Let the interval $[a, b]$ be bisected to obtain a bisection point $x(= c)$ given by

$$c = \frac{a+b}{2} \tag{2.4}$$

Let $f(c)$ be the value of $f(x)$ at $x = c$. Now three possible conditions exist:

1. If $f(c) = 0$ then $x = c$ is the root.
2. If $f(c) \neq 0$ and $f(a) \cdot f(c) < 0$, then the root lies in the new interval $[a, c]$, so we replace b by c.
3. If $f(c) \neq 0$ and $f(a) \cdot f(c) > 0$, then the root lies in the new interval $[c, b]$, so we replace a by c.

By repeatedly bisecting the new intervals obtained in Condition (2) or (3), the size of the search interval is reduced to the value $(b - a)/2^n$ in n iterations.

If ε is the value of the degree of accuracy in the determination of the root, then the iteration cycle terminates when Condition 3 is satisfied.

The number of iterations n can be calculated by setting $(b - a)/2^n < \varepsilon$. Taking logs of the above inequality,

$$\ln (b - a) - n \ln 2 \leq \ln \varepsilon$$

Hence the number of iterations is given by

$$n \geq \frac{\ln (b-a) - \ln \varepsilon}{\ln 2}$$

Convergence of the Bisection Method

The given equation $f(x) = 0$ can be written as $x = \psi(x)$. If x takes the values $x_0, x_1, x_2, \ldots, x_n$, we can write

$$\begin{aligned} x_1 &= \psi(x_0) \\ x_2 &= \psi(x_1) \\ &\vdots \\ x_n &= \psi(x_{n-1}) \end{aligned}$$

If α is the root, then

$$\alpha = \psi(\alpha)$$

On subtraction, we get

$$x_n - \alpha = \psi(x_{n-1}) - \psi(\alpha)$$

Using the mean value theorem of differential calculus, we can write

$$\psi(x_{n-1}) - \psi(\alpha) = (x_{n-1} - \alpha)\psi'(\eta), \text{ where } x_{n-1} < \eta < \alpha$$

Thus, $$x_n - \alpha = (x_{n-1} - \alpha)\psi'(\eta)$$

Let $|\psi'(x)| \le p$ for all values of x in $[x_0, x_n]$.

Therefore, $$(|x_n - \alpha|) \le (|x_{n-1} - \alpha|)p$$

Similarly, $$(|x_{n-1} - \alpha|) \le (|x_{n-2} - \alpha|)p$$

$$\vdots$$

$$(|x_1 - \alpha|) \le (|x_0 - \alpha|)p$$

Multiplying the LHS and RHS of the above equations, we get

$$(|x_n - \alpha|) \le (|x_0 - \alpha|)p^n$$

when $p < 1$, p^n goes to zero as n tends to infinity.

Therefore, $$(|x_n - \alpha|) \to 0 \text{ as } n \to \infty$$

Thus, $$x_n \to \alpha \text{ as } n \to \infty$$

From the preceding analysis we conclude that the bisection method surely converges though slowly as its rate of convergence is linear and the sufficient condition for convergence is

$$\text{for all } x \qquad \psi'(x) < 1 \tag{2.5}$$

2.9 Numerical Examples (Bisection Method)

EXAMPLE 2.2 Using the bisection method, find a root of the equation $f(x) = x^3 - 9x + 1 = 0$, correct up to three significant digits.

Solution

To obtain the root interval we construct Table 2.3 by assuming different values of x.

Table 2.3 Example 2.2

x	1	2	3	4
$f(x)$	–7	–9	1	29

Since the product $f(2) \cdot f(3) < 0$, the root must lie between $x = a = 2$ and $x = b = 3$. We construct Table 2.4, according to the values calculated for the function $f(x)$ and using the bisection method. In this table, we use $c = (a + b)/2$ and replace a by c when $f(a) \cdot f(c) > 0$ and b by c when $f(b) \cdot f(c) > 0$. For example, in iteration $i = 0$, $f(a) = f(2) = -9$, $f(b) = f(3) = 1$, $f(c) = f(2.5) = -5.88$. So we replace a by c in the next iteration $i = 1$.

Table 2.4 Table of iterations—Example 2.2

i	a	b	c	$f(a)$	$f(b)$	$f(c)$
0	2	3	2.5	–ve	+ve	–ve
1	2.5	3	2.75	–ve	+ve	–ve
2	2.75	3	2.88	–ve	+ve	–ve
3	2.88	3	2.94	–ve	+ve	–ve
4	2.94	3	2.97	–ve	+ve	+ve
5	2.94	2.97	2.955	–ve	+ve	+ve
6	2.94	2.955	2.9475	–ve	+ve	+ve
7	2.94	2.9475	2.9438	–ve	+ve	+ve
8	2.94	2.9438	2.9419	–ve	+ve	–ve
9	2.9419	2.9438	2.9428	–ve	+ve	–ve

Thus, the root of the given equation is $x = c = 2.94$, correct up to three significant digits.

EXAMPLE 2.3 Using the bisection method, find a root of the following equation, correct up to three decimal places.

$$f(x) = 2x - 3 \sin x - 5 = 0$$

Solution

To obtain the root interval, we construct Table 2.5 by assuming different values of x.

Table 2.5 Example 2.3

x	0	1	2	3
$f(x)$	–5	–5.5	–3.7	0.57

Since the product $f(2) \cdot f(3) < 0$, the root must lie between $x = a = 2$ and $x = b = 3$. We construct Table 2.6, according to the values calculated for the function $f(x)$ and using the bisection method. In this table, we use $c = (a + b)/2$ and replace a by c when $f(a) \cdot f(c) > 0$ and b by c when $f(b) \cdot f(c) > 0$. For example, at $i = 0$, $f(a) = f(2) = -3.7$, $f(b) = f(3) = 0.57$, $f(c) = f((2 + 3)/2) = f(2.5) = 2 \times 2.5 - 3 \times \sin 2.5 - 5 = 5 - 3 \times 0.6 - 5 = -1.8$.

Table 2.6 Table of iterations—Example 2.3

i	a	b	c	$f(a)$	$f(b)$	$f(c)$
0	2	3	2.5	–ve	+ve	–ve
1	2.5	3	2.75	–ve	+ve	–ve
2	2.75	3	2.875	–ve	+ve	–ve
3	2.875	3	2.938	–ve	+ve	+ve
4	2.875	2.938	2.906	–ve	+ve	+ve
5	2.875	2.906	2.8905	–ve	+ve	+ve

(Contd.)

Table 2.6 Table of iterations—Example 2.3 (*Contd.*)

i	a	b	c	$f(a)$	$f(b)$	$f(c)$
6	2.875	2.8905	2.8828	–ve	+ve	–ve
7	2.8828	2.8905	2.8866	–ve	+ve	+ve
8	2.8826	2.8866	2.8847	–ve	+ve	+ve
9	2.8828	2.8847	2.8838	–ve	+ve	+ve
10	2.8828	2.8838	2.8833	–ve	+ve	+ve

Thus, the root of the given equation is $x = c = 2.883$, correct up to three decimal places.

EXAMPLE 2.4 Using the bisection method, find a root of the following equation, correct up to three decimal places.

$$f(x) = x + \ln(x) - 2 = 0$$

Solution

To obtain the root interval, we construct Table 2.7 by assuming different values of x.

Table 2.7 Example 2.4

x	1	2	3
$f(x)$	–1	0.69	2.09

Since $f(1)\cdot f(2) < 0$, the root lies between $x = a = 1$ and $x = b = 2$. We construct Table 2.8, according to the values calculated for the function $f(x)$ and using the bisection method. In this table we use $c = (a + b)/2$ and replace a by c when $f(a)\cdot f(c) > 0$ and b by c when $f(b)\cdot f(c) > 0$.

Table 2.8 Table of iterations—Example 2.4

i	a	b	c	$f(a)$	$f(b)$	$f(c)$
0	1	2	1.5	–ve	+ve	–ve
1	1.5	2	1.75	–ve	+ve	+ve
2	1.5	1.75	1.625	–ve	+ve	+ve
3	1.5	1.625	1.562	–ve	+ve	+ve
4	1.5	1.562	1.531	–ve	+ve	–ve
5	1.531	1.562	1.5465	–ve	+ve	–ve
6	1.5465	1.562	1.5542	–ve	+ve	–ve
7	1.5542	1.562	1.5581	–ve	+ve	+ve
8	1.5542	1.5581	1.5562	–ve	+ve	–ve
9	1.5562	1.5581	1.55715	–ve	+ve	+ve
10	1.5562	1.55715	1.55668	–ve	+ve	–ve

Thus, the root of the given equation is $x = c = 1.557$, correct up to three decimal places.

EXAMPLE 2.5 Using the bisection method, find a root of the following equation, correct up to three decimal places.

$$f(x) = x - \cos x = 0$$

Solution

To obtain the root interval, we construct Table 2.9 by assuming different values of x.

Table 2.9 Example 2.5

x	0	0.5	1.0
$f(x)$	–1	–0.38	0.46

Since $f(0.5)\cdot f(1) < 0$, the root lies between $x = a = 0.5$ and $x = b = 1$. We construct the following Table 2.10 according to the values calculated for the function $f(x)$ and using the bisection method. In this table we use $c = (a + b)/2$ and replace a by c when $f(a)\cdot f(c) > 0$ and b by c when $f(b)\cdot f(c) > 0$.

Table 2.10 Table of iterations—Example 2.5

i	a	b	c	$f(a)$	$f(b)$	$f(c)$
0	0.5	1.0	0.75	–ve	+ve	+ve
1	1.5	0.75	0.625	–ve	+ve	–ve
2	0.625	0.75	0.688	–ve	+ve	–ve
3	0.688	0.75	0.719	–ve	+ve	–ve
4	0.719	0.75	0.734	–ve	+ve	–ve
5	0.734	0.75	0.742	–ve	+ve	+ve
6	0.734	0.742	0.738	–ve	+ve	–ve
7	0.738	0.742	0.74	–ve	+ve	+ve
8	0.738	0.740	0.739	–ve	+ve	+ve

Thus, the root of the given equation is $x = c = 0.739$ correct up to three decimal places.

EXAMPLE 2.6 Using the bisection method, find the negative root of the following equation, correct up to two decimal places.

$$f(x) = x^3 - 4x + 9 = 0$$

Solution

The –ve root of the given equation $f(x) = 0$ is the +ve root of the function $f(-x) = \phi(x) = -x^3 + 4x + 9 = 0$, for which Table 2.11 can be constructed.

Table 2.11 Example 2.6

x	2	3	4
$f(x)$	–9	6	39

Since $f(2) \cdot f(3) < 0$, the root lies between $x = a = 2$ and $x = b = 3$. We construct Table 2.12, according to the values calculated for the function $f(x)$ and using the bisection method. In this table we use $c = (a + b)/2$ and replace a by c when $f(a) \cdot f(c) > 0$ and b by c when $f(b) \cdot f(c) > 0$.

Table 2.12 Table of iterations—Example 2.6

i	a	b	c	$f(a)$	$f(b)$	$f(c)$
0	2	3	2.5	–ve	+ve	–ve
1	2.5	3	2.75	–ve	+ve	+ve
2	2.5	2.75	2.63	–ve	+ve	–ve
3	2.63	2.75	2.69	–ve	+ve	–ve
4	2.69	2.75	2.72	–ve	+ve	+ve
5	2.69	2.72	2.72	–ve	+ve	–ve
6	2.7	2.72	2.72	–ve	+ve	–ve

Thus, the –ve root of the given function $f(x)$ is $x = c = -2.72$ correct up to two decimal places.

2.10 Algorithm (AL23) for the Bisection Method

This algorithm is transformed to a computer program written in C++ language and presented at the end of this chapter (see **p23.cpp**).

Let a and b be the initial and final values of the interval over which $y = f(x)$ is to be tabulated for finding the root value.

1. Define the inline function $f(x) = x^3 - 4x - 9$.
2. Define eps = 0.0001.
3. Declare/define the function/subprogram **bisec** to find the root.
4. Start the (main) function.
5. Define the main function which calls the subprogram/function according to given choice.
6. Stop (main).

Details of function/subprogram **bisec**:

1. Start
2. Input the initial root interval a, b
3. If $f(a) \cdot f(b) < 0$

```
        count = 0
        do
           c = (a + b)/2
           If f (a) · f (c) < 0
              b = c
           else
              a = c
           endif
```

```
        count = count+1
       while ((count <= 20) or (f (c) > eps)
       output 'root=', c
       output count, f (c)
    else
       output 'initial interval incorrect'
4. Return
```

2.11 The False Position Method (Regula–Falsi Method)

In this method too, the first step is to find the search interval $[a, b]$ which contains the root of the equation $f(x) = 0$ by graphical/tabulation methods such that the product $f(a) \cdot f(b) < 0$. But unlike the bisection method the root-search interval is not halved in each iteration but is chosen between a computed new approximation and one of the initial positions. Thus, in this method the position of the root lies somewhere between the initial position of the preceding iteration and a new calculated approximation of each iteration.

Consider the graph of the function $f(x)$ vs x as shown in Figure 2.2.

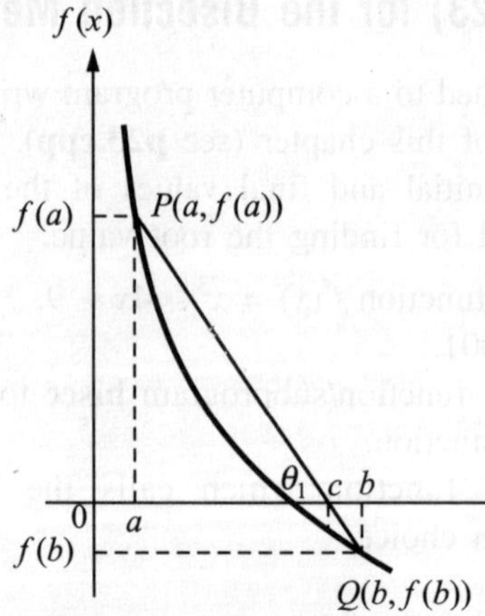

Figure 2.2 Regula–Falsi method.

Let $P(a, f(a))$ and $Q(b, f(b))$ be any two points on the curve $y = f(x)$. Joining the points P and Q by a straight line, we get a point of intersection c, on the x-axis. The slope of the chord PQ is given by

$$\tan \theta_1 = \frac{0 - f(a)}{c - a}$$

Also, the value of the slope is given by

$$\tan \theta_1 = \frac{f(a) - f(b)}{a - b}$$

Equating the above slope values gives

$$c = \frac{af(b) - bf(a)}{f(b) - f(a)} \tag{2.6}$$

The value $x = c$ gives the first approximation to the value of the root.

Depending upon the sign of the products $f(a) \cdot f(c)$ or $f(b) \cdot f(c)$ the next approximation to the root is made.

If $f(a) \cdot f(c) < 0$, then the root lies in $[a, c]$, so b is replaced by c in Eq. (2.6) and the second approximation to the root is $x = c$.

If $f(b) \cdot f(c) < 0$, then the root lies in $[b, c]$, so a is replaced by c in Eq. (2.6) and the second approximation to the root is $x = c$.

2.12 Numerical Examples (False Position Method)

EXAMPLE 2.7 Find the root of the equation $f(x) = 3x - \cos x - 1 = 0$, using the false position method up to four significant digits.

Solution

To get at the root interval, we construct Table 2.13 using the function $f(x)$.

Table 2.13 Example 2.7

x	0	1	2
$f(x)$	–2	1.46	5.42

Thus, the root lies in [0, 1] with $a = 0$ and $b = 1$. Using Eq. (2.6), we calculate the value of the approximate root c, in each iteration and construct Table 2.14, in which a is replaced by c, if the product $f(b) \cdot f(c) < 0$ in an iteration.

Table 2.14 Table of iterations—Example 2.7

i	a	b	c	$f(b) \cdot f(c)$
0	0	1	0.578	–ve
1	0.578	1	0.605	–ve
2	0.605	1	0.607	–ve
3	0.607	1	0.60708	–ve
4	0.60708	1	0.60710	–ve
5	0.60710	1	0.60710	–ve

Thus, the root is $x = c = 0.6071$, correct up to four decimal digits.

EXAMPLE 2.8 Find the root of the equation $f(x) = 2x - \log_{10} x - 7 = 0$, using the false position method up to four significant digits.

Solution

Construct Table 2.15 to find the root interval [a, b].

Table 2.15 Example 2.8

x	2	3	4
$f(x)$	–3.3	–1.48	0.4

Thus, the root lies in the interval [3, 4]. Using the initial values $a = 3$ and $b = 4$, we calculate the value of c using Eq. (2.6) and construct Table 2.16 of iterations.

Table 2.16 Table of iterations—Example 2.8

i	a	b	c	$f(c)$
0	3	4	3.79	+ve
1	3	3.79	3.789	–ve
2	3.789	3.79	3.789278	–ve
3	3.789278	3.79	3.78927	–ve

Thus, the root is $x = c = 3.789$, correct up to three decimal places.

EXAMPLE 2.9 Find the root of the equation $f(x) = xe^x - 2 = 0$ that lies in the interval [0, 1] using the false position method up to four significant digits.

Solution

Using the given initial values $a = 0$ and $b = 1$, Table 2.17 of iterations can be constructed.

Table 2.17 Table of iterations—Example 2.9

i	a	b	c	$f(c)$
0	0	1	0.735759	–ve
1	0.735759	1	0.839521	–ve
2	0.839521	1	0.851184	–ve
3	0.851184	1	0.852452	–ve
4	0.852452	1	0.85261	–ve
5	0.85261	1	0.85261	–ve

Thus, the root is $x = c = 0.8526$, correct up to four significant digits.

EXAMPLE 2.10 Find a root of the equation $f(x) = x^3 + 2x - 2 = 0$ using the false position method up to three significant digits.

Solution

At $x = 0$, $f(0) = -2$ and at $x = 1$, $f(1) = 1$. Therefore, the root lies in the interval [a, b] = [0, 1]. Construct Table 2.18 using the false position method by replacing a by c, whenever $f(c) < 0$.

Table 2.18 Table of iterations—Example 2.10

i	a	b	c	$f(c)$
0	0	1	0.67	–ve
1	0.67	1	0.757	–ve
2	0.757	1	0.769	–ve
3	0.769	1	0.771	–ve
4	0.771	1	0.771	–ve

Thus the root is $x = c = 0.771$, correct upto three significant digits.

2.13 Algorithm (AL24) for False Position Method

This algorithm is transformed to a computer program written in C++ language and presented at the end of this chapter (see **p24.cpp**).

Let a and b be the initial and final values of the interval over which $y = f(x)$ is to be tabulated for finding the root value.

1. Define the inline function $f(x) = x^3 - 4x - 9$.
2. Define eps = 0.0001.
3. Declare/define the function/subprogram **regfal** to find the root.
4. Start the (main) function.
5. Define the main function which calls the subprogram/function according to given choice.
6. Stop (main).

Details of function/subprogram **regfal**:

```
1. Start
2. Input the initial root interval a, b.
3. If f(a)*f(b)<0
      count = 0
      do
         c = (af(b) – bf(a))/(f(b) – f(a))
         if f(a)*f(c) < 0
            b = c
         else
            a = c
         endif
      count = count + 1
      while ((count <= 20) or (f(c) > eps)
      output 'root =', c
      output count, f(c)
   else
   output 'initial interval incorrect'
4. Return
```

2.14 Newton–Raphson (N–R) Method

This is an iteration method to find the root of an equation $f(x) = 0$ by correcting the value of the approximate root $x = x_0$ in each iteration. Let h be the small correction to the value of the assumed approximate root so that the next approximation is

$$x_1 = x_0 + h \tag{2.7}$$

Thus, $$f(x_1) = f(x_0 + h) = 0$$

Using the Taylor's series expansion for the above function, we get

$$f(x_0 + h) = f(x_0) + h\,f'(x_0) + (h^2/2!)\,f''(x_0) + \cdots = 0$$

As h is a very small number, so we can neglect the terms with higher powers in h.

Therefore, $$f(x_0) + h\,f'(x_0) \simeq 0$$

Thus $$h = -\frac{f(x_0)}{f'(x_0)}$$

Using Eq. (2.7),

$$x_1 = x_0 - \frac{f(x_0)}{f'(x_0)} \tag{2.8}$$

The next approximation to the root will be given by $x_2 = x_1 + h_1$.

Therefore, $$f(x_2) = f(x_1 + h_1) = 0$$

Using Taylor's series expansion about $x = x_1$,

$$f(x_1 + h_1) = f(x_1) + h_1\,f'(x_1) + (h_1^2/2!)\,f''(x_1) + \cdots = 0$$

As h_1 is a very small number, so we can neglect the terms with higher powers in h_1.

Therefore, $$f(x_1) + h_1\,f'(x_1) \simeq 0.$$

Thus $$h_1 = -\frac{f(x_1)}{f'(x_1)}$$

Therefore, $$x_2 = x_1 - \frac{f(x_1)}{f'(x_1)} \tag{2.9}$$

By induction, the $(n + 1)$th iterated value of the root is given by

$$x_{n+1} = x_n - \frac{f(x_n)}{f'(x_n)} \tag{2.10}$$

Equation (2.10) is called the *iteration formula for the Newton–Raphson Method.*

Note that this method would fail when $f'(x) = 0$ as evident from Eq. (2.10). The initial approximation to the root should be taken near the value of the actual root to avoid the divergent values of the root in iterations.

The iterations should terminate when $|x_{n+1} - x_n| \le \varepsilon$.

Geometrical Significance of the N–R Method

Consider a plot of the function $f(x)$ vs x as shown in Figure 2.3.

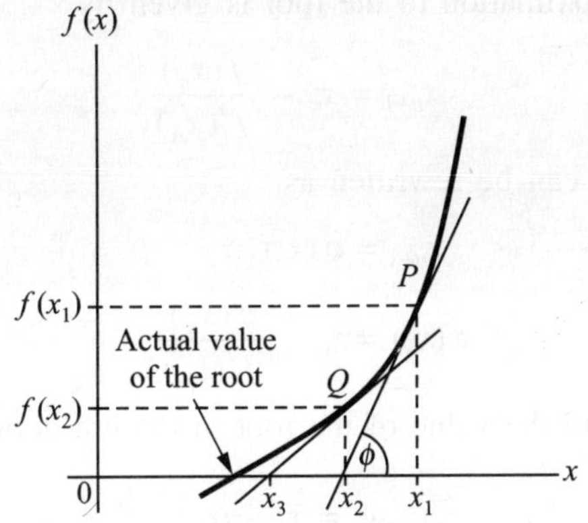

Figure 2.3 N–R method.

To begin with the initial approximation to the root is given by $x = x_1$. A tangent drawn at this point cuts the x-axis at point $x = x_2$, which can be taken as the second approximation to the root. The slope of the tangent drawn at point P is given by

$$\tan \phi = \frac{f(x_1)}{x_1 - x_2} = f'(x_1)$$

Solving for x_2 gives

$$x_2 = x_1 - \frac{f(x_1)}{f'(x_1)}$$

which is the same as Eq. (2.9) obtained from Taylor's series expansion.

By drawing again a tangent at the point $x = x_2$, another point $x = x_3$ is obtained at which the tangent cuts the x-axis. The slope of this tangent at point Q can be written as

$$\tan \phi = \frac{f(x_2)}{x_2 - x_3} = f'(x_2)$$

Solving for x_3 gives

$$x_3 = x_2 - \frac{f(x_2)}{f'(x_2)}$$

Continuing like this, the $(n + 1)$th approximation to the root is given by

$$x_{n+1} = x_n - \frac{f(x_n)}{f'(x_n)}$$

As expected, this equation is the same as Eq. (2.10).

Convergence of the N–R Method

The $(n + 1)$th approximation to the root is given by

$$x_{n+1} = x_n - \frac{f(x_n)}{f'(x_n)}$$

The above formula can be rewritten as

$$x_{n+1} = \phi(x_n) \tag{2.11}$$

where $$\phi(x_n) = x_n - \frac{f(x_n)}{f'(x_n)}$$

Let e_n be the error in the value of the root in the nth iteration so that we can write

$$e_n = x_n - \alpha \tag{2.12}$$

where α is the value of the actual root.

Rewriting Eq. (2.11), we get

$$x_{n+1} = \phi(x_n) = \phi(e_n + \alpha)$$

Expanding by Taylor's series,

$$x_{n+1} = \alpha + e_n \cdot \frac{\phi'(\alpha)}{1!} + e_n^2 \cdot \frac{\phi''(\alpha)}{2!} + \cdots$$

or $$x_{n+1} - \alpha = e_n \cdot \frac{\phi'(\alpha)}{1!} + e_n^2 \cdot \frac{\phi''(\alpha)}{2!} + \cdots \tag{2.13}$$

From Eq. (2.12), we get

$$e_{n+1} = x_{n+1} - \alpha$$

Using this in Eq. (2.13),

$$e_{n+1} = e_n \cdot \frac{\phi'(\alpha)}{1!} + e_n^2 \cdot \frac{\phi''(\alpha)}{2!} + \cdots \tag{2.14}$$

Since $$\phi(x) = x - \frac{f(x)}{f'(x)} \tag{2.15}$$

$$\phi'(x) = f(x) \cdot \frac{f''(x)}{[f'(x)]^2} \tag{2.16}$$

At $x = \alpha$, $f(\alpha) = 0$ and $\phi'(\alpha) = 0$.

Similarly, from Eq. (2.15)

$$\phi''(\alpha) = \frac{f''(\alpha)}{f'(\alpha)} \qquad \text{(using } f(\alpha) = 0\text{)}$$

From Eq. (2.14) (neglecting the higher powers in e_n)

$$e_{n+1} = [e_n]^2 \cdot \frac{f''(\alpha)}{[2 \cdot f'(\alpha)]} \tag{2.17}$$

Equation (2.17) implies that the error at any iteration in the N–R method is proportional to the square of the error in the preceding iteration. Thus, the convergence in this method is said to be of order 2.

Condition of Convergence

The sequence of approximations $x_1, x_2, x_3, x_4, \ldots, x_n$ converges to the root if $|\phi'(x)| < 1$.

Using (2.16), we get

$$\phi(x) \cdot \frac{f''(x)}{[f'(x)]^2} < 1$$

Rewriting the above inequality,

$$f(x) \cdot [f''(x)] < [f'(x)]^2 \tag{2.18}$$

Equation (2.18) gives the condition for convergence of the N–R method.

2.15 Numerical Examples (N–R Method)

EXAMPLE 2.11 Using the N–R method, find a root of the following equation correct up to three decimal places.

$$x^2 + 2x - 2 = 0$$

Solution

Using the function $f(x) = x^2 + 2x - 2$, we construct Table 2.19.

Table 2.19 Example 2.11

x	0.5	0.7	0.8	1.0
$f(x)$	−0.75	−0.11	0.24	1.0

The root lies in the interval [0.7, 0.8] and let the initial value be $x_0 = 0.7$. Also $f'(x) = 2x + 2$ and checking $f'(x_0) = 3.4$ ($\neq 0$), we construct Table 2.20 to find the value of x at which $f(x) = 0$.

Table 2.20 Table of iterations—Example 2.11

n	x_n	$f(x_n)$	$f'(x_n)$	$h_n(=-f(x_n)/f'(x_n)$	$x_{n+1}(=x_n+h_n)$
0	0.7	– 0.11	3.4	0.03	0.73
1	0.73	– 0.0071	3.46	0.00205	0.73205
2	0.73205	– 0.0000028	3.4641	0.0000008	0.732051

Therefore, the root is $x = 0.732$, correct up to three decimal places.

EXAMPLE 2.12 Using the N–R method, find a root of the following equation up to five decimal places.

$$x + \ln x - 2 = 0$$

Solution

From the given equation we have the function $f(x) = x + \ln x - 2$. Using this function, we construct Table 2.21.

Table 2.21 Example 2.12

x	1.0	1.5	2.0
$f(x)$	– 1.0	−0.09	0.69

The root lies in the interval [1.5, 2.0] and let the initial value be $x_0 = 1.5$. Also $f'(x) = 1 + (1/x)$ and checking $f'(x_0) = 1.67$ ($\neq 0$), we construct Table 2.22 to find the value of x at which $f(x) = 0$.

Table 2.22 Table of iterations—Example 2.12

n	x_n	$f(x_n)$	$f'(x_n)$	$h_n(=-f(x_n)/f'(x_n))$	$x_{n+1}(=x_n+h_n)$
0	1.5	−0.019	1.67	0.04	1.554
1	1.554	−0.00517	1.6435	0.003146	1.557146
2	1.557146	0.00007	1.6422	−0.0000004	1.5571456
3	1.5571456	−0.00005	1.6422	0.00000003	1.5571459

Therefore, the root is $x = 1.55715$, correct up to five decimal places.

EXAMPLE 2.13 Using the N–R method, find a root of the following equation up to four decimal places.

$$x^x + x - 4 = 0$$

Solution

From the given equation, we have the function $f(x) = x^x + x - 4$. Using this function, we determine that the root lies in the interval [1.6, 1.7]. Also, checking $f'(x_0) = 4.12$ ($\neq 0$), we construct Table 2.23 to find the value of x at which $f(x) = 0$.

Table 2.23 Table of iterations—Example 2.13

n	x_n	$f(x_n)$	$f'(x_n)$	$h_n(= -f(x_n)/f'(x_n))$	$x_{n+1}(= x_n + h_n)$
0	1.6	−0.27	4.12	0.066	1.666
1	1.666	0.0065	4.5352	−0.00143	1.66457
2	1.66457	0.0000318	4.525536	−0.00007	1.664563
3	1.664563	0.0000002	4.5254887	−0.0000004	1.664563

Therefore, the root is $x = 1.6646$, correct up to four decimal places.

2.16 *s*th Root of a Real Number Using the N–R Method

Let the nonlinear equation be given by

$$x^s - R = 0$$

or

$$x = (R)^{1/s} \tag{2.19}$$

where R is any positive real number.

According to the N–R method, the root of the above equation is given by

$$x_{n+1} = x_n - \frac{f(x_n)}{f'(x_n)}$$

$$x_{n+1} = \frac{(s-1)(x_n)^s + R}{s(x_n)^{s-1}} \tag{2.20}$$

Equation (2.20) gives the value of the sth root of the real number, R.

For example, if $s = 2$, the square root of R is given by

$$x_{n+1} = \frac{x_n + \dfrac{R}{x_n}}{2} \tag{2.21}$$

if $s = 3$, the cube root of R is given by

$$x_{n+1} = \frac{2x_n + \dfrac{R}{x_n^2}}{3} \tag{2.22}$$

if $s = 5$, the value of the 5th root is given by

$$x_{n+1} = \frac{4x_n + \dfrac{R}{x_n^4}}{5} \tag{2.23}$$

2.17 Numerical Examples (*s*th Root by N–R Method)

EXAMPLE 2.14 Find the value of $\sqrt{8}$ by the N–R method.

Solution

Using Eq. (2.21),

$$x_{n+1} = \frac{x_n + \dfrac{8}{x_n}}{2}$$

We now construct the following Table 2.24 with initial value $x_0 = 2.5$ for $n = 0$ iteration.

Table 2.24 Example 2.14

n	x_n	x_{n+1}
0	2.5	2.85
1	2.85	2.8285
2	2.8285	2.8284271
3	2.8284271	2.8284271

Therefore, the root is 2.828427.

EXAMPLE 2.15 Find the value of $(3)^{1/5}$ by the N–R method.

Solution

Using Eq. (2.23),

$$x_{n+1} = \frac{4x_n + \dfrac{R}{x_n^4}}{5} = \frac{4x_n + \dfrac{3}{x_n^4}}{5}$$

we construct the following Table 2.25 with initial value $x_0 = 1.0$ for $n = 0$ iteration.

Table 2.25 Example 2.15

n	x_n	x_{n+1}
0	1.0	1.4
1	1.4	1.276
2	1.276	1.2471
3	1.2471	1.2457
4	1.2457	1.2457301

Therefore, the root is 1.2457.

2.18 Generalized Newton's Method

This method is a slight improvement over the Newton–Raphson method when a given function $f(x)$ has the multiplicity p. This means that the equation $f(x) = 0$ has a double root ($p = 2$) or a triple root ($p = 3$). We rewrite the N–R formula to account for the multiplicity, in the form

$$x_{n+1} = x_n - \frac{p\, f(x_n)}{f'(x_n)} \tag{2.24}$$

This formula is called the *generalized Newton's formula.*

Let α be the root of the equation $f(x) = 0$ with multiplicity p. This implies that α is also the root of the equation $f'(x) = 0$ with multiplicity $(p - 1)$ and that of $f''(x) = 0$ with multiplicity $(p - 2)$, and so on. This means that the following expressions for the root will give the same value.

$$x_{n+1} = x_n - \frac{p\, f(x_n)}{f'(x_n)} = x_n - (p-1)\frac{f'(x_n)}{f''(x_n)} = x_n - (p-2)\frac{f''(x_n)}{f'''(x_n)} \cdots$$

and so on for higher derivatives of the function $f(x)$.

2.19 Numerical Examples (Generalized Newton Method)

EXAMPLE 2.16 Determine the double root of the equation

$$x^3 - 5.39x^2 + 9.23x - 5.1 = 0$$

given that the root is close to 1.49.

Solution

Given $f(x) = x^3 - 5.39x^2 + 9.23x - 5.1$.

$$f'(x) = 3x^2 - 10.78x + 9.23$$

With $p = 2$, we write the root value in the $(i + 1)$th iteration as

$$x_{i+1} = x_i - \frac{2f(x_i)}{f'(x_i)}$$

and construct the following Table 2.26 for different iterations.

Table 2.26 Example 2.16

i	x_i	x_{i+1}
0	1.49	1.395
1	1.395	1.397
2	1.397	1.402
3	1.402	1.421
4	1.421	1.419

Thus, the root of the given equation is 1.42.

2.20 Algorithm (AL25) for Newton–Raphson Method

This algorithm is transformed to a computer program written in C++ language and presented at the end of this chapter (see **p25.cpp**).

Let a be the initial value of the root for which $y = f(x)$ is to be tabulated for finding the root value.

1. Define the inline function $f(x) = x^2 + x - 2$.
2. Define the inline function derf = $2x + 1$ for derivative of $f(x)$.
3. Define eps = 0.0001.
4. Declare/define the function/subprogram **ntrp** to find the root.
5. Start the (main) function.
6. Define the main function which calls the subprogram/function according to the given choice.
7. Stop (main).

Details of function/subprogram **ntrp**:

```
1. Start
2. Input the initial root value, a
3. count = 0
       do
          if derf(a) > 0
          h1 = f(a)/(derf(a))
          c = a–h1
          count = count +1
       if (|((c–a)/c)| < eps and f(c) = 0)
          exit while loop
       else
          a = c
       endif
       while ((count =50) or (f(c)>eps)
4. Output 'root=', c
   output count, f(c)
5. Return
```

The algorithm for the generalized Newton's method is the same as that for the N–R method with the inclusion of multiplicity factor p, in the expression for x_{n+1}.

2.21 Secant Method

This iteration method is used for finding the root of a nonlinear equation $f(x) = 0$, without requiring the initial approximation to bracket the root value. The method is based on the construction of a secant between two positions on the curve $f(x)$ vs x as shown in Figure 2.4. Let x_1 and x_2 be the initial approximations to the root corresponding to points P and Q on the curve. On the extension side, the secant PQ cuts the x-axis at $x = x_3$ at the point R.

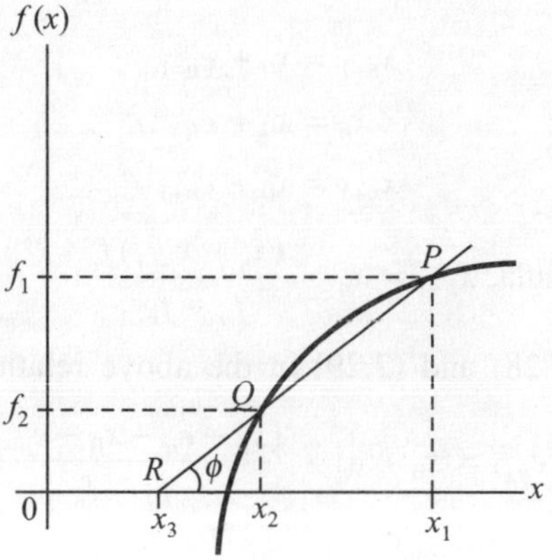

Figure 2.4 Secant method.

To obtain the value of the root in the $(n + 1)$th iteration the slope of the secant PQ is given by

$$\tan \phi = \frac{f_1}{x_1 - x_3} = \frac{f_2}{x_2 - x_3}$$

where $f_1 = f(x_1)$, $f_2 = f(x_2)$ and ϕ is the angle the secant PQR makes with the x-axis. Solving for x_3, which represents the new approximation to the value of the root,

$$x_3 = \frac{x_1 f_2 - x_2 f_1}{f_2 - f_1} \tag{2.25}$$

Adding and subtracting $x_2 f_2$ on the RHS in the above equation,

$$x_3 = x_2 - \frac{(x_2 - x_1) f_2}{f_2 - f_1}$$

In the next iteration replacing x_1 by x_2, x_2 by x_3, x_3 by x_4, f_1 by f_2 and f_2 by f_3, we obtain the next approximation to the root as

$$x_4 = x_3 - \frac{(x_3 - x_2) f_3}{f_3 - f_2}$$

In the $(n + 1)$th iteration the value of the root is given by

$$x_{n+1} = x_n - \frac{(x_n - x_{n-1}) f_n}{f_n - f_{n-1}} \qquad \text{(for } n \geq 2\text{)} \tag{2.26}$$

Equation (2.26) is called the secant formula.

Convergence of Secant Method

Let $x = x_0$ be the root of the equation $f(x) = 0$ and e be the error in its estimation during iterations. The root value in $(n - 1)$th, nth and $(n + 1)$th iterations is given by

$$x_{n-1} = x_0 + e_{n-1} \tag{2.27}$$

$$x_n = x_0 + e_n \tag{2.28}$$

$$x_{n+1} = x_0 + e_{n+1} \tag{2.29}$$

From the secant formula, $x_{n+1} = x_n - \dfrac{(x_n - x_{n-1})f_n}{f_n - f_{n-1}}$

Using Eqs. (2.27), (2.28) and (2.29) in the above relation, we get

$$x_0 + e_{n+1} = x_0 + e_n - \frac{(x_0 - e_n - x_0 - e_{n-1})f_n}{f_n - f_{n-1}}$$

This simplifies to

$$e_{n+1} = \frac{e_{n-1}f_n - e_n f_{n-1}}{f_n - f_{n-1}} \tag{2.30}$$

Using the mean value theorem, there exists at least one point $x = m_n$ in the interval $[x_n, x_0]$ such that

$$f'_{m(n)} = \frac{f_n - f_0}{x_n - x_0}$$

Since $f_0 = 0$ and $x_n - x_0 = e_n$, we get

$$f'_{m(n)} = \frac{f_n}{e_n}$$

or
$$f_n = f'_{m(n)}e_n \tag{2.31}$$

Similarly, we can write

$$f_{n-1} = f'_{m(n-1)}e_{n-1} \tag{2.32}$$

Using Eqs. (2.31) and (2.32) in Eq. (2.30), we get

$$e_{n+1} = \frac{e_{n-1}e_n(f'_{m(n)} - f'_{m(n-1)})}{f_n - f_{n-1}} \tag{2.33}$$

Thus, the error in the $(n + 1)$th iteration is proportional to the errors in the previous iterations. That is,

$$e_{n+1} \propto e_{n-1} \cdot e_n$$

Let p be the order of convergence such that

$$e_n \propto (e_{n-1})^p \tag{2.34}$$

and
$$e_{n+1} \propto (e_n)^p \tag{2.35}$$

Thus,
$$(e_n)^p \propto (e_{n-1})^{p+1}$$

or
$$e_n \propto (e_{n-1})^{(p+1)/p} \tag{2.36}$$

Comparing Eqs. (2.34) and (2.36), we get

$$p = \frac{p+1}{p}$$

or

$$p^2 - p - 1 = 0$$

On solving the preceding equation we get the order of convergence in secant method as $p = 1.618$. As this is lower than the value obtained for the N–R method, therefore, we conclude that the secant method is slower than the N–R method.

2.22 Numerical Examples (Secant Method)

EXAMPLE 2.17 Using the secant method, find a root of the following equation up to two decimal places.

$$f(x) = \cos x - xe^x = 0$$

Solution

Let us assume that the interval [0.5, 2.0] contains the root of the given equation.

We construct Table 2.27 to obtain the function values.

Table 2.27 Example 2.17

x	0.5	1.0	2.0
$f(x)$	0.05322	–2.1780	–15.194

We now construct Table 2.28 using the secant formula (2.26). For example, for $n = 2$, $x_1 = 0.5$, $x_2 = 1.0$, we obtain using Eq. (2.26) value of root $x_3 = 0.5119$. In the next iteration replacing x_1 by x_2 and x_2 by x_3 we get $x_4 = 0.5158$.

Table 2.28 Table of iterations—Example 2.17

n	x_{n-1}	x_n	x_{n+1}	f_{n-1}	f_n	f_{n+1}
2	0.5	1.0	0.5119	0.05322	–2.1780	0.0177
3	1.0	0.5119	0.5158	–2.1780	0.0177	0.0058
4	0.5119	0.5158	0.5178	0.0177	0.0058	0.0000

Thus, the root is $x = x_{n+1} = 0.5178$.

EXAMPLE 2.18 Using the secant method, find a root of the equation

$$f(x) = x^3 - 3x^2 + x + 1 = 0$$

given the interval $[x_1, x_2]$ as [0, 1.5] to contain the root up to two decimal places.

Solution

Taking $x_1 = 0$, $x_2 = 1.5$, we substitute $n = 2$ in secant formula (2.26) to obtain the next approximation to the root as $x_3 = 0.8$.

We construct Table 2.29, using the secant formula.

Table 2.29 Table of iterations—Example 2.18

n	x_{n-1}	x_n	x_{n+1}	f_{n-1}	f_n	f_{n+1}
2	0	1.5	0.8	1.0	–0.875	0.392
3	1.5	0.8	1.0165	–0.875	0.392	–0.0319
4	0.8	1.0165	0.999	0.392	–0.0319	0.0015
5	1.0165	0.999	0.9999	–0.0319	0.0015	0.0001
6	0.999	0.9999	1.0	0.0015	0.0001	0.00

Thus, the root is $x = x_{n+1} = 1.0$.

2.23 Algorithm (AL26) for Secant Method

This algorithm is transformed to a computer program written in C++ language and presented at the end of this chapter (see **p26.cpp**).

Let a be the initial value of the root for which $y = f(x)$ is to be tabulated for finding the root value. We make use of formula (2.25) to implement the secant method on computer.

1. Define the inline function $f(x) = x^2 + x - 2$.
2. Define eps = 0.0001.
3. Declare/define the function/subprogram **scnt** to find the root.
4. Start the (main) function.
5. Define the main function which calls the subprogram/function according to given choice.
6. Stop (main).

Details of function/subprogram **scnt**:

```
1. Start
2. Input the initial root interval a, b
3. If (f(b) – f(a)) > eps
      count=0
      do
      c = (a*f(b) – b*f(a))/(f(b) – f(a))
      if |(c–b)/c| < eps and f(c) = 0
      exit do loop
      else
          a = b
          b = c
      endif
```

count = count +1
while ((count =50) or (f(c)!=0)
4. Output 'root=', c
output count, f(c)
5. Return

2.24 Muller's Method

Consider a nonlinear equation $f(x) = 0$. Let the value of $f(x)$ at x_1, x_2, x_3 be f_1, f_2 and f_3 respectively.

In this method we assume a quadratic polynomial $p(x)$ to pass through three intersecting coordinate points (x_1, f_1), (x_2, f_2) and (x_3, f_3) of the $f(x)$ vs x plot as shown in Figure 2.5.

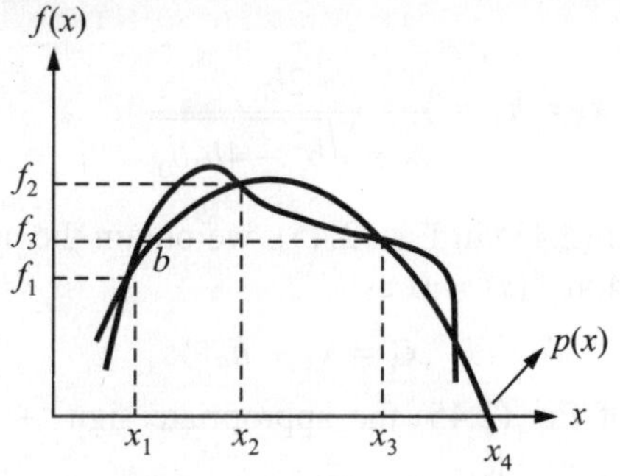

Figure 2.5 Muller's method.

The point $x = x_4$ represents an approximation to the root of the function $f(x)$.

Let the polynomial $p(x)$ be written as

$$p(x) = b_0 + b_1(x - x_a) + b_2(x - x_a)^2 \tag{2.37}$$

where $x = x_a$ can be any point x_1, x_2 or x_3.

Let $\quad x_a = x_3$

$$p(x_1) = b_0 + b_1(x_1 - x_3) + b_2(x_1 - x_3)^2 = f_1$$

$$p(x_2) = b_0 + b_1(x_2 - x_3) + b_2(x_2 - x_3)^2 = f_2$$

$$p(x_3) = b_0 + b_1(0) + b_2(0) = f_3$$

Let

$$\left.\begin{aligned} x_1 - x_3 &= h_1 \\ x_2 - x_3 &= h_2 \end{aligned}\right\} \tag{2.38}$$

Rewriting the above equations, we obtain

$$f_1 = b_2h_1^2 + b_1h_1 + b_0$$

$$f_2 = b_2h_2^2 + b_1h_2 + b_0$$

$$f_3 = b_0 \tag{2.39}$$

Now
$$f_1 - f_3 = d_1 = b_2h_1^2 + b_1h_1 \tag{2.40}$$
$$f_2 - f_3 = d_2 = b_2h_2^2 + b_1h_2 \tag{2.41}$$

Solving Eqs. (2.40) and (2.41) for b_1 and b_2, we get

$$b_1 = \frac{h_1^2 d_2 - h_2^2 d_1}{h_1 h_2 (h_1 - h_2)} = \frac{h_1^2 d_2 - h_2^2 d_1}{D} \tag{2.42}$$

$$b_2 = \frac{h_2 d_1 - h_1 d_2}{h_1 h_2 (h_1 - h_2)} = \frac{h_2 d_1 - h_1 d_2}{D} \tag{2.43}$$

where
$$D = h_1 h_2 (h_1 - h_2) \tag{2.44}$$

At $x = x_4$, Eq. (2.37) gives

$$p(x_4) = b_0 + b_1(x_4 - x_3) + b_2(x_4 - x_3)^2 = 0$$

Solving this, we get

$$x_4 - x_3 = h_4 = \frac{-2b_0}{b_1 \pm \sqrt{b_1^2 - 4b_2 b_0}} \tag{2.45}$$

Using Eqs. (2.42) and (2.43) in Eq. (2.45), we obtain the approximate value of the root of the equation $f(x) = 0$ as

$$x_4 = x_3 + h_4$$

In the denominator of Eq. (2.45) the appropriate sign '+' or '–' is chosen to make h_4 as small as possible.

The above steps are repeated with initial values chosen as x_2, x_3 and x_4 to obtain the next approximation to the root value $x_5 = x_4 + h_5$.

The process ends when sufficient condition for accuracy is satisfied.

EXAMPLE 2.19 Solve the following nonlinear equation by Muller's method.

$$f(x) = x^3 + 2x^2 + 10x - 20 = 0$$

given the initial values $x_1 = 0$, $x_2 = 1$, $x_3 = 2$.

Solution

Let
$$x_a = x_3 = 2$$

Therefore, the polynomial $p(x)$ is

$$p(x) = b_0 + b_1(x - 2) + b_2(x - 2)^2$$
$$f(x_1) = f_1 = -20$$
$$f(x_2) = f_2 = -7$$
$$f(x_3) = f_3 = 16$$
$$h_1 = x_1 - x_3 = -2,\ h_2 = x_2 - x_3 = -1,\ d_1 = f_1 - f_3 = -36$$
$$d_2 = f_2 - f_3 = -23,\ D = h_1 h_2 (h_1 - h_2) = -2$$

We can now estimate b_0, b_1 and b_2 as follows:

From Eq. (2.39), we get $b_0 = f_3 = 16$

From Eq. (2.42), we get $b_1 = h_1^2 d_2 - h_2^2 d_1/D = 28$

From Eq. (2.43), we get $b_2 = (h_2 d_1 - h_1 d_2)/D = 5$

Therefore, from Eq. (2.45), we get $h_4 = -0.646$ (using '+' sign).

The next approximation to the root is $x_4 = x_3 + h_4 = 1.354$.

For the next iteration, we choose $x_1 = 1$, $x_2 = 2$, $x_3 = 1.354$ and repeat the steps as above.

The final value of the root obtained after four iterations is $x = 1.369$.

2.25 Algorithm (AL27) for Muller's Method

1. Define the function f(x), ε
2. Assume three values x_1, x_2, and x_3 close to the approximate root.
3. $f(x_1) = f_1$, $f(x_2) = f_2$ and $f(x_3) = f_3$.
4. $h_1 = x_1 - x_3$, $h_2 = x_2 - x_3$, $d_1 = f_1 - f_3$, $d_2 = f_2 - f_3$, $D = h_1 h_2 (h_1 - h_2)$
5. $b_0 = f_3$, $b_1 = (d_2 h_1^2 - d_1 h_2^2)/D$, $b_2 = (d_1 h_2 - d_2 h_1)/D$
6. $h_4 = -2b_0 \Big/ \left(b_1 \pm \sqrt{b_1^2 - 4b_2 b_0}\right)$
7. $x_4 = x_3 + h_4$
8. If $f(x_4) \le \varepsilon$
   go to end
9. $x_1 = x_2$, $x_2 = x_3$, $x_3 = x_4$
10. go to step 3
11. End
12. Output x_4

2.26 Comments and Conclusions

In this chapter we discussed the following numerical methods—Fixed-point iteration method, Bisection method, False position method, N–R method, Secant method and Muller's method. There are merits and demerits of each of these methods with respect to their following parameters:

1. Efficiency
2. Rates of convergence to the root
3. Dependence on initial approximation of the root value.

By efficiency we mean the amount of calculation required to be done by the computer in an iteration.

The convergence to the root can be slow or fast depending upon the rate of convergence of the method concerned.

In some of the methods the initial approximation to the value of the root can be very critical for convergence to the root.

The fixed-point method is easy to program but convergence is not guaranteed. It is an efficient method as only one calculation of the function is required per iteration.

The convergence is guaranteed in the bisection method but the rate of convergence is slow. It is efficient as only one calculation of the function is required per iteration.

The false-position method is slow to converge but convergence is guaranteed. It is faster than the bisection method and equally efficient.

In the N–R method the convergence is not guaranteed. It is the fastest of all methods to converge to the root but least efficient of all because two calculations per iteration are required. Also in this method, convergence depends strongly on the initial value of the root. If a suitable initial value of the root is made, the N–R method converges faster than the false-position and the secant methods. But the N–R method may diverge if the initial choice is not made nearer to the actual value of the root.

The secant method is more efficient than the N–R method as it requires only one calculation per iteration. In the secant method the root may not bracket the initial approximation interval and the method is even faster than the false-position method but convergence is not assured and, therefore, in using this method a limit on the maximum number of iterations to be performed should be specified. The Muller's method being an extension of the secant method, uses a quadratic polynomial to determine the root. The Muller's method is more accurate than the secant method though slow to converge.

Exercises

1. Solve the following equations for a root by (a) the bisection method and (b) the false-position method.

(i) $2x - 3 \sin x - 5 = 0$ [**Ans.** 2.883]

(ii) $x^3 + x^2 - 1 = 0$ [**Ans.** 0.755]

(iii) $x - \ln (2(x + 1)) = 0$ [**Ans.** 1.68]

2. Solve the following equations for a root by the N–R method.

(i) $x^7 - 5 = 0$ [**Ans.** 1.258]

(ii) $x^9 - 87 = 0$ [**Ans.** 1.647]

(iii) $x^3 + 7x^2 + 9 = 0$ [**Ans.** –7.175]

(iv) $2x - 3 \sin x - 5 = 0$ [**Ans.** 2.883]

(v) $\tan x + x = 0$ [**Ans.** 2.03]

3. Solve the following equations for a root by the secant method.

(i) $2x - 6 - \log_{10} x = 0$ [**Ans.** 3.256]

(ii) $x^4 - x - 9 = 0$ [**Ans.** 1.813]

(iii) $2x - \cos x - 3 = 0$ [**Ans.** 1.524]

4. Solve the following equations for a root by the fixed-point iteration method.

(i) $2x - 7 - \log_{10} x = 0$ [**Ans.** 3.79]

(ii) $x^2 - \sin x = 0$ [**Ans.** 0.877]

(iii) $3x - \cos x - 1 = 0$ [**Ans.** 0.607]

(iv) $x^2 + \ln x - 2 = 0$ [**Ans.** 1.31]

5. Solve the following equation for a root by the generalized Newton's method.

$f(x) = x^3 - x^2 - x + 1 = 0$ by choosing an initial value 0.8

[**Ans.** 1.0001]

C++ Programs

The C++ programs can be implemented on any O/S, namely

1. Windows O/S using Turbo C++, Dev C++ and Visual C++ compilers.
2. Linux-based Ubuntu/Knoppix/Redhat O/S using GNU C++ compiler.

These compilers have been discussed in Chapter 0. No change is required if Ubuntu is used.

While using Turbo C++, Dev C++ and Visual C++ compilers, note the following points for every program.

- Use header file `#include <iostream.h>` (for Turbo C++ only)
- Use header file `#include <math.h>`
- Use header file `#include <conio.h>`
- Use `getch()` function before the closing bracket '}' of the `main()` function.

Program: p21.cpp

```
//Search interval by tabulation method
#include <iostream>
#include<iomanip>
using namespace std;
inline float func(float x)
   {
     return (x*x*x-4*x-9);
     }
void sit()
   {
     float xi,xf,dx,x,y;
     char option;
   cout<<"For default input values enter 'y' else 'n'\n";
   cin>>option;
   if (option=='y')
     {
       xi=1; xf=4; dx=1;
     }
   else
   {
     cout<<"input initial,final,step-size values, xi xf dx\n";
     cin>>xi>>xf>>dx;
     }
     x=xi;
     cout<<"x   y\n";
     while (x<xf)
```

```
      {
         y=func(x);
       cout<<x<<"    "<<setprecision(4)<<y<<endl;
         x=x+dx;
      }
    }
main()
{
   sit();
}
```

Program: p22.cpp

```
//FIXED-point iteration method
#include <iostream>
#include <cmath>
#define eps 0.0001
using namespace std;
inline float f(float x)
   {
     return 1/(9-x*x);
     }
void fpt()
   {
     float a,c;
     int count,maxit;
     char option;
     cout<<"For default input values enter 'y' else 'n'\n";
     cin>>option;
     if (option=='y')
     a=0;
     else
     {
     cout<<"input initial root value\n";
     cin>>a;
     }
     maxit=50;
     for (count=1;count<=maxit;count++)
       {
         c=f(a);
         if (fabs((c-a)/c)>eps)
           a=c;
           else
           break;
       }
```

```
      cout<<"root=  "<<c<<endl;
      cout<<"f(root)=  "<<f(c)<<endl;
      cout<<"iterations=  "<<count<<endl;
      }
main()
{
   fpt();
}
```

Program: p23.cpp

```
//Bisection method
#include <iostream>
#include <cmath>
#define eps 0.0001
using namespace std;
inline float f(float x)
   {
     return x*x*x-9*x+1;
     }
void bisec()
   {
     float a,b,c;
     int count;
     char option;
     cout<<"For default input values enter 'y' else 'n'\n";
     cin>>option;
   if (option=='y')
     {
       a=2; b=3;
     }
   else
   {
     cout<<"input initial root interval a, b\n";
     cin>>a>>b;
   }
   if ((f(a)*f(b))<0)
     {
       count=0;
       do
       {
         c=(a+b)*0.5;
         if (f(a)*f(c)<0)
            b=c;
         else
            a=c;
```

```
        count=count+1;
        } while ((count<=20) && fabs(f(c))>eps);
      cout<<"root=  "<<c<<endl;
      cout<<"f(root)=  "<<f(c)<<endl;
      cout<<"iterations=  "<<count<<endl;
      }
      else
        cout<<"initial interval incorrect\n";
}
main()
{
   bisec();
}
```

Program: p24.cpp

```
//Regula-Falsi/false position method
#include <iostream>
#include <cmath>
#define eps 0.0001
using namespace std;
inline float f(float x)
   {
     return x*x*x-9*x+1;
   }
void regfal()
   {
     float a,b,c;
     int count=0;
     char option;
     cout<<"For default input values enter 'y' else 'n'\n";
     cin>>option;
   if (option=='y')
     {
       a=2; b=3;
     }
   else
   {
     cout<<"input initial root interval a, b\n";
     cin>>a>>b;
   }
   if ((f(a)*f(b))<0)
     {
     count=0;
     do
```

```
    {  c=(a*f(b)-b*f(a))/(f(b)-f(a));
       if  (f(a)*f(c)<0)
         b=c;
         else
           a=c;
           count=count+1;
    } while  ((count<=20)  &&  fabs(f(c))>eps);
  cout<<"root=  "<<c<<endl;
  cout<<"f(root)=  "<<f(c)<<endl;
  cout<<"iterations=  "<<count<<endl;
  }
}
main()
{
  regfal();
 }
```

Program: p25.cpp

```
//Newton-Raphson method
#include <iostream>
#include <cmath>
#define eps 0.00001
using namespace std;
inline float f(float x)
  {
    return x*x*x-9*x+1;
    }
inline float derf(float x)
  {
    return (3*x*x-9);
    }
void ntrp()
  {
    float a,c,h1;
    int count;
    char option;
    cout<<"For default input values enter 'y' else 'n'\n";
    cin>>option;
  if (option=='y')
    {
      a=2;
    }
  else
  {
  cout<<"input initial root value a\n";
```

```
    cin>>a;
    }
    count=0;
     do
     {
       if (derf(a)>0)
         h1=f(a)/derf(a);
         c=a-h1;
         count=count+1;
       if ((fabs((c-a)/c)<eps) && (f(c)==0))
       break;
       else
       a=c;
         }
       while ((count<=20) && fabs(f(c))>eps);
    cout<<"root=  "<<c<<endl;
    cout<<"f(c)=  "<<f(c)<<endl;
    cout<<"iterations=  "<<count<<endl;
}
main()
{
    ntrp();
}
```

Program: p26.cpp

```
//Secant method
#include <iostream>
#include <cmath>
#define eps 0.0001
using namespace std;
inline float f(float x)
    {
      return x*x*x-9*x+1;
      }
void scnt()
    {
      float a,b,c;
      int count;
        char option;
      cout<<"For default input values enter 'y' else 'n'\n";
      cin>>option;
    if (option=='y')
      {
        a=2; b=3;
      }
```

```
   else
   {
     cout<<"input  initial  root  interval  a,  b\n";
     cin>>a>>b;
   }
   if  ((f(b)-f(a))>eps)
     {
       count=0;
       do
       {  c=(a*f(b)-b*f(a))/(f(b)-f(a));
          if  ((fabs((c-b)/c)<eps)  &&  (f(c)==0))
            break;
          else
            {a=b;
            b=c;
          }
          count=count+1;
       } while  ((count<=20)  &&  fabs(f(c))>eps);
     cout<<"root=  "<<c<<endl;
     cout<<"f(root)=  "<<f(c)<<endl;
     cout<<"iterations=  "<<count<<endl;
     }
}
main()
{
   scnt();
}
```

3

Solution of Simultaneous Linear Equations

3.1 Introduction

In the field of science and engineering the system of simultaneous linear algebraic equations occurs quite often in areas like mechanics, electric circuits, heat transfer, etc. For example, a system of three simultaneous equations in three unknowns x, y and z is given by

$$4x + 3y - 2z = 5$$
$$x - 3y - 2z = 2$$
$$3x - 5y - z = 8$$

If a system of equations contains as many equations as there are unknowns in it, then a unique solution is said to exist.

In general, a system of m-equations which are algebraic, linear and homogeneous or non-homogeneous containing n-unknowns $(x_1, x_2, x_3, \ldots, x_n)$, can be written as

$$\left.\begin{aligned} a_{11}x_1 + a_{12}x_2 + \cdots + a_{1n}x_n &= b_1 \quad (1)\\ a_{21}x_1 + a_{22}x_2 + \cdots + a_{2n}x_n &= b_2 \quad (2)\\ &\vdots\\ a_{m1}x_1 + a_{m2}x_2 + \cdots + a_{mn}x_n &= b_m \quad (n) \end{aligned}\right\} \qquad (3.1)$$

If $m = n$, then the above system of equations has a unique solution. Thus, we have to solve n-equations in n-unknowns. The above equations can also be written in matrix form as

$$AX = B$$

$$\text{where } A = \begin{vmatrix} a_{11} & a_{12} & \cdots & a_{1n} \\ a_{21} & a_{22} & \cdots & a_{2n} \\ \vdots & \vdots & & \vdots \\ a_{n1} & a_{n2} & \cdots & a_{nn} \end{vmatrix} \text{ is called the coefficient matrix.}$$

$$X = \begin{vmatrix} x_1 \\ x_2 \\ \vdots \\ x_n \end{vmatrix} \text{ is called the solution vector.}$$

$$B = \begin{vmatrix} b_1 \\ b_2 \\ \vdots \\ b_n \end{vmatrix} \text{ is called the column vector.}$$

In the augmented form the matrix A can be written by including the B matrix elements as follows:

$$\text{aug } A = \begin{vmatrix} a_{11} & a_{12} & \cdots & a_{1n} & a_{1\,n+1} \\ a_{21} & a_{22} & \cdots & a_{2n} & a_{2\,n+1} \\ \vdots & \vdots & & \vdots & \vdots \\ a_{n1} & a_{n2} & \cdots & a_{nn} & a_{n\,n+1} \end{vmatrix}$$

where $a_{1\,n+1} = b_1$, $a_{2\,n+1} = b_2$, ..., $a_{n\,n+1} = b_n$.

A solution to the above equations can be found by the following common algebraic methods:

1. Using the elimination of variables method which is suitable only if the number of unknowns is not more than three.
2. Using the determinant method (Cramer's rule) which is also only suitable when the determinant A is a nonzero and has an inverse.

The numerical methods to solve the above set of equations are of two types.

Direct Methods (also called elimination methods)

In these methods, the system of equations is manipulated to a form from which the solution is obtained by simple back substitution. The direct methods include the following methods:

(a) Gauss elimination method (with and without pivoting)
(b) Gauss–Jordan method
(c) Matrix inversion method
(d) Crout's method (LU decomposition)

Indirect Methods (also called iteration methods)

In these methods, an approximate solution of the system of equations is assumed and then the sequence of computation is repeated to obtain the solution of desired accuracy.

Iteration methods are more useful when the coefficient matrix contains many zeros but with a necessary condition that the diagonal elements should have large magnitudes compared to the other elements of the matrix. The following methods are covered under this category.

(a) Jacobi's method

(b) Gauss–Seidel method

3.2 Gauss Elimination Method

This method consists of the following two steps to solve a system of n-equations in n-unknowns.

Step 1: Triangularization

Step 2: Back substitution

In Step 1, the system of equations is reduced to a triangular form by eliminating successively variables $x_1, x_2, x_3, \ldots, x_{n-1}$ from the given equations.

The procedure of elimination is illustrated below:

1. First, eliminate x_1 from equations (2), (3), …, (n) of the set of Eqs. (3.1) using the following steps:

I. Multiply (1) by (a_{21}/a_{11}) and subtract from (2) to get (2i) modified as $(a_{21} - (a_{21}/a_{11})a_{11})x_1 + (a_{22} - (a_{21}/a_{11})a_{12})x_2 + \cdots + (a_{2n} - (a_{21}/a_{11})a_{1n})x_1 = b_2 - (a_{21}/a_{11})b_1$, which simplifies to

$$a_{22}x_2 + a_{23}x_3 + \cdots + a_{2n}x_n = b_2 \qquad \text{(2i)}$$

Note that (2i) is the modified form of (2).

II. Multiply (1) by (a_{31}/a_{11}) and subtract from (3) to get (3i) modified as $(a_{31} - (a_{31}/a_{11})a_{11})x_1 + (a_{32} - (a_{21}/a_{11})a_{12})x_2 + \cdots + (a_{2n} - (a_{21}/a_{11})a_{1n})x_n = b_3 - (a_{21}/a_{11})b_1$, which simplifies to

$$a_{32}x_2 + a_{33}x_3 + \cdots + a_{3n}x_n = b_3 \qquad \text{(3i)}$$

Now continuing this process up to the nth equation, we obtain

$$\begin{array}{ll} a_{42}x_2 + a_{43}x_3 + \cdots + a_{4n}x_n = b_4 & \text{(4i)} \\ \vdots \qquad \vdots \qquad \vdots \qquad \vdots & \\ a_{n2}x_2 + a_{n3}x_3 + \cdots + a_{nn}x_n = b_n & (ni) \end{array}$$

Note that in modified equations (2i), (3i), …, (ni) the coefficients a_{ij} and b_i are modified from their initial values because of the algebraic manipulations in Steps I and II.

2. Second, eliminate x_2 from equations (2i), (3i), ..., (*n*i) using the following steps:

I. Multiply (2i) by (a_{32}/a_{22}) and subtract from (3i) to get (3ii) modified as

$$a_{33}x_3 + a_{34}x_4 + \cdots + a_{3n}x_n = b_3 \qquad \text{(3ii)}$$

II. Multiply (2i) by (a_{42}/a_{22}) and subtract from (4i) to get (4ii) modified as

$$a_{43}x_3 + a_{44}x_4 + \cdots + a_{4n}x_n = b_4 \qquad \text{(4ii)}$$

and continue this process up to the *n*th equation,

$$a_{n3}x_3 + a_{n4}x_4 + \cdots + a_{nn}x_n = b_n \qquad (n\text{ii})$$

Note that in the above equations the coefficients a_{ij} and b_i are modified from their previous values because of the algebraic manipulations in Steps I and II.

3. Repeating the above procedure of elimination up to the x_{n-1} unknowns so that the last equation contains only one unknown x_n, we obtain the following triangular form of *n*-equations.

$$\left.\begin{aligned}
a_{11}x_1 + a_{12}x_2 + \cdots + a_{1n}x_n &= b_1 && (1)\\
a_{22}x_2 + a_{23}x_3 + \cdots + a_{2n}x_n &= b_2 && (2)\\
a_{33}x_3 + a_{34}x_4 + \cdots + a_{3n}x_n &= b_3 && (3)\\
&\vdots\\
a_{n-1\,n-1}x_{n-1} + a_{n-1\,n}x_n &= b_{n-1} && (n-1)\\
a_{nn}x_n &= b_n && (n)
\end{aligned}\right\} \qquad (3.2)$$

The above procedure is termed *triangularization*. In matrix form the above set of equations can be written as

$$\text{aug } A = \begin{vmatrix}
a_{11} & a_{12} & \cdots & a_{1n} & a_{1\,n+1}\\
0 & a_{22} & \cdots & a_{2n} & a_{2\,n+1}\\
0 & 0 & a_{33} & a_{3n} & a_{3\,n+1}\\
 & & & \vdots & \\
0 & 0 & 0 & a_{nn} & a_{n\,n+1}
\end{vmatrix}$$

where $a_{1\,n+1} = b_1$, $a_{2\,n+1} = b_2$, ..., $a_{n\,n+1} = b_n$.

In Step 2 involving back-substitution, the value of x_n is obtained from the above (*n*)th equation as

$$x_n = \frac{b_n}{a_{nn}}$$

Substituting this into the $(n-1)$th equation gives the value of x_{n-1} as

$$x_{n-1} = \frac{b_{n-1} - a_{n-1\,n}x_n}{a_{n-1\,n-1}}$$

Continuing this procedure of back-substitution into the triangular form of the equations, we obtain values of all the unknowns. In general, the value of the *i*th unknown is given by

$$x_i = \frac{b_i - \Sigma a_{ik} x_k}{a_{ii}}$$

where the Σ is from $k = i + 1$ to $k = n$.

Note that the values of the coefficients a_{ij} and b_i of the matrix equation $AX = B$, are modified during triangularization as

$$a_{ij} = a_{ij} - a_{kj}\frac{a_{ik}}{a_{kk}}$$

where $k = 1$ to $n - 1$, $i = k + 1$ to n, $j = k$ to $n + 1$ and $a_{kk} \neq 0$.

3.3 Numerical Examples (Based on Gauss Elimination Method)

EXAMPLE 3.1 Solve the following system of equations using the Gauss elimination method.

$$x_1 + \frac{x_2}{2} + \frac{x_3}{3} = 1 \qquad (R_1)$$

$$\frac{x_1}{2} + \frac{x_2}{3} + \frac{x_3}{4} = 0 \qquad (R_2)$$

$$\frac{x_1}{3} + \frac{x_2}{4} + \frac{x_3}{5} = 0 \qquad (R_3)$$

Solution

The coefficients of the matrix A are:

$$a_{11} = 1 \quad a_{12} = \frac{1}{2} \quad a_{13} = \frac{1}{3} \quad a_{14} = 1$$

$$a_{21} = \frac{1}{2} \quad a_{22} = \frac{1}{3} \quad a_{23} = \frac{1}{4} \quad a_{24} = 0$$

$$a_{31} = \frac{1}{3} \quad a_{32} = \frac{1}{4} \quad a_{33} = \frac{1}{5} \quad a_{34} = 0$$

For elimination of x_1 from (R_2) and (R_3):

Operation: $(R_2) - \frac{a_{21}}{a_{11}}(R_1)$ gives $\frac{x_2}{12} + \frac{x_3}{12} = -\frac{1}{2}$ $(R_2\text{i})$

Operation: $(R_3) - \frac{a_{31}}{a_{11}}(R_1)$ gives $\frac{x_2}{12} + \frac{4x_3}{45} = -\frac{1}{3}$ $(R_3\text{i})$

The modified coefficients are:

$$a_{22} = \frac{1}{12} \quad a_{23} = \frac{1}{12} \quad a_{24} = -\frac{1}{2}$$

$$a_{32} = \frac{1}{12} \quad a_{33} = \frac{4}{55} \quad a_{34} = -\frac{1}{3}$$

For elimination of x_2 from (R_3i),

Operation: $(R_3\text{i}) - \frac{a_{32}}{a_{22}}(R_2\text{i})$ gives $\frac{x_3}{180} = \frac{1}{6}$ (R_3ii)

The triangular form of the given system of equations is given by

$$x_1 + \frac{x_2}{2} + \frac{x_3}{3} = 1 \qquad (R_1)$$

$$\frac{x_2}{12} + \frac{x_3}{12} = -\frac{1}{2} \qquad (R_2)$$

$$\frac{x_3}{180} = \frac{1}{6} \qquad (R_3)$$

The back-substitution of the values into the equations gives

$$x_3 = 30, \quad x_2 = -36, \quad x_1 = 9$$

EXAMPLE 3.2 Solve the following system of equations using the Gauss elimination method.

$$2x_1 + 8x_2 + 2x_3 = 14 \qquad (R_1)$$
$$x_1 + 6x_2 - x_3 = 13 \qquad (R_2)$$
$$2x_1 - x_2 + 2x_3 = 5 \qquad (R_3)$$

Solution

For elimination of x_1 from (R_2) and (R_3):

Operation: $(R_2) - \frac{a_{21}}{a_{11}}(R_1)$ gives $2x_2 - 2x_3 = 6$ (R_2i)

Operation: $(R_3) - \frac{a_{31}}{a_{11}}(R_1)$ gives $-9x_2 + 0x_3 = -9$ (R_3i)

For elimination of x_2 from (R_3i):

Operation: $(R_3) - \frac{a_{32}}{a_{22}}(R_2\text{i})$ gives $-9x_3 = 18$ (R_3ii)

The back-substitution of the values into the equations gives

$$x_3 = -2, \quad x_2 = 1, \quad x_1 = 5$$

3.4 Algorithm (AL31) for Triangularization in Gauss Elimination Method

This algorithm is transformed to a computer program written in C++ language and presented at the end of this chapter (see **p31.cpp**).

1. Define the error limit eps = 0.00001.
2. Declare/define the function/subprogram **gel** to implement the method for triangularization and back-substitution.
3. Start the (main) function.
4. Define the main function which calls the appropriate subprogram/function according to given choice.
5. Stop (main).

Details of function/subprogram **gel**:

1. Start
2. Input the number of equations/rows/columns/unknowns, n
3. For i = 1 to n do
   For j = 1 to (n + 1) do
   read (a_{ij})
   end {for}
4. For k = 1 to (n – 1) do
   For i = (k + 1) to n do
   aik = a_{ik}/a_{kk}
   For j = k to (n + 1) do
   $a_{ij} = a_{ij} - a_{kj} * aik$
   end {for}
   end {for}
   end {for} (triangularization complete)
   back-substitution start
5. Compute $x_n = a_{nn+1}/a_{nn}$
6. For i = (n – 1) to 1 do
   s = 0
   For j = (i + 1) to n do
   $s = s + a_{ij} x_j$
   end {for}
   $x_i = (a_{in+1} - s)/a_{ii}$
   end {for}
7. For i = 1 to n do
   output solution x_i
8. Return

In the above algorithm we have used the augmented matrix elements $a_{i\,n+1} = b_i$ for $i = 1$ to n.

3.5 Gauss Elimination Method (with Pivoting)

The basic Gauss elimination method fails to solve a given system of equations if the diagonal element a_{ii} is zero in any of the equations.

In such a situation the Gauss elimination method (with pivoting) is used in which that equation (or row of the coefficient matrix) is interchanged with the equation (or row) having the largest absolute (called the pivot element) value of the coefficient in the given position. The method is illustrated in the following steps:

(a) From the first column of the coefficient matrix the coefficient with the largest absolute value (pivot element) is located.
(b) The row corresponding to the largest coefficient [of step (a)] is then interchanged with the first row of the coefficient matrix.
(c) From this system of equations the first variable is eliminated from the second equation using the basic Gauss elimination method.
(d) Now from the second column of the second row to the nth row of the coefficient matrix, the coefficient having the largest absolute value (pivot element) is searched.
(e) The second row is interchanged with the row containing the largest absolute coefficient found in step (d).
(f) The above procedure is continued till the $(n - 1)$ unknowns are eliminated from the equations.

This procedure is called *pivoting*. Note that the partial pivoting procedure can be used even if the pivot element is nonzero in order to improve the accuracy of the result.

3.6 Numerical Examples [Gauss Elimination (with Pivoting) Method]

EXAMPLE 3.3 Using the Gauss Elimination method, solve the following system of equations:

$$2x_1 + 2x_2 + x_3 = 6 \qquad (R_1)$$

$$4x_1 + 2x_2 + 3x_3 = 4 \qquad (R_2)$$

$$x_1 - x_2 + x_3 = 0 \qquad (R_3)$$

Solution

The coefficient matrix is given by

$$\begin{vmatrix} 2 & 2 & 1 & 6 \\ 4 & 2 & 3 & 4 \\ 1 & -1 & 1 & 0 \end{vmatrix}$$

From the first column of the above matrix, the pivot element (the largest absolute value element) is 4. Interchanging the row corresponding to this element with the first row, we obtain

$$\begin{vmatrix} 4 & 2 & 3 & 4 \\ 2 & 2 & 1 & 6 \\ 1 & -1 & 1 & 0 \end{vmatrix}$$

Eliminating the first variable from the second row onwards using the basic Gauss elimination method, the coefficient matrix of the new system of equations is obtained as

$$\begin{vmatrix} 4 & 2 & 3 & 4 \\ 0 & 1 & -\dfrac{1}{2} & 4 \\ 0 & -\dfrac{3}{2} & \dfrac{1}{4} & -1 \end{vmatrix}$$

From the second row onwards the pivot element is searched in the second column. It can be seen that it is –3/2.

Interchanging the second row with the pivot element row,

$$\begin{vmatrix} 4 & 2 & 3 & 4 \\ 0 & -\dfrac{3}{2} & \dfrac{1}{4} & -1 \\ 0 & 1 & -\dfrac{1}{2} & \dfrac{10}{3} \end{vmatrix}$$

Eliminating the second variable from the second row onwards using the basic Guass elimination method, we get the new coefficient matrix as

$$\begin{vmatrix} 4 & 2 & 3 & 4 \\ 0 & -\dfrac{3}{2} & \dfrac{1}{4} & -1 \\ 0 & 0 & -\dfrac{1}{3} & \dfrac{10}{3} \end{vmatrix}$$

which gives the third row as $-\dfrac{1}{3}x_3 = \dfrac{10}{3}$ or $x_3 = -10$

Back substituting the value of x_3 into the second row,

$$-\frac{3}{2}x_2 + \frac{1}{4}x_3 = -1 \quad \text{or} \quad -\frac{3}{2}x_2 - \frac{10}{4} = -1 \quad \text{or} \quad x_2 = -1$$

Similarly, we can get $x_1 = 9$.

3.7 Algorithm (AL32) for Gauss Elimination Method with Pivoting

Starting with the basic Gauss elimination method, the following steps are to be inserted at step 4 between the first two lines of the algorithm (AL31) of the basic method. The complete algorithm is as follows.

This algorithm is transformed to a computer program written in C++ language and presented at the end of this chapter (see **p32.cpp**).

1. Define the error limit eps = 0.00001.
2. Declare/define the function/subprogram **gelp** to implement the method for triangularization with pivoting and back-substitution.
3. Start the (main) function.
4. Define the main function which calls the appropriate subprogram/ function according to given choice.
5. Stop (main).

Details of function/subprogram **gelp**:

```
1. Start
2. Input the number of equations/rows/columns/unknowns, n
3. For i = 1 to n do
      For j = 1 to (n + 1) do
      read (a_ij)
   end {for}
4. For k = 1 to (n – 1) do
   begin
      max = |a_kk|
      p = k
      for m = (k + 1) to n
      begin
         if (|a_mk| > max) then
         begin
            max = |a_mk|
            p = m
         endif
      end
   if p ≠ k then
   begin
      For q = k to (n + 1) do
      begin
         temp = a_kq
         a_kq = a_pq
         a_pq = temp
         end {for}
      endif (pivoting complete)
```

```
        For i = (k + 1) to n do
        begin
           aik = a_ik/a_kk
           For j = k to (n + 1) do
           a_ij = a_ij − a_kj*aik
        end {for}
     end {for}
     end {for} (triangularization with pivoting complete)
     back-substitution start
  5. Compute x_n = a_nn+1/a_nn
  6. For i = (n − 1) to 1 do
     s = 0
     For j = (i + 1) to n do
     s = s + a_ij x_j
     end {for}
     x_i = (a_in+1 − s)/a_ii
     end {for}
  7. For i = 1 to n do
     output solution x_i
  8. Return
```

In the above algorithm we have used the augmented matrix elements $a_{i\,n+1} = b_i$ for i = 1 to n.

3.8 Gauss–Jordan Method

This method is an improvement over the Gauss elimination method. In this method the need for back-substitution of the values of unknowns is not required. During the procedure of triangularization itself the system of equations resukts in a diagonal matrix from which the solution is obtained trivially. This method is illustrated in the following steps:

1. Given the set of equations (3.3):

$$\left.\begin{aligned} a_{11}x_1 + a_{12}x_2 + \cdots + a_{1n}x_n &= b_1 \qquad (1)\\ a_{21}x_1 + a_{22}x_2 + \cdots + a_{2n}x_n &= b_2 \qquad (2)\\ &\vdots\\ a_{n1}x_1 + a_{n2}x_2 + \cdots + a_{nn}x_n &= b_n \qquad (n) \end{aligned}\right\} \quad (3.3)$$

For elimination of variable x_1 from the second equation onwards, we do the following opertions:

$$(2) - \left(\frac{a_{12}}{a_{11}}\right) * (1)$$

$$(3) - \left(\frac{a_{31}}{a_{11}}\right) * (1)$$

$$(4) - \left(\frac{a_{41}}{a_{11}}\right) * (1)$$

$$\vdots$$

$$(n) - \left(\frac{a_{n1}}{a_{11}}\right) * (1)$$

The above steps give the following set of equations:

$$\left.\begin{array}{ll} x_1 + a_{12}x_2 + \cdots + a_{1n}x_n = b_1 & (1) \\ 0x_1 + a_{22}x_2 + \cdots + a_{2n}x_n = b_2 & (2) \\ 0x_1 + a_{32}x_2 + \cdots + a_{3n}x_n = b_3 & (3) \\ \vdots & \\ 0x_1 + a_{n2}x_2 + \cdots + a_{nn}x_n = b_n & (n) \end{array}\right\} \quad (3.4)$$

2. To eliminate x_2 from all equations except the second equation, we do the following operations:

$$(1) - \left(\frac{a_{12}}{a_{22}}\right) * (2)$$

$$(3) - \left(\frac{a_{32}}{a_{22}}\right) * (2)$$

$$(4) - \left(\frac{a_{42}}{a_{22}}\right) * (2)$$

$$\vdots$$

$$(n) - \left(\frac{a_{n2}}{a_{22}}\right) * (2)$$

This results in the following equations:

$$\left.\begin{array}{ll} x_1 + 0x_2 + \cdots + a_{1n}x_n = b_1 & (1) \\ 0x_1 + x_2 + \cdots + a_{2n}x_n = b_2 & (2) \\ 0x_1 + 0x_2 + \cdots + a_{3n}x_n = b_3 & (3) \\ \vdots & \\ 0x_1 + 0x_2 + \cdots + a_{nn}x_n = b_n & (n) \end{array}\right\} \quad (3.5)$$

Continuing the above process, we eliminate

All x's from the first equation except x_1
All x's from the second equation except x_2
All x's from the third equation except x_3

and so on.

Thus, we get the following sets of equations

$$\left.\begin{array}{lr} x_1 + 0x_2 \quad + \cdots + 0x_n = b_1 & (1) \\ 0x_1 + x_2 \quad + \cdots + 0x_n = b_2 & (2) \\ 0x_1 + 0x_2 + x_3 + \cdots + 0x_n = b_3 & (3) \\ \vdots & \\ 0x_1 + 0x_2 \quad + \cdots + x_n = b_n & (n) \end{array}\right\} \tag{3.6}$$

The solution is now trivial

$$x_1 = b_1,\ x_2 = b_2,\ x_3 = b_3,\ \ldots\ x_n = b_n$$

where b_1, b_2, b_3, ..., b_n are the modified coefficients of Eqs. (1), (2), …, (n) of the set of Eqs. (3.6).

3.9 Numerical Examples (Gauss–Jordan Method)

EXAMPLE 3.4 Solve the following system of equations using the Gauss–Jordan method.

$$\left.\begin{array}{lr} x + 2y - 3z = -4 & (1) \\ x + 3y + z = 10 & (2) \\ 2x - 4y - 2z = -12 & (3) \end{array}\right\} \tag{3.7}$$

Solution

Using $a_{21} = 1$, $a_{11} = 1$ in Step 1 of Gauss–Jordan method for elimination of x from equation (2), we get

$$x + 3y + z - 10 - (1/1)(x + 2y - 3z + 4) = y + 4z - 14 = 0$$

or $$y + 4z = 14 \qquad (2)$$

Similarly, eliminating x from Eq. (3), we get

$$-8y + 4z = -4 \qquad (3)$$

The above steps give the following new set of equations:

$$\left.\begin{array}{lr} x + 2y - 3z = -4 & (1) \\ y + 4z = 14 & (2) \\ -8y + 4z = -4 & (3) \end{array}\right\} \tag{3.8}$$

Now using step 2 of G–J method to eliminate y for Eq. (1), we do the following:

$$(x + 2y - 3z) - 2(y + 4z) = -4 - 2 \times 14$$

or $$x - 11z = -32 \qquad (1)$$

Similarly, for eliminating y from Eq. (3), we do the following:

$$-8y + 4z + 8(y + 4z) = -4 + 8 \times 14$$

or

$$36z = 108 \quad \text{or} \quad z = 3 \qquad (3)$$

The new set of equations is thus

$$\left.\begin{aligned} x - 11z &= -32 & (1) \\ y + 4z &= 14 & (2) \\ z &= 3 & (3) \end{aligned}\right\} \qquad (3.9)$$

Now eliminating z, from Eqs. (1) and (2) except Eq. (3), we get

$$x = 1, \qquad y = 2, \qquad z = 3$$

3.10 Algorithm (AL33) for Triangularization in Gauss–Jordan Method

This algorithm is transformed to a computer program written in C++ language and presented at the end of this chapter (see **p33.cpp**).

1. Define the error limit eps = 0.00001.
2. Declare/define the function/subprogram to implement the method for triangularization and back-substitution.
3. Start the (main) function.
4. Define the main function which calls the appropriate subprogram/function according to given choice.
5. Stop (main).

Details of function/subprogram **gjel**:

1. Start
2. Input the number of equations/rows/columns/unknowns, n
3. For i = 1 to n do
   For j = 1 to (n + 1) do
   read (a_{ij})
   end {for}
4. For k = 1 to n do
   temp = a_{kk}
   For j = k to n + 1 do
   a_{kk} = a_{kj}/temp
   if (i ≠ k) then
   aik = a_{ik}
   for j = k to n + 1 do
   a_{ij} = a_{ij} – a_{kj}*aik
   end for
   endif
   end {for}
   end {for}

5. For i = 1 to n do
   output solution $x_i = a_{in+1}$
6. Return

In the above algorithm, we have used the augmented matrix elements $a_{in+1} = b_i$ for $i = 1$ to n.

3.11 LU Decomposition/Factorization Methods

These are very popular methods of solving simultaneous equations in numerical analysis because of their simplicity and ease of application. In these methods the set of equations is represented in matrix form as

$$AX = B$$

For example, consider a set of three simultaneous equations:

$$a_{11}x_1 + a_{12}x_2 + a_{13}x_3 = b_1$$
$$a_{21}x_1 + a_{22}x_2 + a_{23}x_3 = b_2$$
$$a_{31}x_1 + a_{32}x_2 + a_{33}x_3 = b_3$$

Here the matrix

$$A = \begin{bmatrix} a_{11} & a_{12} & a_{13} \\ a_{21} & a_{22} & a_{23} \\ a_{31} & a_{32} & a_{33} \end{bmatrix}$$

$$X = \begin{bmatrix} x_1 \\ x_2 \\ x_3 \end{bmatrix}$$

$$B = \begin{bmatrix} b_1 \\ b_2 \\ b_3 \end{bmatrix}$$

We need to solve the above equations for the unknowns x_1, x_2 and x_3.

In LU decomposition methods, the matrix A is factorized into two matrices as

$$A = LU$$

where

L = the lower tridiagonal matrix
U = the upper tridiagonal matrix.

Also one of these matrices is chosen to be having unity diagonal components.

Here we discuss three methods based on LU decomposition.

1. Dolittle LU decomposition method.
2. Crout LU decomposition method.
3. Cholesky LU decomposition method.

Dolittle LU Decomposition Method

Consider the set of equations

$$a_{11}x_1 + a_{12}x_2 + a_{13}x_3 = b_1$$
$$a_{21}x_1 + a_{22}x_2 + a_{23}x_3 = b_2$$
$$a_{31}x_1 + a_{32}x_2 + a_{33}x_3 = b_3$$

Equivalently, we can write as

$$AX = B \tag{3.10}$$

where
$$A = \begin{bmatrix} a_{11} & a_{12} & a_{13} \\ a_{21} & a_{22} & a_{23} \\ a_{31} & a_{32} & a_{33} \end{bmatrix}$$

$$X = \begin{bmatrix} x_1 \\ x_2 \\ x_3 \end{bmatrix}$$

$$B = \begin{bmatrix} b_1 \\ b_2 \\ b_3 \end{bmatrix}$$

Let the matrix A be factorized into the product of two matrices as

$$A = LU \tag{3.11}$$

where
$$L = \begin{bmatrix} 1 & 0 & 0 \\ l_{21} & 1 & 0 \\ l_{31} & l_{32} & 1 \end{bmatrix}$$

$$U = \begin{bmatrix} u_{11} & u_{12} & u_{13} \\ 0 & u_{22} & u_{23} \\ 0 & 0 & u_{33} \end{bmatrix}$$

Note that the diagonal elements of L are unity.

From Eq. (3.11), we get

$$\begin{bmatrix} a_{11} & a_{12} & a_{13} \\ a_{21} & a_{22} & a_{23} \\ a_{31} & a_{32} & a_{33} \end{bmatrix} = \begin{bmatrix} u_{11} & u_{12} & u_{13} \\ l_{21}u_{11} & l_{21}u_{11} + u_{22} & l_{21}u_{13} + u_{23} \\ l_{31}u_{11} & l_{31}u_{12} + l_{32}u_{22} & l_{31}u_{13} + l_{32}u_{23} + u_{33} \end{bmatrix}$$

Since the matrix A is known, we can determine the three components l_{21}, l_{31} and l_{32} of L and the six components u_{11}, u_{12}, u_{13}, u_{22}, u_{23} and u_{33} of U by equating the components on both sides.

That is,

$$u_{11} = a_{11},\ u_{12} = a_{12},\ u_{13} = a_{13}$$

$$a_{21} = l_{21}u_{11}$$

$$\Rightarrow \qquad l_{21} = \frac{a_{21}}{a_{11}}$$

and

$$a_{31} = l_{31}u_{11}$$

$$\Rightarrow \qquad l_{31} = \frac{a_{31}}{a_{11}}$$

$$a_{22} = l_{21}u_{11} + u_{22}$$

$$\Rightarrow \qquad u_{22} = a_{22} - \frac{a_{21}}{a_{11}}a_{12}$$

$$a_{23} = l_{21}u_{13} + u_{23}$$

$$\Rightarrow \qquad u_{23} = a_{23} - \frac{a_{21}}{a_{11}}a_{13}$$

$$a_{32} = l_{31}u_{12} + l_{32}u_{22}$$

$$\Rightarrow \qquad l_{32} = \frac{a_{32} - (a_{31}/a_{11})a_{12}}{a_{22} - (a_{21}/a_{11})a_{12}}$$

Similarly,

$$a_{33} = l_{31}u_{13} + l_{32}u_{23} + u_{33}$$

$$\Rightarrow \qquad u_{33} = a_{33} - l_{31}u_{13} - l_{32}u_{23}$$

u_{33} can be obtained since all the components of R.H.S. are known in terms of the components of A.

Using Eq. (3.11) in Eq. (3.10), we get

$$(LU)X = B \tag{3.12}$$

Let

$$UX = Y \tag{3.13}$$

and then Eq. (3.12) becomes

$$LY = B \tag{3.14}$$

From Eq. (3.14), we can write

$$\begin{bmatrix} 1 & 0 & 0 \\ l_{21} & 1 & 0 \\ l_{31} & l_{32} & 1 \end{bmatrix} \begin{bmatrix} y_1 \\ y_2 \\ y_3 \end{bmatrix} = \begin{bmatrix} b_1 \\ b_2 \\ b_3 \end{bmatrix}$$

Hence, $y_1 = b_1, y_2 = b_2 - l_{21}y_1, y_3 = b_3 - l_{31}y_1 - l_{32}y_2$

From Eq. (3.13), we get

$$\begin{aligned} u_{11}x_1 + u_{12}x_2 + u_{13}x_3 &= y_1 \\ u_{22}x_2 + u_{23}x_3 &= y_2 \\ u_{33}x_3 &= y_3 \end{aligned}$$

Thus, x_1, x_2, x_3 can be determined from the above equations.

EXAMPLE 3.5 Using the *LU*-decomposition method, determine the unknowns x_1, x_2 and x_3 from the following equations.

$$\begin{aligned} x_1 + 5x_2 + x_3 &= 14 \\ 2x_1 + x_2 + 3x_3 &= 13 \\ 3x_1 + x_2 + 4x_3 &= 17 \end{aligned}$$

Solution

Let the above equations be written in matrix form

$$AX = B$$

where

$$A = \begin{bmatrix} 1 & 5 & 1 \\ 2 & 1 & 3 \\ 3 & 1 & 4 \end{bmatrix}$$

$$X = \begin{bmatrix} x_1 \\ x_2 \\ x_3 \end{bmatrix}$$

$$B = \begin{bmatrix} 14 \\ 13 \\ 17 \end{bmatrix}$$

Decomposing A gives

$$A = LU = \begin{bmatrix} 1 & 0 & 0 \\ l_{21} & 1 & 0 \\ l_{31} & l_{32} & 1 \end{bmatrix} \begin{bmatrix} u_{11} & u_{12} & u_{13} \\ 0 & u_{22} & u_{23} \\ 0 & 0 & u_{33} \end{bmatrix} = \begin{bmatrix} 1 & 5 & 1 \\ 2 & 1 & 3 \\ 3 & 1 & 4 \end{bmatrix}$$

Equating the coefficients, we get

$$u_{11} = 1,\ u_{12} = 5,\ u_{13} = 1$$

$$u_{22} = -9,\ u_{23} = 1,\ u_{33} = -\frac{5}{9}$$

$$l_{21} = 2,\ l_{31} = 3,\ l_{32} = \frac{14}{9}$$

Now, $LY = B$ gives y_1, y_2 and y_3 as

$$\begin{bmatrix} 1 & 0 & 0 \\ 2 & 1 & 0 \\ 3 & \frac{14}{9} & 1 \end{bmatrix} \begin{bmatrix} y_1 \\ y_2 \\ y_3 \end{bmatrix} = \begin{bmatrix} 14 \\ 13 \\ 17 \end{bmatrix}$$

$$y_1 = 14,\ y_2 = -15,\ y_3 = -\frac{5}{3}$$

Now, $UX = Y$ gives

$$\begin{bmatrix} 1 & 5 & 1 \\ 0 & -9 & 1 \\ 0 & 0 & -\frac{5}{9} \end{bmatrix} = \begin{bmatrix} x_1 \\ x_2 \\ x_3 \end{bmatrix} = \begin{bmatrix} 14 \\ -15 \\ -\frac{5}{3} \end{bmatrix}$$

$\Rightarrow$ $$x_1 = 1,\ x_2 = 2,\ x_3 = 3$$

Crout LU Decomposition/Factorization Method

This method is similar to the Dolittle method but with a small difference that the diagonal elements of the U matrix are chosen as unity instead of those of the L matrix.

Thus, we have

$$L = \begin{bmatrix} l_{11} & 0 & 0 \\ l_{21} & l_{22} & 0 \\ l_{31} & l_{32} & l_{33} \end{bmatrix}$$

and

$$U = \begin{bmatrix} 1 & u_{12} & u_{13} \\ 0 & 1 & u_{23} \\ 0 & 0 & 1 \end{bmatrix}$$

so that

$$A = LU \tag{3.15}$$

and the matrix equation is

$$AX = B \tag{3.16}$$

or

$$(LU)X = B \tag{3.17}$$

Proceeding in the similar manner as in the Dolittle method, we obtain the following equation,

$$\begin{bmatrix} a_{11} & a_{12} & a_{13} \\ a_{21} & a_{22} & a_{23} \\ a_{31} & a_{32} & a_{33} \end{bmatrix} = \begin{bmatrix} l_{11} & 0 & 0 \\ l_{21} & l_{22} & 0 \\ l_{31} & l_{32} & l_{33} \end{bmatrix} \begin{bmatrix} 1 & u_{12} & u_{13} \\ 0 & 1 & u_{23} \\ 0 & 0 & 1 \end{bmatrix}$$

or
$$\begin{bmatrix} a_{11} & a_{12} & a_{13} \\ a_{21} & a_{22} & a_{23} \\ a_{31} & a_{32} & a_{33} \end{bmatrix} = \begin{bmatrix} l_{11} & l_{11}u_{12} & l_{11}u_{13} \\ l_{21} & l_{21}u_{12} + l_{22} & l_{21}u_{13} + l_{22}u_{23} \\ l_{31} & l_{31}u_{12} + l_{32} & l_{31}u_{13} + l_{32}u_{23} + l_{33} \end{bmatrix}$$

Equating coefficients on both the sides,

$$l_{11} = a_{11}, \quad l_{21} = a_{21}, \quad l_{31} = a_{31}$$

$$u_{12} = \frac{a_{12}}{a_{11}}$$

$$u_{13} = \frac{a_{13}}{a_{11}}$$

$$l_{22} = a_{22} - l_{21}u_{12}$$

$$l_{32} = a_{32} - l_{31}u_{12}$$

$$u_{23} = \frac{a_{23} - l_{21}u_{13}}{l_{22}}$$

$$l_{33} = a_{33} - l_{31}u_{13} - l_{32}u_{23}$$

Using
$$LY = B \tag{3.18}$$

i.e.
$$\begin{bmatrix} l_{11} & 0 & 0 \\ l_{21} & l_{22} & 0 \\ l_{31} & l_{32} & l_{33} \end{bmatrix} \begin{bmatrix} y_1 \\ y_2 \\ y_3 \end{bmatrix} = \begin{bmatrix} b_1 \\ b_2 \\ b_3 \end{bmatrix}$$

and solving the above equation, we get

$$y_1 = \frac{b_1}{a_{11}}$$

$$y_2 = \frac{b_2 - l_{21}y_1}{l_{22}}$$

$$y_3 = \frac{b_3 - l_{31}y_1 - l_{32}y_2}{l_{33}}$$

Using
$$UX = Y \tag{3.19}$$

i.e.
$$\begin{bmatrix} 1 & u_{12} & u_{13} \\ 0 & 1 & u_{23} \\ 0 & 0 & 1 \end{bmatrix} \begin{bmatrix} x_1 \\ x_2 \\ x_3 \end{bmatrix} = \begin{bmatrix} y_1 \\ y_2 \\ y_3 \end{bmatrix}$$

and solving the above equation, we get

$$x_3 = y_3$$
$$x_2 + x_3 u_{23} = y_2$$
$$x_1 + x_2 u_{12} + x_3 u_{13} = y_3$$

The solution x_1, x_2 and x_3 thus becomes known.

EXAMPLE 3.6 Solve the following system of equations using the Crout's method.

$$x_1 + x_2 + x_3 = 3$$
$$2x_1 - x_2 + 3x_3 = 16$$
$$3x_1 + x_2 - x_3 = -3$$

Solution

In Crout's method, $AX = B$

where
$$A = \begin{bmatrix} 1 & 1 & 1 \\ 2 & -1 & 3 \\ 3 & 1 & -1 \end{bmatrix}$$

$$B = \begin{bmatrix} 3 \\ 16 \\ -3 \end{bmatrix}$$

$$X = \begin{bmatrix} x_1 \\ x_2 \\ x_3 \end{bmatrix}$$

Now,
$$(LU)X = B$$

$$L = \begin{bmatrix} l_{11} & 0 & 0 \\ l_{21} & l_{22} & 0 \\ l_{31} & l_{32} & l_{33} \end{bmatrix}$$

$$U = \begin{bmatrix} 1 & u_{12} & u_{13} \\ 0 & 1 & u_{23} \\ 0 & 0 & 1 \end{bmatrix}$$

Using formulae of the Crout's method, we obtain

$$L = \begin{bmatrix} 1 & 0 & 0 \\ 2 & -3 & 0 \\ 3 & -2 & -\frac{14}{3} \end{bmatrix} \text{ and } U = \begin{bmatrix} 1 & 1 & 1 \\ 0 & 1 & -\frac{1}{3} \\ 0 & 0 & 1 \end{bmatrix}$$

Using $LY = B$, we get

$$y_1 = 3,\ y_2 = -\frac{10}{3},\ y_3 = 4$$

Using $UX = Y$, we get

$$x_1 = 1,\ x_2 = -2,\ x_3 = 4$$

Cholesky Method (modified LU-decomposition method)

Consider a set of equations in matrix form

$$AX = B \tag{3.20}$$

where
$$A = \begin{bmatrix} a_{11} & a_{12} & a_{13} \\ a_{21} & a_{22} & a_{23} \\ a_{31} & a_{32} & a_{33} \end{bmatrix}$$

is a symmetric matrix. The factorization of A can be simplified to take the product of L and its transpose or U and its transpose as follows:

$$A = LL^T$$

or
$$A = U^T U \tag{3.21}$$

We thus determine the matrix U from Eq. (3.21). Equation (3.20) can be written as

$$(U^T U)X = B \tag{3.22}$$

Let
$$U^T Y = B \tag{3.23}$$

We determine Y from Eq. (3.23). Now from Eq. (3.22), we have

$$UX = Y \tag{3.24}$$

Thus, we determine X from Eq. (3.24). The solution x_1, x_2 and x_3 for the set of Eqs. (3.20) is thus completely determined.

3.12 Matrix Inversion Method

Given the set of equations

$$a_{11}x_1 + a_{12}x_2 + a_{13}x_3 = b_1$$
$$a_{21}x_1 + a_{22}x_2 + a_{23}x_3 = b_2$$
$$a_{31}x_1 + a_{32}x_2 + a_{33}x_3 = b_3$$

We can write in matrix form as

$$AX = B \tag{3.25}$$

Pre-multiplying Eq. (3.25) by A^{-1},

$$A^{-1}AX = A^{-1}B$$

or

$$IX = A^{-1}B \qquad (\because \quad A^{-1}A = I)$$

or

$$X = A^{-1}B$$

where $I = \begin{bmatrix} 1 & 0 & 0 \\ 0 & 1 & 0 \\ 0 & 0 & 1 \end{bmatrix}$ is the identity matrix.

We can write

$$IX = A^{-1}B$$

or

$$X = A^{-1}B \tag{3.26}$$

If A^{-1} is known, we can determine the solution x_1, x_2, x_3 of the given system of equations.

We may use the Crout's method for computing A^{-1}. In Crout's method, A is decomposed as $A = LU$

where

L = the lower triangular matrix
U = the upper unit triangular matrix.

Taking the inverse of A, we get

$$A^{-1} = (LU)^{-1}$$

or

$$A^{-1} = U^{-1}L^{-1} \tag{3.27}$$

where U^{-1} is also the upper triangular matrix and L^{-1} is also the lower triangular matrix.

If L and U are determined using the Crout method, we can determine L^{-1} and U^{-1} by the following relations

$$LL^{-1} = I \tag{3.28}$$

$$UU^{-1} = I \tag{3.29}$$

where I is the identity matrix.

Using Eq. (3.27), we can now determine A^{-1}. Substituting in Eq. (3.26), we finally get the solution vector (X) of the given set of equations.

EXAMPLE 3.7 Solve the following system of equations by the matrix inversion method.

$$\begin{aligned} 3x - y + z &= 1 \\ -15x + 6y - 5z &= 2 \\ 5x - 2y + 2z &= -1 \end{aligned}$$

Solution

The solution is given by $X = A^{-1}B$. To compute A^{-1}, we use the Crout's method

$$A^{-1} = U^{-1}L^{-1}$$

Since
$$A = LU$$

we get
$$\begin{bmatrix} 3 & -1 & 1 \\ -15 & 6 & -5 \\ 5 & -2 & 2 \end{bmatrix} = \begin{bmatrix} l_{11} & 0 & 0 \\ l_{21} & l_{22} & 0 \\ l_{31} & l_{32} & l_{33} \end{bmatrix} \begin{bmatrix} 1 & u_{12} & u_{13} \\ 0 & 1 & u_{23} \\ 0 & 0 & 1 \end{bmatrix}$$

Equating the coefficients and solving, we get

$$l_{11} = 3,\ l_{21} = -15,\ l_{31} = 5$$

$$l_{22} = 1,\ l_{32} = -\frac{1}{3},\ l_{33} = \frac{1}{3}$$

$$u_{12} = -\frac{1}{3},\ u_{13} = \frac{1}{3},\ u_{23} = 0$$

Thus $L = \begin{bmatrix} 3 & 0 & 0 \\ -15 & 1 & 0 \\ 5 & -\frac{1}{3} & \frac{1}{3} \end{bmatrix}$ and $U = \begin{bmatrix} 1 & -\frac{1}{3} & \frac{1}{3} \\ 0 & 1 & 0 \\ 0 & 0 & 1 \end{bmatrix}$

Let $L^{-1} = \begin{bmatrix} il_{11} & 0 & 0 \\ il_{21} & il_{22} & 0 \\ il_{31} & il_{32} & il_{33} \end{bmatrix}$ and $U^{-1} = \begin{bmatrix} iu_{11} & iu_{12} & iu_{13} \\ 0 & iu_{22} & iu_{23} \\ 0 & 0 & iu_{33} \end{bmatrix}$

Using $LL^{-1} = I$, we get

$$\begin{bmatrix} 3 & 0 & 0 \\ -15 & 1 & 0 \\ 5 & -1/3 & 1/3 \end{bmatrix} \begin{bmatrix} il_{11} & 0 & 0 \\ il_{21} & il_{22} & 0 \\ il_{31} & il_{32} & il_{33} \end{bmatrix} = \begin{bmatrix} 1 & 0 & 0 \\ 0 & 1 & 0 \\ 0 & 0 & 1 \end{bmatrix}$$

Equating coefficients and solving, we get

$$il_{11} = \frac{1}{3}$$

$$il_{21} = 5,\ il_{22} = 1$$

$$il_{31} = 0,\ il_{32} = 1,\ il_{33} = 3$$

Thus, $$L^{-1} = \begin{bmatrix} \frac{1}{3} & 0 & 0 \\ 5 & 1 & 0 \\ 0 & 1 & 3 \end{bmatrix}$$

Similarly, using $UU^{-1} = I$, we get

$$U^{-1} = \begin{bmatrix} 1 & \frac{1}{3} & -\frac{1}{3} \\ 0 & 1 & 0 \\ 0 & 0 & 1 \end{bmatrix}$$

Now $$A^{-1} = U^{-1}L^{-1} = \begin{bmatrix} 1 & \frac{1}{3} & -\frac{1}{3} \\ 0 & 1 & 0 \\ 0 & 0 & 1 \end{bmatrix}\begin{bmatrix} \frac{1}{3} & 0 & 0 \\ 5 & 1 & 0 \\ 0 & 1 & 3 \end{bmatrix} = \begin{bmatrix} 2 & 0 & -1 \\ 5 & 1 & 0 \\ 0 & 1 & 3 \end{bmatrix}$$

and $$X = A^{-1}B$$

$$\begin{bmatrix} x_1 \\ x_2 \\ x_3 \end{bmatrix} = \begin{bmatrix} 2 & 0 & -1 \\ 5 & 1 & 0 \\ 0 & 1 & 3 \end{bmatrix}\begin{bmatrix} 1 \\ 2 \\ -1 \end{bmatrix} = \begin{bmatrix} 2\times1+0+1 \\ 5\times1+2+0 \\ 0\times1+2-3 \end{bmatrix} = \begin{bmatrix} 3 \\ 7 \\ -1 \end{bmatrix}$$

$\therefore$ $$x_1 = 3, \quad x_2 = 7, \quad x_3 = -1$$

3.13 Jacobi's Method

In this method each of the given equations is rearranged initially such that the value of one variable can be expressed in terms of the other variables. For example, let the given equations be as follows:

$$\begin{aligned} a_{11}x_1 + a_{12}x_2 + \cdots + a_{1n}x_n &= b_1 \\ a_{21}x_1 + a_{22}x_2 + \cdots + a_{2n}x_n &= b_2 \\ \vdots \qquad\qquad & \quad \vdots \\ a_{n1}x_1 + a_{n2}x_2 + \cdots + a_{nn}x_n &= b_n \end{aligned}$$

Rearrangement of the above equations gives:

$$x_1 = \frac{b_1 - (a_{12}x_2 + a_{13}x_3 + \cdots + a_{1n}x_n)}{a_{11}}$$

$$x_2 = \frac{b_2 - (a_{21}x_1 + a_{23}x_3 + \cdots + a_{2n}x_n)}{a_{22}}$$

$$\vdots$$

$$x_n = \frac{b_n - (a_{n1}x_1 + a_{n2}x_2 + \cdots + a_{n\,n-1}x_{n-1})}{a_{nn}}$$

In the first iteration the initial trial values for $x_k (k = 1, 2, \ldots, n)$ are chosen to be zero and substituted into the above relations. Then the so-obtained new values of x_k are taken as trial values for the second iteration. The values obtained in the second iteration are taken as trial values for the third iteration, and so on. For example, for a system of three equations, the values of the unknowns in the $(i + 1)$th iteration are given by

$$(x_1)^{i+1} = \frac{b_1 - a_{12}(x_2)^i - a_{13}(x_3)^i}{a_{11}}$$

$$(x_2)^{i+1} = \frac{b_2 - a_{21}(x_1)^i - a_{23}(x_2)^i}{a_{22}}$$

$$(x_3)^{i+1} = \frac{b_3 - a_{31}(x_1)^i - a_{32}(x_2)^i}{a_{33}}$$

The Jacobi's method is illustrated in Figure 3.1.

Iteration 0: $\begin{cases} x_1 = 0 \\ x_2 = 0 \\ x_3 = 0 \end{cases}$

Iteration 1: $\begin{cases} x_1 = \dfrac{b_1 - a_{12}(x_2) - a_{13}(x_3)}{a_{11}} \\ x_2 = \dfrac{b_2 - a_{21}(x_1) - a_{23}(x_3)}{a_{22}} \\ x_3 = \dfrac{b_3 - a_{31}(x_1) + a_{32}(x_2)}{a_{33}} \end{cases}$

Iteration 2: $\begin{cases} x_1 = \dfrac{b_1 - a_{12}(x_2) - a_{13}(x_3)}{a_{11}} \\ x_2 = \dfrac{b_2 - a_{21}(x_1) - a_{23}(x_3)}{a_{22}} \\ x_3 = \dfrac{b_3 - a_{31}(x_1) + a_{32}(x_2)}{a_{33}} \end{cases}$

$\vdots \qquad \vdots$

Figure 3.1 Jacobi's method.

The iterations would stop when the difference between the values of x_i for the $(i + 1)$th and ith iterations becomes smaller than the prescribed limit.

The Jacobi's method is convergent and leads to the solution of simultaneous equations in a finite number of iterations when the diagonal elements of the coefficient matrix are dominant,

$$| a_{ii} | > \Sigma | a_{ij} |$$

where the Σ is from $j = 1$ to $j = n$ and $i \neq j$.

3.14 Numerical Examples (Jacobi's Method)

EXAMPLE 3.8 Solve the following system of equations using the Jacobi's method.

$$\begin{aligned} x_1 + \quad x_2 + 4x_3 &= 9 \\ 8x_1 - \quad 3x_2 + 2x_3 &= 20 \\ 4x_1 + 11x_2 - \quad x_3 &= 33 \end{aligned}$$

Solution

The given system of equations is not diagonally dominated because

$$|a_{11}| < |a_{12}| + |a_{13}|$$

To make $|a_{11}| > |a_{12}| + |a_{13}|$ the given system of equations should be rearranged as

$$\begin{aligned} 8x_1 - \quad 3x_2 + 2x_3 &= 20 \\ 4x_1 + 11x_2 - \quad x_3 &= 33 \\ x_1 + \quad x_2 + 4x_3 &= 9 \end{aligned}$$

Now $|a_{11}|$ (= 8) > $|a_{12}| + |a_{13}|$ (= 3 + 2).

Following the Jacobi's method, construct Table 3.1 of values for iterations by taking the initial solution as $x_{01} = x_{02} = x_{03} = 0$.

Table 3.1 Example 3.8

i	$(x_1)^i$	$(x_2)^i$	$(x_3)^i$
0	0	0	0
1	2.5	3.0	2.25
2	3.06	2.30	0.88
3	3.142	1.967	0.91
4	3.0101	1.9402	0.9728
5	2.9844	1.9938	1.0124
6	2.9946	2.0068	1.0054
7	3.0012	2.0024	0.9996

The solution up to two decimal places is given by $x_1 = 3.00$, $x_2 = 2.00$, $x_3 = 1.00$.

3.15 Algorithm (AL34) for the Jacobi's Method

This algorithm is transformed to a computer program written in C++ language and presented at the end of this chapter (see **p34.cpp**).

1. Define the error limit eps = 0.00001.
2. Declare/define the function/subprogram **jcb** to implement the method.
3. Start the (main) function.
4. Define the main function which calls the appropriate subprogram/function.
5. Stop (main).

Details of function/subprogram **jcb**:

```
1. Start
2. Input n, a_ij, b_i (=a_i n+1)
3. Input itrmax, er
4. For i=1 to n do
     x0_i = 0
5. For k=1 to itrmax
     for i=1 to n
       s=0
       for j=1 to n
         if i ≠ j then
           s=s+a_ij x0_j
         endif
       xi=(a_in+1 – s)/a_ii
       er=|(x_i – x0_i)/x_i|
     if er ≤ eps then
     go to stp
     for i=1 to n do
       x0_i=x_i
     end
     if (er > eps) then
     write "non-convergent solution"
     return
     stp: write "convergent solution"
       For i=1 to n do
         write x_i
6. Return
```

3.16 Gauss–Seidel Method

This method is an extension of the Jacobi's method to obtain a more accurate solution of the system of equations. The basic idea in this method is to use improved values of the unknowns within the same iteration.

For example, for a system of three equations,

$$a_{11}x_1 + a_{12}x_2 + a_{13}x_3 = b_1$$

$$a_{21}x_1 + a_{22}x_2 + a_{23}x_3 = b_2$$

$$a_{31}x_1 + a_{32}x_2 + a_{33}x_3 = b_3$$

in the Jacobi's method, the initial values $x_1 = x_2 = x_3 = 0$ are chosen as initial values for the unknowns in the 0th iteration and improved values obtained in this iteration are used in the next iteration, and so on.

In the Guass–Seidel method, for a system of three equations, the initial values for $x_2 = x_3 = 0$ are chosen and substituted in the 0th iteration for calculating the value of x_1 from the first equation. The improved value of x_1 so obtained is then used in the 0th iteration itself to get improved value of x_2, taking $x_3 = 0$, from the second equation. The value of x_3 is improved in the 0th iteration by using improved values of x_1 and x_2 in the third equation. In the next iteration, the improved values of x_2 and x_3 of 0th iteration are used to calculate the value of x_1. This value of x_1 and that of x_3 (of 0th iteration) are then used for the calculation of x_2. The improved values of x_2 and x_3 so obtained are used in this iteration itself to get the improved value of x_3. Then in the next iteration the above process is repeated till the desired accuracy is obtained. The Guass–Seidel method is shown in Figure 3.2 by considering a system of three equations. In iteration 0, the initial values for $x_2 = x_3 = 0$.

Iteration 0:

$$x_1 = \frac{b_1 - a_{12}(x_2) - a_{13}(x_3)}{a_{11}}$$

$$x_2 = \frac{b_2 - a_{21}(x_1) - a_{23}(x_3)}{a_{22}}$$

$$x_3 = \frac{b_3 - a_{31}(x_1) + a_{32}(x_2)}{a_{33}}$$

Iteration 1:

$$x_1 = \frac{b_1 - a_{12}(x_2) - a_{13}(x_3)}{a_{11}}$$

$$x_2 = \frac{b_2 - a_{21}(x_1) - a_{23}(x_3)}{a_{22}}$$

$$x_3 = \frac{b_3 - a_{31}(x_1) + a_{32}(x_2)}{a_{33}}$$

Iteration 2:

$$x_1 = \frac{b_1 - a_{12}(x_2) - a_{13}(x_3)}{a_{11}}$$

$$x_2 = \frac{b_2 - a_{21}(x_1) - a_{23}(x_3)}{a_{22}}$$

$$x_3 = \frac{b_3 - a_{31}(x_1) + a_{32}(x_2)}{a_{33}}$$

⋮ ⋮

Figure 3.2 Gauss–Seidel method.

For example, for a system of three equations, the values of unknowns in the $(i + 1)$th iteration are given by

$$(x_1)^{i+1} = \frac{b_1 - a_{12}(x_2)^i - a_{13}(x_3)^i}{a_{11}}$$

$$(x_2)^{i+1} = \frac{b_2 - a_{21}(x_1)^{i+1} - a_{23}(x_3)^i}{a_{22}}$$

$$(x_3)^{i+1} = \frac{b_3 - a_{31}(x_1)^{i+1} - a_{32}(x_2)^{i+1}}{a_{33}}$$

The Gauss–Seidel method is convergent and leads to the solution of simultaneous equations in a finite number of iterations when the diagonal elements of the coefficient matrix are dominant, i.e. when

$$| a_{ii} | > \Sigma | a_{ij} |$$

where the Σ is from $j = 1$ to $j = n$ and $i \neq j$.

3.17 Numerical Examples (Gauss–Seidel Method)

EXAMPLE 3.9 Solve the following system of equations using the Gauss–Seidel method.

$$\begin{aligned} 8x_1 - 3x_2 + 2x_3 &= 20 \\ 4x_1 + 11x_2 - x_3 &= 33 \\ x_1 + x_2 + 4x_3 &= 9 \end{aligned}$$

Solution

Using the iteration equations of the Gaus–Seidel method,

$$(x_1)^{i+1} = \frac{20 + 3(x_2)^i - 2(x_3)^i}{8}$$

$$(x_2)^{i+1} = \frac{33 - 4(x_1)^{i+1} + (x_3)^i}{11}$$

$$(x_3)^{i+1} = \frac{9 - (x_1)^{i+1} - (x_2)^{i+1}}{4}$$

Using the initial approximations $x_1 = x_2 = x_3 = 0$ in the 0th iteration, from the Gauss–Seidel method we get from the first equation $x_1 = 20/8 = 2.5$. Using this value of x_1 and $x_3 = 0$ in the second equation, we get $x_2 = 2.0909$. Using this value of x_2 and that of x_1 in the third equation, we get $x_3 = 1.1023$. Now these are the values in 0th iteration. For successive iterations we construct Table 3.2 using the above set of equations.

Table 3.2 Example 3.9

i	$(x_1)^i$	$(x_2)^i$	$(x_3)^i$
0	2.5	2.0909	1.1023
1	3.0085	2.0062	0.9963
2	3.0032	1.9985	0.9996
3	3.0	2.0	1.0

Therefore, the solution is $x_1 = 3$, $x_2 = 2$, $x_3 = 1$.

EXAMPLE 3.10 Solve the following system of equations using the Gauss–Seidel method.

$$3x_1 + 9x_2 - 2x_3 = 11 \qquad (R_1)$$

$$4x_1 + 2x_2 + 13x_3 = 24 \qquad (R_2)$$

$$4x_1 - 2x_2 + x_3 = -8 \qquad (R_3)$$

Solution

Rearranging to get the diagonally dominated system of equations,

$$4x_1 - 2x_2 + x_3 = -8 \qquad (R_1)$$

$$3x_1 + 9x_2 - 2x_3 = 11 \qquad (R_2)$$

$$4x_1 + 2x_2 + 13x_3 = 24 \qquad (R_3)$$

In the above system of equations,

$$4 > (2 + 1 = 3) \text{ in } R_1$$

$$9 > (3 + 2 = 5) \text{ in } R_2$$

$$13 > (4 + 2 = 6) \text{ in } R_3$$

Using the iteration equations of the Gauss–Seidel method,

$$(x_1)^{i+1} = \frac{-8 + 2(x_2)^i - (x_3)^i}{4}$$

$$(x_2)^{i+1} = \frac{11 - 3(x_1)^{i+1} + 2(x_3)^i}{9}$$

$$(x_3)^{i+1} = \frac{24 - 4(x_1)^{i+1} - 2(x_2)^{i+1}}{13}$$

Using the initial approximations $x_1 = x_2 = x_3 = 0$ in the 0th iteration and using the Gauss–Seidel method, we calculate the values in the 0th iteration as $x_1 = -2$, $x_2 = 1.89$, $x_3 = 2.17$. For successive iterations, we construct Table 3.3 using the above set of equations.

Table 3.3 Example 3.10

i	$(x_1)^i$	$(x_2)^i$	$(x_3)^i$
0	–2.0	1.89	2.17
1	–1.6	2.24	1.99
2	–1.38	2.12	1.94
3	–1.425	2.128	1.957
4	–1.4252	2.1322	1.9566
5	–1.4230	2.1314	1.9561
6	–1.4233	2.1313	1.9562

Therefore, the solution is $x_1 = -1.423$, $x_2 = 2.131$, $x_3 = 1.956$.

3.18 Algorithm (AL35) Gauss–Seidel Method

This algorithm is transformed to a computer program written in C++ language and presented at the end of this chapter (see **p35.cpp**).

1. Define the error limit eps = 0.00001.
2. Declare/define the function/subprogram **gs** to implement the method.
3. Start the (main) function.
4. Define the main function which calls the appropriate subprogram/ function.
5. Stop (main).

Details of function/subprogram **gs**:

1. For i=1 to n do
   For j=1 to (n+1) do
   read a_{ij}
   {n represents the number of equations; a_{in+1} represents the RHS elements b_i}
2. input itrmax
   {itrmax represents maximum number of iterations}
3. For i=1 to n do
   set $x0_i$=0
4. For k=1 to itrmax do
   for i=1 to n do
   s=0
   for j=1 to n do
   if (i ≠ j) then
   begin
   s=s+$a_{ij}x0_j$
   endif

```
        xi=(ain+1 – s)/aii
        er=|(xi – x0j)|/|xi|
        end
        if (er<eps) then
        go to stp
        endif
        for i=1 to n do
        x0i = xi
        end for
        if (er > eps) then
        write 'non-convergent solution'
        return
   stp: write 'convergent solution in k iterations'
        for i=1 to n do
        write xi
        end
     5. Return
```

3.19 Eigenvalue and Eigenvector of a Matrix of a Given System of Linear Homogeneous Equations by the Power Method

Let a system of equations be given by

$$\begin{aligned} a_{11}x_1 + a_{12}x_2 + \cdots + a_{1n}x_n &= 0 \\ a_{21}x_1 + a_{22}x_2 + \cdots + a_{2n}x_n &= 0 \\ \vdots \qquad\qquad\qquad & \vdots \\ a_{n1}x_1 + a_{n2}x_2 + \cdots + a_{nn}x_n &= 0 \end{aligned}$$

or

$$AX = 0$$

This system of equations can be solved by using a special technique called the **eigenvalue technique**. In this method the above system of equations is transformed to the following form by subtracting from the diagonal coefficients of the matrix A a constant λ called the eigenvalue of the system of equations.

$$\left.\begin{aligned} (a_{11} - \lambda)x_1 + a_{12}x_2 + \cdots + a_{1n}x_n &= 0 \\ a_{21}x_1 + (a_{22} - \lambda)x_2 + \cdots + a_{2n}x_n &= 0 \\ \vdots \qquad\qquad\qquad & \vdots \\ a_{n1}x_1 + a_{n2}x_2 + \cdots + (a_{nn} - \lambda)x_n &= 0 \end{aligned}\right\} \tag{3.30}$$

In the matrix form, we can write

$$\begin{vmatrix} a_{11}-\lambda & a_{12} & \cdots & a_{1n} \\ a_{21} & a_{22}-\lambda & \cdots & a_{2n} \\ \vdots & \vdots & & \vdots \\ a_{n1} & a_{n2} & \cdots & a_{nn}-\lambda \end{vmatrix} \begin{vmatrix} x_1 \\ x_2 \\ \vdots \\ x_n \end{vmatrix} = 0$$

or $$(A - \lambda I)X = 0$$

where I = identity matrix.

Setting the $$\det (A - \lambda I) = 0$$

From this, we obtain the following polynomial equation which can be solved for λ

$$\lambda^n - p_1\lambda^{n-1} - p_2\lambda^{n-2} - \cdots - p_{n-1}\lambda - p_n = 0$$

where p_i's are constants.

The above equation is called the **characteristic polynomial** or **characteristic equation**. The roots (λ's) of this equation are called **eigenvalues** or **characteristic values** of the matrix A. After solving for λ's the solution to the given set of equations, that is, the unknowns x_1, x_2, ..., x_n can be found for each value of λ. The column matrix of the x_i's is called the **eigenvector corresponding to a value of λ.**

An iterative method called the **power method** can determine the largest as well as the smallest eigenvalue of the system of equations. Rewriting the matrix Eq. (3.30) as

$$AX = \lambda X \tag{3.31}$$

the power method is explained in the following steps:

1. Assume a unit column matrix $[X_0] = [1]$ as the first approximation to the solution of the given set of equations.
2. Using this unit matrix in Eq. (3.31) and carrying out the matrix multiplication gives the next approximate solution of the RHS of Eq. (3.31).
3. The vector $\lambda|X|$ is divided by the magnitude of the first component which makes it unity. This step is called **normalization.**
4. The normalized vector of step 3 is used on the LHS of Eq. (3.31) again for multiplication to get the next approximate eigenvector matrix on the RHS of Eq. (3.31).
5. The above steps are repeated till there is negligible variation in the values of the eigenvector components in two successive iterations.
6. The normalization factor of the iteration gives the value of the largest eigenvalue ($\lambda_{\max}$) and the associated eigenvector is the solution of the system of equations corresponding to this eigenvalue.
7. The smallest eigenvalue can be calculated by multiplying both sides of Eq. (3.31) by the inverse $A(= A^{-1})$

i.e. $$A^{-1}(AX) = A^{-1}\lambda X$$

or $$X = \lambda A^{-1}X$$

or $$A^{-1}X = (1/\lambda)X \tag{3.32}$$

Following the steps 1 through 5, using Eq. (3.32) the maximum value of $(1/\lambda)$ can be obtained which gives the minimum value of λ.

3.20 Numerical Examples (Eigenvalues and Eigenvectors)

EXAMPLE 3.11 Find the eigenvalues and eigenvectors of the following matrix:

$$A = \begin{bmatrix} 1 & 2 & 3 \\ 0 & -4 & 2 \\ 0 & 0 & 7 \end{bmatrix}$$

Solution

The characteristic equation is given by

$$\det(A - \lambda I) = 0$$

or
$$\begin{vmatrix} 1-\lambda & 2 & 3 \\ 0 & -4-\lambda & 2 \\ 0 & 0 & 7-\lambda \end{vmatrix} = 0$$

Expanding the determinant, we get

$$(1 - \lambda)[(-4 - \lambda)(7 - \lambda)] = 0$$

This gives the eigenvalues, $\lambda = 1, -4, 7$.

For eigenvalue $\lambda = 1$, the eigenvector is given by solving $(A - \lambda I)x = 0$, i.e. by solving

$$\begin{pmatrix} 0 & 2 & 3 \\ 0 & -5 & 2 \\ 0 & 0 & 6 \end{pmatrix} \begin{pmatrix} x_1 \\ x_2 \\ x_3 \end{pmatrix} = \begin{pmatrix} 0 \\ 0 \\ 0 \end{pmatrix}$$

we get $x_2 = 0$, $x_3 = 0$ and $x_1 = c$ (a constant real number).

Thus $(c, 0, 0)$ is the eigenvector corresponding to the eigenvalue $\lambda = 1$.

Similarly, the eigenvector corresponding to $\lambda = -4$ is $(-2c/5, c, 0)$ and the eigenvector corresponding to $\lambda = 7$ is $(37c/66, 2c/11, c)$.

EXAMPLE 3.12 Find the largest eigenvalue and the associated eigenvector of the following system of equations correct up to two decimal places.

$$10x_1 + 4x_2 - x_3 = 0$$
$$4x_1 + 2x_2 + 3x_3 = 0$$
$$-x_1 + 3x_2 + x_3 = 0$$

Solution

Let us re-write the above system of equations in matrix form as

$$AX = \lambda X \tag{3.33}$$

and assume the solution to be

$$X = X_0 = \begin{bmatrix} 1 \\ 1 \\ 1 \end{bmatrix}$$

In iteration 0th,

$$AX_0 = \begin{bmatrix} 10 & 4 & -1 \\ 4 & 2 & 3 \\ -1 & 3 & 1 \end{bmatrix} \begin{bmatrix} 1 \\ 1 \\ 1 \end{bmatrix}$$

$$= \begin{bmatrix} 13 \\ 9 \\ 3 \end{bmatrix}$$

$$= 13 \begin{bmatrix} 1 \\ 0.6923 \\ 0.2308 \end{bmatrix}$$

In iteration 1, we take

$$X = \begin{bmatrix} 1 \\ 0.6923 \\ 0.2308 \end{bmatrix}$$

From Eq. (3.33), we get

$$AX = \begin{bmatrix} 10 & 4 & -1 \\ 4 & 2 & 3 \\ -1 & 3 & 1 \end{bmatrix} \begin{bmatrix} 1 \\ 0.6923 \\ 0.2308 \end{bmatrix}$$

$$= \begin{bmatrix} 12.5385 \\ 6.0769 \\ 1.3080 \end{bmatrix}$$

$$= 12.5385 \begin{bmatrix} 1.0 \\ 0.4847 \\ 0.1043 \end{bmatrix}$$

In iteration 2, we take

$$X = \begin{bmatrix} 1.0 \\ 0.4847 \\ 0.1043 \end{bmatrix}$$

and obtain

$$AX = 11.8344 \begin{bmatrix} 1 \\ 0.4463 \\ 0.4717 \end{bmatrix}$$

In iteration 3, we take

$$X = \begin{bmatrix} 1 \\ 0.4463 \\ 0.4717 \end{bmatrix}$$

and obtain

$$AX = 11.7382 \begin{bmatrix} 1 \\ 0.4289 \\ 0.0329 \end{bmatrix}$$

In iteration 4, we take

$$X = \begin{bmatrix} 1 \\ 0.4289 \\ 0.0329 \end{bmatrix}$$

and obtain

$$AX = 11.6826\begin{bmatrix}1\\0.4243\\0.02734\end{bmatrix}$$

In iteration 5, we take

$$X = \begin{bmatrix}1\\0.4243\\0.02734\end{bmatrix}$$

and obtain

$$AX = 11.6697\begin{bmatrix}1\\0.4225\\0.02572\end{bmatrix}$$

In iteration 6, we take

$$X = \begin{bmatrix}1\\0.4225\\0.02572\end{bmatrix}$$

and obtain

$$AX = 11.6643\begin{bmatrix}1\\0.42199\\0.02514\end{bmatrix}$$

In iteration 7, we take

$$X = \begin{bmatrix}1\\0.42199\\0.02514\end{bmatrix}$$

and obtain

$$AX = 11.6628 \begin{bmatrix} 1 \\ 0.4218 \\ 0.025 \end{bmatrix}$$

Thus up to two decimal places the maximum eigenvalue is λ_{max} = 11.66. The solution vector components are x_1 = 1.0, x_2 = 0.42, x_3 = 0.025.

3.21 Algorithm (AL36) Power Method

This algorithm is transformed to a computer program written in C++ language and presented at the end of this chapter (see **p36.cpp**).

1. Define the error limit eps = 0.00001.
2. Declare/define the function/subprogram pmegn to implement the method.
3. Start the (main) function.
4. Define the main function which calls the appropriate subprogram/ function.
5. Stop (main).

Details of function/subprogram **pmegn**:

1. Input matrix A, initial eigenvector (X) and error (eps)
2. Initialization

   For i=1 to n do

       $x0_i$ =1
3. k=0

   Repeat

   For i=1 to n do

       s_i=0

       for j=1 to n do

       $s_i=s_i+a_{ij}x0_j$

       endfor

   endfor

   $\lambda=|s_1|$

   For i=1 to n do

       $x_i=s_i/\lambda$

   endfor

```
        er2=|x2–x02|
        er3=|x3–x03|
        xi=tmp
        if (er2 < eps) and (er3 < eps) then
        exit (repat loop)
      For i=1 to n do
        x0i=xi
        endfor
        k=k+1
      until (k >= kmax)
      stp: write 'convergent solution in k iterations'
      write 'largest eigenvalue λ
        for i=1 to n do
        write 'xi'
        return
   4. Write 'non-convergent solution'
   5. Return
```

Exercises

1. Solve the following equations using the Gauss elimination and Gauss–Jordan methods:

(a) $2x + 6y - z = -12$

$5x - y + z = 11$

$4x - y + 3z = 10$ [**Ans.** $x = 1.63$, $y = -2.49$, $z = 0.32$]

(b) $x + 3y + 10z = 24$

$2x + 17y + 4z = 35$

$28x + 4y - z = 32$ [**Ans.** $x = 1.0$, $y = 1.49$, $z = 1.82$]

(c) $3x + y - z = 3$

$2x - y + z = -5$

$x - 2y + 9z = 8$ [**Ans.** $x = 1$, $y = 1$, $z = 1$]

(d) $x + y + z = 1$

$3x + y + z = 1$

$4x + 3y + 2z = -1$ [**Ans.** $x = 1$, $y = -1$, $z = -1$]

(e) $x - y + z = 6$

$2x + 4y + z = 3$

$3x + 2y - 2z = -2$ [**Ans.** $x = 2$, $y = -1$, $z = 3$]

2. Find the solution of the following equations using the *LU* decomposition methods:

(a)
$$\begin{aligned} x + y + z &= 1 \\ 4x + 3y - z &= 6 \\ 3x + 5y + 3z &= 4 \end{aligned}$$
[**Ans.** $x = 1, y = -0.5, z = 0.5$]

(b)
$$\begin{aligned} 2x + 8y + 2z &= 14 \\ x + 6y - z &= 13 \\ 2x - y + 2z &= 5 \end{aligned}$$
[**Ans.** $x = 5, y = 1, z = -2$]

3. Find the inverse of the following matrices. Choose any matrix *B* and solve for *X* using matrix equation $AX = B$.

(a) $A = \begin{bmatrix} 1 & -2 & 3 \\ 0 & -1 & 4 \\ -2 & 2 & 0 \end{bmatrix}$ $\left(\textbf{Ans. } A^{-1} = \begin{bmatrix} -4 & 3 & -\frac{5}{2} \\ -4 & 3 & -2 \\ -1 & 1 & -\frac{1}{2} \end{bmatrix}\right)$

(b) $A = \begin{bmatrix} 3 & -3 & 4 \\ 2 & -3 & 4 \\ 0 & -1 & 1 \end{bmatrix}$ $\left(\textbf{Ans. } A^{-1} = \begin{bmatrix} 1 & -1 & 0 \\ -2 & 3 & -4 \\ -2 & 3 & -3 \end{bmatrix}\right)$

4. Solve the following equations using the Jacobi and Gauss–Seidel methods.

(a)
$$\begin{aligned} 10x - 5y - 2z &= 3 \\ 4x - 10y + 3z &= -3 \\ x + 6y + 10z &= -3 \end{aligned}$$
[**Ans.** $x = 0.34, y = 0.29, z = -0.51$]

(b)
$$\begin{aligned} 8x + y + z &= 8 \\ 2x + 4y + z &= 4 \\ x + 3y + 3z &= 5 \end{aligned}$$
[**Ans.** $x = 0.82, y = 0.33, z = 1.06$]

(c)
$$\begin{aligned} 5x - y - z &= 3 \\ -x + 10y - 2z &= 7 \\ -x - y + 10z &= 8 \end{aligned}$$
[**Ans.** $x = 1, y = 1, z = 1$]

5. Find the largest eigenvalue and the corresponding eigenvector of the following matrices using the matrix equation $AX = \lambda X$.

(a) $\begin{pmatrix} 2 & -1 & 0 \\ -1 & 2 & -1 \\ 0 & -1 & 2 \end{pmatrix}$ [**Ans.** 3.41; (1, –1.414, 1)]

(b) $\begin{pmatrix} -13 & 3 & -5 \\ 0 & -4 & 0 \\ 15 & -9 & 7 \end{pmatrix}$ [**Ans.** 8; (–1, 0, 1)]

(c) $\begin{pmatrix} 1 & 2 & 4 \\ 3 & 1 & 2 \\ 4 & 2 & 5 \end{pmatrix}$ [**Ans.** 8.66; (1, 0.79, 1.52)]

(d) $\begin{pmatrix} 6.4 & 5.9 & 2.3 \\ 3.1 & 2.7 & 6.3 \\ 2.1 & 1.3 & 5.6 \end{pmatrix}$ [**Ans.** 11.65; (1, 0.69, 0.49)]

C++ Programs

The C++ programs can be implemented on any O/S, namely

1. Windows O/S using Turbo C++, Dev C++ and Visual C++ compilers.
2. Linux-based Ubuntu/Knoppix/Redhat O/S using GNU C++ compiler.

These compilers have been discussed in Chapter 0. No change is required if Ubuntu is used.

While using Turbo C++, Dev C++ and Visual C++ compilers, note the following points for every program.

- Use header file `#include <iostream.h>` (for Turbo C++ only)
- Use header file `#include <math.h>`
- Use header file `#include <conio.h>`
- Use `getch()` function before the closing bracket '}' of the `main()` function.

Program: p31.cpp

```
//Gauss elimination method
#include <iostream>
#include <cmath>
//#define eps 0.00001
using namespace std;
void gel()
{
   int i,j,k,n;
   float a[20][20],x[10],aik,s;
   char option;
   cout<<"enter y for default values of a[i][j] else enter n\n";
   cin>>option;
   if (option=='y')
{
   n=3;
   a[1][1]=1; a[1][2]=-2; a[1][3]=5; a[1][4]=2;
   a[2][1]=4; a[2][2]=9; a[2][3]=-1; a[2][4]=3;
   a[3][1]=3; a[3][2]=7; a[3][3]=2; a[3][4]=7;
   }
   else
{
   cout<<"input the number of rows/columns\n";
   cin>>n;
   //input coefficients
   for (i=1; i<=n;i++)
     for (j=1; j<=n+1; j++)
```

```
      { cout<<"a["<<i<<j<<"]= ";
        cin>>a[i][j];
      }
    }
//elimination/triangularization procedure
for (k=1; k<=n-1; k++)
    {
      for (i=k+1; i<=n; i++)
      {aik=a[i][k]/a[k][k];
      for (j=k; j<=n+1; j++)
      a[i][j]=a[i][j]-a[k][j]*aik;
    }
}
//back-substitution
x[n]=a[n][n+1]/a[n][n];
for (i=n-1;i>=1;i--)
    {
      s=0;
      for (j=i+1;j<=n;j++)
        { =s+a[i][j]*x[j];}
          x[i]=(a[i][n+1]-s)/a[i][i];
        }
    for (i=1;i<=n;i++)
      cout<<"x["<<i<<"]= "<<x[i]<<endl;
        //output: x1=-2.57;x2=1.65;x3=1.57
    }
    main()
{
    gel();
}
```

Program: p32.cpp

```
//Gauss elimination (with pivoting) method
#include <iostream>
#include <cmath>
//#define eps 0.00001
using namespace std;
void gelp()
{
    int i,j,k,q,p,m,n;
    char option;
    float a[20][20],x[10],s,tmp,max;
    cout<<"enter y for default values of a[i][j] else enter n\n";
    cin>>option;
```

```
    if (option=='y')
    {
      n=3;
      a[1][1]=2; a[1][2]=2; a[1][3]=1; a[1][4]=6;
      a[2][1]=4; a[2][2]=2; a[2][3]=3; a[2][4]=4;
      a[3][1]=1; a[3][2]=1; a[3][3]=1; a[3][4]=0;
    }
    else
    {
      cout<<"input the number of rows/columns\n";
      cin>>n;
    //input coefficients of the augmented matrix
      for (i=1; i<=n;i++)
        for (j=1; j<=n+1; j++)
        { cout<<"a["<<i<<j<<"]= ";
          cin>>a[i][j];
        }
    }
//pivoting procedure
for (k=1; k<=n-1; k++)
    {
      max=fabs(a[k][k]);
        p=k;
        for (m=k+1;m<=n;m++)
          {
            if (fabs(a[m][k]>max))
              {
                max=fabs(a[m][k]);
                  p=m;
              }
          }
        if (p != k) //triangularization
    {
      for (q=k; q<=n+1; q++)
          {
            tmp=a[k][q];
            a[k][q]=a[p][q];
            a[p][q]=tmp;
          }
    }
    for (i=k+1;i<=n;i++)
      {
        tmp=a[i][k]/a[k][k];
```

```
         for  (j=k;j<=n+1;j++)
         a[i][j]=a[i][j]-tmp*a[k][j];
      }
   }
   //back  substitution
x[n]=a[n][n+1]/a[n][n];
for  (i=n-1;i>=1;i--)
   {
      s=0;
      for  (j=i+1;j<=n;j++)
   {
      s=s+a[i][j]*x[j];
      }
   x[i]=(a[i][n+1]-s)/a[i][i];
   }
//output  of  solution
cout<<"solution  is\n";
for  (i=1;i<=n;i++)
   cout<<"x["<<i<<"]=  "<<x[i]<<endl;
      //output:  x1=5;x2=1;x3=-6
   }
   main()
{
   gelp();
}
```

Program: p33.cpp

```
//Gauss-Jordan  elimination  method
#include  <iostream>
#include  <cmath>
using  namespace  std;
void  gjel()
{
   char  option;
   int  i,j,k,n;
   float  a[20][20],x[10],aik,tmp;
   cout<<"enter y for default values of a[i][j] else enter n\n";
   cin>>option;
   if  (option=='y')
   {
   n=3;
   a[1][1]=1;  a[1][2]=-2;  a[1][3]=5;  a[1][4]=2;
   a[2][1]=4;  a[2][2]=9;  a[2][3]=-1;  a[2][4]=3;
   a[3][1]=3;  a[3][2]=7;  a[3][3]=2;  a[3][4]=7;
   }
```

```
    else
    {
      cout<<"input the number of rows/columns\n";
      cin>>n;
    // input coefficients of augmented matrix [A]
      for (i=1; i<=n;i++)
        for (j=1; j<=n+1; j++)
        { cout<<"a["<<i<<j<<"]= ";
          cin>>a[i][j];
        }
    }
 //elimination/triangularization procedure
 for (k=1; k<=n; k++)
    {
      tmp=a[k][k];
      for (j=k; j<=n+1; j++)
        a[k][j]=a[k][j]/tmp;
        for (i=1; i<=n; i++)
          {
            if (i != k)
              {
                 aik=a[i][k];
               for (j=k;j<=n+1;j++)
               a[i][j]=a[i][j]-a[k][j]*aik;
              }
          }
    }
 //output solution
 for (i=1;i<=n;i++)
    cout<<"x["<<i<<"]= "<<a[i][n+1]<<endl;
      //output: x1=-2.57;x2=1.65;x3=1.57
    }
    main()
 {
    gjel();
 }
```

Program: p34.cpp

```
//Jacobi's method
//Jacobi iteration method
#include <iostream>
#include <cmath>
#include <iomanip>
# define eps 0.001
```

```
using namespace std;
void jcb()
{
   char option;
   int i,j,k,n,itrmax=10;
   float a[20][20],x[10],x0[10],er,s;
   cout<<"enter y for default values of a[i][j] else enter n\n";
   cin>>option;
   if (option=='y')
   {
     n=3;
     a[1][1]=20; a[1][2]=1; a[1][3]=-2; a[1][4]=17;
     a[2][1]=3; a[2][2]=20; a[2][3]=-1; a[2][4]=-18;
     a[3][1]=2; a[3][2]=-3; a[3][3]=20; a[3][4]=25;
   }
   else
   {
     cout<<"input the number of rows/columns\n";
     cin>>n;
   //input coefficients of augmented matrix [A]
     for (i=1; i<=n;i++)
       for (j=1; j<=n+1; j++)
         {
           cout<<"a["<<i<<j<<"]= ";
           cin>>a[i][j];
         }
   }
//initialization
for (i=1; i<=n; i++)
   x0[i]=0;
for (k=1;k<=itrmax;k++)
   {
     for (i=1; i<=n;i++)
     {
       s=0;
       for (j=1;j<=n;j++)
         {
           if (i != j)
           s=s+a[i][j]*x0[j];
         }
       x[i]=(a[i][n+1]-s)/a[i][i];
       er=fabs((x[i]-x0[i])/x[i]);
     if (er < eps)
       goto stp;
     }
```

```
      for (i=1;i<=n;i++)
        x0[i]=x[i];
    }
    if (er > eps)
    cout<<"non-convergent solution\n";
    return;
stp: {cout<<"convergent solution in "<<k<<" iterations\n";
      //output solution
      for (i=1;i<=n;i++)
      cout<<"x["<<i<<"]= "<<setprecision(4)<<x[i]<<endl;
      //output: x1=1;x2=-1;x3=1
      }
    }
    main()
{
    jcb();
}
```

Program: p35.cpp

```
//Gauss-Seidal iteration method
#include <iostream>
#include <cmath>
#include <iomanip>
# define eps 0.001
using namespace std;
void gs()
{
    int n;
    char option;
    int i,j,k,itrmax=10;
    float a[20][20],x[10],x0[10],er,s;
    cout<<"enter y for default values of a[i][j] else enter n\n";
    cin>>option;
    if (option=='y')
    {
      n=3;
      a[1][1]=20; a[1][2]=1; a[1][3]=-2; a[1][4]=17;
      a[2][1]=3; a[2][2]=20; a[2][3]=-1; a[2][4]=-18;
      a[3][1]=2; a[3][2]=-3; a[3][3]=20; a[3][4]=25;
    }
    else
    {
      cout<<"input the number of rows/columns\n";
      cin>>n;
```

```
    //input coefficients of augmented matrix [A]
      for (i=1; i<=n;i++)
        for (j=1; j<=n+1; j++)
          {
            cout<<"a["<<i<<j<<"]= ";
            cin>>a[i][j];
          }
    }
//initialization
    for (i=1; i<=n; i++)
      x0[i]=0;
    //iteration values
    for (k=1;k<=itrmax;k++)
      {
        for (i=1; i<=n;i++)
        {
          s=0;
          for (j=1;j<=n;j++)
            {
              if (i != j)
              s=s+a[i][j]*x0[j];
            }
          x[i]=(a[i][n+1]-s)/a[i][i];
          er=fabs((x[i]-x0[i])/x[i]);
          if (er < eps)
            goto stp;
        }
        for (i=1;i<=n;i++)
          x0[i]=x[i];
    }
    if (er > eps)
    cout<<"non-convergent solution\n";
    return;
stp: { cout<<"convergent solution in "<<k<<" iterations\n";
        //output solution
      for (i=1;i<=n;i++)
      cout<<"x["<<i<<"]= "<<setprecision(4)<<x[i]<<endl;
      //output: x1=1;x2=-1;x3=1
      }
}
    main()
{
    gs();
}
```

Program: p36.cpp

```
//Power method for maximum eigenvalue
#include <iostream>
#include <cmath>
#include <iomanip>
# define eps 0
using namespace std;
void pmegn()
{
   int n=3;
   char option;
   int i,j,k,kmax=20;
   float a[20][20],x[10],x0[10],s[10],lma,er2,er3;
   //input coefficients of augmented matrix [A]
   cout<<"enter y for default values of a[i][j] else enter n\n";
   cin>>option;
   if (option=='y')
   {
     a[1][1]=10; a[1][2]=4; a[1][3]=-1;
     a[2][1]=4; a[2][2]=2; a[2][3]=3;
     a[3][1]=-1; a[3][2]=3; a[3][3]=1;
   }
   else
   {
     for (i=1; i<=n;i++)
       for (j=1; j<=n; j++)
         { cout<<"a["<<i<<j<<"]= ";
           cin>>a[i][j];
         }
   }
//initialization
   for (i=1; i<=n; i++)
     x0[i]=1;
     k=0;
//iteration values
do
   {
     for (i=1; i<=n;i++)
       {
         s[i]=0;
           for (j=1;j<=n;j++)
             s[i]=s[i]+a[i][j]*x0[j];
       }
```

```
      lma=fabs(s[1]);
for (i=1; i<=n;i++)
   x[i]=s[i]/lma;
      er2=fabs(x[2]-x0[2]);
      er3=fabs(x[3]-x0[3]);
      if ((er2 < eps) && (er3 < eps))
      break;
      for (i=1;i<=n;i++)
      x0[i]=x[i];
      k+=1;
   }
   while (k <= kmax);
stp: { cout<<"convergent solution in "<<k<<" iterations\n";
         //output solution
      cout<<"largest eigenvalue is= "<<lma<<endl;
      for (i=1;i<=n;i++)
      cout<<"x["<<i<<"]= "<<setprecision(4)<<x[i]<<endl;
      //output: x1=1;x2=0.4217;x3=-0.02487,lmbda=11.662
      return;
      }
   cout<<"non-convergent solution\n";
}
   main()
{
   pmegn();
}
```

4

Interpolation

4.1 Introduction

Let a function $y = f(x)$ be given in a tabulated form in the interval $[x_1, x_n]$ as shown in Table 4.1.

Table 4.1 Tabulated function

x_i	x_1	x_2	x_3	. . .	x_n
$y_i = f(x_i)$	y_1	y_2	y_3	. . .	y_n

where the x_i's are assumed to be equally spaced at small interval h.

If the value of the function $f(x)$ is required to be calculated at a point that is not one of the tabulated points, then a numerical method called **interpolation** is required. If the value of the function is required at a point outside the interval $[x_1, x_n]$ tabulated above, then the numerical procedure called **extrapolation** is required. For example, if the point lies between x_1 and x_2, then interpolation is required, and if the point lies beyond x_n, then extrapolation is necessary.

The technique of interpolation is very useful in making statistical predictions of census surveys, in performing calculation of the values of known mathematical functions, such as Bessel's function, at some non-tabulated points, etc. Interpolation is also used for calculating the derivatives of a function at a given point, for finding the integral of a function and for finding the solution of a differential equation.

The method of interpolation involves the determination of the function $y(x)$ such that the given tabulated function agrees with the values of the function $y(x)$ at all the specified tabulated points. The function $y(x)$ can be a polynomial function, trigonometric function, etc. But the simplest form of a function is the polynomial function as it can be easily used for operations like numerical differentiation and integration.

We will discuss the following three methods of interpolation:

1. Lagrange method of interpolation
2. Newton's methods of interpolation based on finite differences:
   (a) Forward difference interpolation formula
   (b) Backward difference interpolation formula
   (c) Divided difference interpolation formula
3. Central difference methods.

4.2 Lagrange Interpolation Method

In this method we assume that the dependent variable $y = f(x)$ is such that it takes the values $y_0 = f(x_0)$, $y_1 = f(x_1)$, $y_2 = f(x_2)$, etc. The independent variable values x_i may be **unequally spaced**. Let the function $y = f(x)$ be given by the polynomial

$$\left.\begin{aligned} y = f(x) = \; & b_0(x - x_1)(x - x_2) \qquad\quad \ldots (x - x_n) \\ & + b_1(x - x_0)(x - x_2)(x - x_3) \ldots (x - x_n) \\ & + b_2(x - x_0)(x - x_1)(x - x_3) \;\; \ldots (x - x_n) \\ & \;\vdots \\ & + b_n(x - x_0)(x - x_1)(x - x_2) \;\; \ldots (x - x_{n-1}) \end{aligned}\right\} \tag{4.1}$$

Using $x = x_0$, $y = y_0$ in Eq. (4.1) gives

$$y_0 = b_0(x_0 - x_1)(x_0 - x_2) \cdots (x_0 - x_n)$$

Thus,
$$b_0 = \frac{y_0}{(x_0 - x_1)(x_0 - x_2) \ldots (x_0 - x_n)}$$

Similarly at $x = x_1$, $y = y_1$ gives

$$b_1 = \frac{y_1}{(x_1 - x_0)(x_1 - x_2) \ldots (x_1 - x_n)}$$

At $x = x_n$, $y = y_n$ gives

$$b_n = \frac{y_n}{(x_n - x_0)(x_n - x_1) \ldots (x_n - x_{n-1})}$$

Using the above values of the coefficients in Eq. (4.1), we obtain

$$\left.\begin{aligned} y = f(x) = \; & \frac{y_0(x - x_1)(x - x_2) \ldots (x - x_n)}{(x_0 - x_1)(x_0 - x_2) \ldots (x_0 - x_n)} \\ & + \frac{y_1(x - x_0)(x - x_2)(x - x_3) \ldots (x - x_n)}{(x_1 - x_0)(x_1 - x_2) \ldots (x_1 - x_n)} \\ & \;\vdots \\ & + \frac{y_n(x - x_0)(x - x_1)(x - x_2) \ldots (x - x_{n-1})}{(x_n - x_0)(x_n - x_1) \ldots (x_n - x_{n-1})} \end{aligned}\right\} \tag{4.2}$$

Equation (4.2) is the general form of **Lagrange's interpolation formula** which is applicable to unequally spaced independent variable values.

For example, for a polynomial of the second order, Eq. (4.1) can be written as

$$\begin{aligned} y = f(x) &= b_0(x - x_1)(x - x_2) \\ &+ b_1(x - x_0)(x - x_2) \\ &+ b_2(x - x_0)(x - x_1) \end{aligned} \tag{4.3}$$

At $x = x_0$, $y = y_0$ in Eq. (4.3) gives

$$y_0 = b_0(x_0 - x_1)(x_0 - x_2)$$

Thus,
$$b_0 = \frac{y_0}{(x_0 - x_1)(x_0 - x_2)}$$

At $x = x_1$, $y = y_1$ in Eq. (4.3) gives

$$b_1 = \frac{y_1}{(x_1 - x_0)(x_1 - x_2)}$$

At $x = x_2$, $y = y_2$ in Eq. (4.3) gives

$$b_2 = \frac{y_2}{(x_2 - x_0)(x_2 - x_1)}$$

Using the above values of the coefficients in Eq. (4.3), we obtain

$$\begin{aligned} y = f(x) = &\frac{y_0(x - x_1)(x - x_2)}{(x_0 - x_1)(x_0 - x_2)} \\ &+ \frac{y_1(x - x_0)(x - x_2)}{(x_1 - x_0)(x_1 - x_2)} \\ &+ \frac{y_2(x - x_0)(x - x_1)}{(x_2 - x_0)(x_2 - x_1)} \end{aligned} \tag{4.4}$$

This polynomial function is said to pass through the points (x_0, y_0), (x_1, y_1) and (x_2, y_2). Using the product and summation notations, Eqs. (4.2) and (4.4) can be rewritten as

$$y = \sum_{i=0}^{n} y_i \prod_{j=0; j \neq i}^{n} \frac{x - x_j}{x_i - x_j} \tag{4.5}$$

The Lagrange interpolation can be used to find the value of the independent variable when the value of the corresponding dependent variable is given. Rewriting Eq. (4.5) as

$$x = \sum_{i=0}^{n} x_i \prod_{j=0; j \neq i}^{n} \frac{y - y_j}{y_i - y_j} \tag{4.6}$$

Equation (4.6) is known as **Lagrange inverse polynomial formula**.

It may be noted that the order of the fitting polynomial is not possible to ascertain in the Lagrange method.

4.3 Numerical Examples

EXAMPLE 4.1 From the given table, find the function $f(x)$ considering it to be a polynomial of order three.

x_i	0	1	2	3
$y_i = f(x_i)$	1	2	11	34

Solution

From the above table $(x_0, y_0) = (0, 1)$; $(x_1, y_1) = (1, 2)$; $(x_2, y_2) = (2, 11)$; $(x_3, y_3) = (3, 34)$

Using Eq. (4.5), we obtain

$$y = f(x) = \frac{y_0(x - x_1)(x - x_2)(x - x_3)}{(x_0 - x_1)(x_0 - x_2)(x_0 - x_3)}$$

$$+ \frac{y_1(x - x_0)(x - x_2)(x - x_3)}{(x_1 - x_0)(x_1 - x_2)(x_1 - x_3)}$$

$$+ \frac{y_2(x - x_0)(x - x_1)(x - x_3)}{(x_2 - x_0)(x_2 - x_1)(x_2 - x_3)}$$

$$+ \frac{y_3(x - x_0)(x - x_1)(x - x_2)}{(x_3 - x_0)(x_3 - x_1)(x_3 - x_2)}$$

$$= \frac{(1)(x-1)(x-2)(x-3)}{(0-1)(0-2)(0-3)}$$

$$+ \frac{(2)(x-0)(x-2)(x-3)}{(1-0)(1-2)(1-3)}$$

$$+ \frac{(11)(x-0)(x-1)(x-3)}{(2-0)(2-1)(2-3)}$$

$$+ \frac{(34)(x-0)(x-1)(x-2)}{(3-0)(3-1)(3-2)}$$

$$= \frac{(x-1)(x-2)(x-3)}{-6}$$

$$+ \frac{(2)(x)(x-2)(x-3)}{2}$$

$$+ \frac{(11)(x)(x-1)(x-3)}{-2}$$

$$+ \frac{(34)(x)(x-1)(x-2)}{6}$$

Therefore, $y = f(x) = x^3 + x^2 - x + 1$

EXAMPLE 4.2 From the given table, find the value of the function $f(x)$ at $x = 2$ considering it to be a polynomial of order three.

x_i	0	1	3	4
$y_i = f(x_i)$	5	6	50	105

Solution

From the above table $(x_0, y_0) = (0, 5)$; $(x_1, y_1) = (1, 6)$; $(x_2, y_2) = (3, 50)$; $(x_3, y_3) = (4, 105)$

Using Eq. (4.5), we obtain

$$y = f(x) = \frac{y_0(x-x_1)(x-x_2)(x-x_3)}{(x_0-x_1)(x_0-x_2)(x_0-x_3)}$$

$$+ \frac{y_1(x-x_0)(x-x_2)(x-x_3)}{(x_1-x_0)(x_1-x_2)(x_1-x_3)}$$

$$+ \frac{y_2(x-x_0)(x-x_1)(x-x_3)}{(x_2-x_0)(x_2-x_1)(x_2-x_3)}$$

$$+ \frac{y_3(x-x_0)(x-x_1)(x-x_2)}{(x_3-x_0)(x_3-x_1)(x_3-x_2)}$$

$$= \frac{(5)(2-1)(2-3)(2-4)}{(0-1)(0-3)(0-4)}$$

$$+ \frac{(6)(2-0)(2-3)(2-4)}{(1-0)(1-3)(1-4)}$$

$$+ \frac{(50)(2-0)(2-1)(2-4)}{(3-0)(3-1)(3-4)}$$

$$+ \frac{(105)(2-0)(2-3)(2-1)}{(4-0)(4-1)(4-3)}$$

$$= -\frac{5}{6} + 4 + \frac{200}{6} - \frac{105}{6}$$

Therefore, $f(2) = 19$

EXAMPLE 4.3 Using the following table, find the value of x at $y = 0.39$.

x_i	20	25	30	35
$y_i = f(x_i)$	0.342	0.423	0.5	0.65

Solution

From the above table, $(x_0, y_0) = (20, 0.342)$; $(x_1, y_1) = (25, 0.423)$; $(x_2, y_2) = (30, 0.5)$; $(x_3, y_3) = (35, 0.65)$

Using Eq. (4.6), we obain

$$x = f(y) = \frac{x_0(y-y_1)(y-y_2)(y-y_3)}{(y_0-y_1)(y_0-y_2)(y_0-y_3)} + \frac{x_1(y-y_0)(y-y_2)(y-y_3)}{(y_1-y_0)(y_1-y_2)(y_1-y_3)} + \frac{x_2(y-y_0)(y-y_1)(y-y_3)}{(y_2-y_0)(y_2-y_1)(y_2-y_3)} + \frac{x_3(y-y_0)(y-y_1)(y-y_2)}{(y_3-y_0)(y_3-y_1)(y_3-y_2)}$$

$$f(0.39) = \frac{(20)(0.39-0.423)(0.39-0.5)(0.39-0.65)}{(0.342-0.423)(0.342-0.5)(0.342-0.65)} + \frac{(25)(0.39-0.342)(0.39-0.5)(0.39-0.65)}{(0.423-0.342)(0.423-0.5)(0.423-0.65)} + \frac{(30)(0.39-0.342)(0.39-0.423)(0.39-0.65)}{(0.5-0.342)(0.5-0.423)(0.5-0.65)} + \frac{(35)(0.39-0.342)(0.39-0.423)(0.39-0.5)}{(0.65-0.342)(0.65-0.423)(0.65-0.5)}$$

Therefore, $x = f(0.39) = 22.84$

4.4 Algorithm (AL41) for Lagrange Interpolation Method

This algorithm is transformed to a computer program written in C++ language and presented at the end of this chapter (see **p41.cpp**).

1. Declare/define the function/subprogram **li** to implement the method.
2. Start the (main) function.
3. Define the main function which calls the appropriate subprogram/function according to given choice.
4. Stop (main).

Details of function/subprogram **li**:

```
1. Start
2. Enter the number of tabulated points, n
3. Enter the point of interpolation, X
4. Enter the coordinates (xi, yi) using for loop
5. sm = 0
   {computation of polynomial}
6. for i = 1 to n do
   begin
   pr=1
   for j = 1 to n do
     begin
       if (i ≠ j) then
       pr = pr · ((X – xj)/xi – xj))
       endif
     endfor
     sm = sm + yi · pr
     endfor
   write sm
7. Return
```

4.5 Methods Based on Finite Differences

The theory of interpolation depends heavily on the construction of **tables of finite differences** from the given set of tabulated points of the function. The subtractions between the successive values of the tabulated function as well as subtractions between the past subtracted values of the function are known as **finite differences**. There are four types of finite differences and their tables used in the theory of interpolation:

1. Forward differences and the forward difference table (for equally spaced x_i points).
2. Backward differences and the backward difference table (for equally spaced x_i points).
3. Divided differences and the divided difference table (for equally/unequally spaced x_i points).
4. Central differences and the central difference table (for equally spaced x_i points).

The method of interpolation involves the development of a polynomial function of the form:

$$y = f(x) = b_1 + b_2(x - x_1) + b_3(x - x_1)(x - x_2) + \cdots + b_n(x - x_1)(x - x_2) \cdots (x - x_n) \tag{4.7}$$

For interpolating the function at a given point x, the selection of an appropriate finite difference from the above four types is required.

4.6 Forward Differences and the Forward Difference Table

Let a function $y = f(x)$ be given in a tabulated form as in Table 4.1. The forward differences are the differences between two successive values of the function $f(x)$ represented by the symbol 'Δ' (called the **forward difference operator**) as follows:

$$\Delta y_1 = y_2 - y_1$$
$$\Delta y_2 = y_3 - y_2$$
$$\Delta y_3 = y_4 - y_3$$
$$\vdots$$
$$\Delta y_{n-1} = y_n - y_{n-1}$$

where $y_1 = f(x_1)$, $y_2 = f(x_2) = f(x_1 + h)$, ..., $y_n = f(x_n) = f(x_1 + nh)$.

The above differences are known as the first-order forward differences.

The second-order forward differences are defined as the differences calculated from the first-order forward differences as follows:

$$\Delta^2 y_1 = \Delta y_2 - \Delta y_1$$
$$\Delta^2 y_2 = \Delta y_3 - \Delta y_2$$
$$\Delta^2 y_3 = \Delta y_4 - \Delta y_3$$
$$\vdots$$
$$\Delta^2 y_{n-1} = \Delta y_n - \Delta y_{n-1}$$

In the same way, the higher-order differences like $\Delta^3 y$, $\Delta^4 y$, etc., can be defined in terms of the previous order differences.

The kth order forward differences at a point $x = x_i$ are given by

$$\Delta^k y_i = \Delta^{k-1} y_{i+1} - \Delta^{k-1} y_i \tag{4.8}$$

The values of higher-order forward differences go on decreasing with the order.

These different orders of differences can be placed in **two** types of tables, namely

(a) The diagonal forward difference table **(DFDT)**
(b) The horizontal forward difference table **(HFDT)**

In DFDT the differences are placed midway between the two arguments as shown in Table 4.2.

The DFDT is termed *diagonal* because the higher-order forward differences are placed along the forward diagonal in each column.

The horizontal forward difference table (HFDT) is a table in which the forward difference values are calculated and placed horizontally along with the points (x_i, y_i) as shown in Table 4.3.

For example, consider a function $y = f(x)$ tabulated at $n = 6$ points.

Table 4.2 Diagonal forward difference table (DFDT)

i	x_i	y_i	Δy_i	$\Delta^2 y_i$	$\Delta^3 y_i$	$\Delta^4 y_i$	$\Delta^5 y_i$
1	x_1	y_1					
			$\Delta y_1 = y_2 - y_1$				
2	x_2	y_2		$\Delta^2 y_1 = \Delta y_2 - \Delta y_1$			
			$\Delta y_2 = y_3 - y_2$		$\Delta^3 y_1 = \Delta^2 y_2 - \Delta^2 y_1$		
3	x_3	y_3		$\Delta^2 y_2 = \Delta y_3 - \Delta y_2$		$\Delta^4 y_1 = \Delta^3 y_2 - \Delta^3 y_1$	
			$\Delta y_3 = y_4 - y_3$		$\Delta^3 y_2 = \Delta^2 y_3 - \Delta^2 y_2$		$\Delta^5 y_1 = \Delta^4 y_2 - \Delta^4 y_1$
4	x_4	y_4		$\Delta^2 y_3 = \Delta y_4 - \Delta y_3$		$\Delta^4 y_2 = \Delta^3 y_3 - \Delta^3 y_2$	
			$\Delta y_4 = y_5 - y_4$		$\Delta^3 y_3 = \Delta^2 y_4 - \Delta^2 y_3$		
5	x_5	y_5		$\Delta^2 y_4 = \Delta y_5 - \Delta y_4$			
			$\Delta y_5 = y_6 - y_5$				
6	x_6	y_6					

Table 4.3 Horizontal forward difference table (HFDT)

i	x_i	y_i	Δy_i	$\Delta^2 y_i$	$\Delta^3 y_i$	$\Delta^4 y_i$	$\Delta^5 y_i$
1	x_1	y_1	$\Delta y_1 = y_2 - y_1$	$\Delta^2 y_1 = \Delta y_2 - \Delta y_1$	$\Delta^3 y_1 = \Delta^2 y_2 - \Delta^2 y_1$	$\Delta^4 y_1 = \Delta^3 y_2 - \Delta^3 y_1$	$\Delta^5 y_1 = \Delta^4 y_2 - \Delta^4 y_1$
2	x_2	y_2	$\Delta y_2 = y_3 - y_2$	$\Delta^2 y_2 = \Delta y_3 - \Delta y_2$	$\Delta^3 y_2 = \Delta^2 y_3 - \Delta^2 y_2$	$\Delta^4 y_2 = \Delta^3 y_3 - \Delta^3 y_2$	
3	x_3	y_3	$\Delta y_3 = y_4 - y_3$	$\Delta^2 y_3 = \Delta y_4 - \Delta y_3$	$\Delta^3 y_3 = \Delta^2 y_4 - \Delta^2 y_3$		
4	x_4	y_4	$\Delta y_4 = y_5 - y_4$	$\Delta^2 y_4 = \Delta y_5 - \Delta y_4$			
5	x_5	y_5	$\Delta y_5 = y_6 - y_5$				
6	x_6	y_6					

4.7 Numerical Examples (Forward Difference Table)

EXAMPLE 4.4 Construct a forward difference table from the following tabulated function.

x_i	0	1	2	3	4	5
$y_i = f(x_i)$	12	15	20	27	39	52

Solution

Using the definition of the forward difference operator, construct Table 4.4 in HFDT form.

Table 4.4 Example 4.4

x_i	$y_i = f(x_i)$	Δy_i	$\Delta^2 y_i$	$\Delta^3 y_i$	$\Delta^4 y_i$	$\Delta^5 y_i$
0	12	3	2	0	3	–10
1	15	5	2	3	–7	
2	20	7	5	–4		
3	27	12	1			
4	39	13				
5	52					

In DFDT form, Table 4.4 can be represented as shown in Table 4.5.

Table 4.5 DFDT form—Example 4.4

x_i	$y_i = f(x_i)$	Δy_i	$\Delta^2 y_i$	$\Delta^3 y_i$	$\Delta^4 y_i$	$\Delta^5 y_i$
0	12					
		3				
1	15		2			
		5		0		
2	20		2		3	
		7		3		–10
3	27		5		–7	
		12		–4		
4	39		1			
		13				
5	52					

EXAMPLE 4.5 Construct the horizontal forward difference table from the following tabulated function.

x_i	0	1	2	3	4
$y_i = f(x_i)$	2	3	12	35	78

Solution

Using the definition of the forward difference operator, the table in HFDT form is constructed as shown in Table 4.6.

Table 4.6 HFDT form—Example 4.5

i	x_i	$y_i = f(x_i)$	Δy_i	$\Delta^2 y_i$	$\Delta^3 y_i$	$\Delta^4 y_i$
1	0	2	1	8	6	0
2	1	3	9	14	6	
3	2	12	23	20		
4	3	35	43			
5	4	78				

4.8 Algorithm (AL42) for Forward Difference Table Construction

This algorithm is transformed to a computer program written in C++ language and presented at the end of this chapter (see **p42.cpp**).

1. Declare/define the function/subprogram **fdt** to implement the method.
2. Start the (main) function.
3. Define the main function which calls the appropriate subprogram/function according to given choice.
4. Stop (main).

Details of function/subprogram **fdt**:

1. Start
2. Enter the number of tabulated points, n
3. Enter the coordinates (x_i, y_i) using for loop
4. Declare a 2-dimensional (fd) array for the forward difference operator, Δ
5. Compute the elements of fd_{ij}

```
for j = 1 to n – 1 do
begin
    for i = 1 to n – j do
    begin
        if (j = 1) then
            fd_ij = y_i+1 – y_i
        else
            fd_ij = fd_i+1j–1 – fd_ij–1
        endif
    endfor
    write fd_ij
endfor
```

6. Return

4.9 Newton's Forward Interpolation Formula for Tabulated Functions

This interpolation formula is based on taking finite forward differences of the given tabulated function. Let a function $y = f(x)$ be given in tabulated form in the interval $[x_1, x_n]$ as shown below.

x_i	x_1	x_2	x_3	...	x_n
$y_i = f(x_i)$	y_1	y_2	y_3	...	y_{n+1}

where the x_i's are assumed to be equally spaced at a small interval h.

Assume that the function $f(x)$ is a polynomial of nth order and is given by

$$y = f(x) = b_1 + b_2(x - x_1) + b_3(x - x_1)(x - x_2) + \cdots + b_{n+1}(x - x_1)(x - x_2) \cdots (x - x_n)$$

At point $x = x_1$ the value of the function is given by

$$y_1 = f(x_1) = b_1$$

At point $x = x_2$ the value of the function is given by

$$y_2 = f(x_2) = b_1 + b_2(x_2 - x_1)$$

At point $x = x_3$ the value of the function is given by

$$y_3 = f(x_3) = b_1 + b_2(x_3 - x_1) + b_3(x_3 - x_1)(x_3 - x_2)$$

and so on.

The points x_i's are equally spaced with an interval size of h, therefore, we can write

$$x_2 = x_1 + h,\ x_3 = x_1 + 2h,\ x_4 = x_1 + 3h,\ \ldots,\ x_n = x_1 + (n - 1)h$$

Rewriting the y_i's in terms of h as

$$y_1 = f(x_1) = b_1$$
$$y_2 = f(x_2) = b_1 + b_2h$$
$$y_3 = f(x_3) = b_1 + b_2(2h) + b_3(2h^2)$$
$$\vdots$$
$$y_{n+1} = f(x_n) = b_1 + b_2(nh) + b_3(nh)((n - 1)h) + \cdots + b_{n+1}(nh)((n - 1)h) \ldots (h)$$

Rearranging the above to evaluate coefficients b_i as

$$b_1 = y_1$$

$$b_2 = \frac{y_2 - b_1}{h} = \frac{y_2 - y_1}{h} = \frac{\Delta y_1}{h}$$

$$b_3 = \frac{y_3 - (2h)b_2 - b_1}{2h^2} = \frac{y_3 - 2(y_2 - y_1) - y_1}{2h^2} = \frac{y_3 - 2y_2 + y_1}{2h^2}$$

$$= \frac{(y_3 - y_2) - (y_2 - y_1)}{2h^2}$$

$$= \frac{\Delta y_2 - \Delta y_1}{2h^2}$$

$$= \frac{\Delta^2 y_1}{h^2 2!}$$

In general, the $(n + 1)$th coefficient is given by

$$b_{n+1} = \frac{y_{n+1} - ny_n + y_1}{h^n n!}$$

$$= \frac{\Delta^n y_1}{h^n n!}$$

The polynomial function $y = f(x)$ can be written as

$$y = f(x)$$

$$y = f(x) = y_1 + \left(\frac{\Delta y_1}{1!h}\right)(x - x_1) + \left(\frac{\Delta^2 y_1}{h^2 2!}\right)(x - x_1)(x - x_2) + \cdots +$$

$$\left(\frac{\Delta^n y_1}{h^n n!}\right)(x - x_1)(x - x_2) \ldots (x - x_n)$$

Defining a dimensionless variable z called *phase*, as

$$z = \frac{x - x_1}{h}$$

$$x - x_1 = hz$$

$$x - x_2 = x - (x_1 + h) = h(z - 1)$$

$$x - x_3 = x - (x_2 + h) = h(z - 2)$$

$$\vdots$$

$$x - x_n = x - (x_{n-1} + h) = h(z - (n - 1))$$

Rewriting the polynomial as

$$y = y_1 + \frac{\Delta y_1 z}{1!} + \frac{\Delta^2 y_1}{2!} z(z - 1) + \cdots +$$

$$\frac{\Delta^n y_1}{n!} z(z-1)(z-2) \ldots (z-(n-1)) \tag{4.9a}$$

The above relation is true for interpolating the polynomial function at any point in the interval $[x_1, x_2]$.

In general, for interpolating the function at any point in the interval $[x_k, x_{k+1}]$, the polynomial function can be rewritten as

$$y = f(x) = y_k + \frac{\Delta y_k z}{1!} + \frac{\Delta^2 y_k}{2!} z(z-1) + \cdots + \frac{\Delta^n y_k}{n!} z(z-1)(z-2) \ldots (z-(n-1)) \tag{4.9b}$$

where $z = (x - x_k)/h$.

Equations (4.9a) and (4.9b) are known as **Newton's forward interpolation formulas**. These are mainly used for interpolation at a point near the beginning of the forward difference table. It should be noted that if the function $f(x)$ is a polynomial of degree n, then the nth order forward/backward difference will be a constant and the $(n + 1)$th difference will be zero. Using this information, we can infer the order of the polynomial function from the difference table of the function.

4.10 Backward Differences and the Backward Difference Table

Let a function $y = f(x)$ be tabulated as in Table 4.1. The backward differences are the differences between two successive values of the function represented by the symbol '∇' called the **backward difference operator**. The first-order backward differences are given by

$$\nabla y_2 = y_2 - y_1$$
$$\nabla y_3 = y_3 - y_2$$
$$\vdots$$
$$\nabla y_n = y_n - y_{n-1}$$

where $y_1 = f(x_1)$, $y_2 = f(x_2) = f(x_1 + h)$, ..., $y_n = f(x_n) = f(x_1 + nh)$

The second-order backward differences are defined as

$$\nabla^2 y_3 = \nabla y_3 - \nabla y_2$$
$$\nabla^2 y_4 = \nabla y_4 - \nabla y_3$$
$$\vdots$$
$$\nabla^2 y_n = \nabla y_n - \nabla y_{n-1}$$

Similarly, the third, fourth, and higher-order backward differences can be defined.

The kth order backward difference at $x = x_i$ is given by

$$\nabla^k y_i = \nabla^{k-1} y_i - \nabla^{k-1} y_{i-1} \tag{4.10}$$

The backward difference tables can be constructed for the tabulated points of the function in two ways: (a) Diagonal backward difference table (DBDT) and (b) Horizontal backward difference table (HBDT).

In DBDT the successive backward differences are placed midway between the preceding values of the differences as shown in Table 4.7.

Table 4.7 Diagonal backward difference table (DBDT)

i	x_i	$y_i = f(x_i)$	∇y_i	$\nabla^2 y_i$	$\nabla^3 y_i$	$\nabla^4 y_i$
1	x_1	y_1				
			$\nabla y_2 = y_2 - y_1$			
2	x_2	y_2		$\nabla^2 y_3 = \nabla y_3 - \nabla y_2$		
			$\nabla y_3 = y_3 - y_2$		$\nabla^3 y_4 = \nabla^2 y_4 - \nabla^2 y_3$	
3	x_3	y_3		$\nabla^2 y_4 = \nabla y_4 \nabla y_3$		$\nabla^4 y_5 = \nabla^3 y_5 - \nabla^3 y_4$
			$\nabla^2 y_4 = y_4 - y_3$		$\nabla^3 y_4 = \nabla^2 y_5 - \nabla^2 y_4$	
4	x_4	y_4		$\nabla^2 y_5 = \nabla y_5 - \nabla y_4$		
			$\nabla^2 y_5 = y_5 - y_4$			
5	x_5	y_5				

In HBDT, the successive backward differences are placed alongside the points (x_i, y_i) as shown in Table 4.8.

Table 4.8 Horizontal backward difference table (HBDT)

i	x_i	$y_i = f(x_i)$	∇y_i	$\nabla^2 y_i$	$\nabla^3 y_i$	$\nabla^4 y_i$
1	x_1	y_1				
2	x_2	y_2	$\nabla y_2 = y_2 - y_1$			
3	x_3	y_3	$\nabla y_3 = y_3 - y_2$	$\nabla^2 y_3 = \nabla y_3 - \nabla y_2$		
4	x_4	y_4	$\nabla y_4 = y_4 - y_3$	$\nabla^2 y_4 = \nabla y_4 - \nabla y_3$	$\nabla^3 y_4 = \nabla^2 y_4 - \nabla^2 y_3$	
5	x_5	y_5	$\nabla y_5 = y_5 - y_4$	$\nabla^2 y_5 = \nabla y_5 - \nabla y_4$	$\nabla^3 y_5 = \nabla^2 y_5 - \nabla^2 y_4$	$\nabla^4 y_5 = \nabla^3 y_5 - \nabla^3 y_4$

We may use either of the two forms of tables to solve numerical problems.

4.11 Numerical Examples (Backward Differences)

EXAMPLE 4.6 Construct a backward difference table from the following tabulated function.

x_i	0	1	2	3	4	5
$y_i = f(x_i)$	12	15	20	27	39	52

Solution

Using the definition of the backward difference operator, we construct the HBDT (Table 4.9) as follows.

Table 4.9 HBDT form—Example 4.6

x_i	$y_i = f(x_i)$	∇y_i	$\nabla^2 y_i$	$\nabla^3 y_i$	$\nabla^4 y_i$	$\nabla^5 y_i$
0	12					
1	15	3				
2	20	5	2			
3	27	7	2	0		
4	39	12	5	3	3	
5	52	13	1	–4	–7	–10

EXAMPLE 4.7 Construct a backward difference table from the following tabulated function.

x_i	0	1	2	3	4
$y_i = f(x_i)$	2	3	12	35	78

Solution

Using the definition of the backward difference operator, we construct the HBDT (Table 4.10) as follows:

Table 4.10 HBDT form—Example 4.7

i	x_i	$y_i = f(x_i)$	∇y_i	$\nabla^2 y_i$	$\nabla^3 y_i$	$\nabla^4 y_i$
1	0	2				
2	1	3	1			
3	2	12	9	8		
4	3	35	23	14	6	
5	4	78	43	20	6	0

4.12 Newton's Backward Interpolation Formula for Tabulated Functions

This interpolation formula is based on taking finite *backward differences* of the given tabulated function. Let a function $y = f(x)$ be given in a tabulated form in the interval $[x_1, x_n]$ as shown below:

x_i	x_1	x_2	x_3	...	x_n
$y_i = f(x_i)$	y_1	y_2	y_3	...	y_n

where the x_i's are assumed to be equally spaced at a small interval h.

Assume that the function $f(x)$ is a polynomial of nth order and is given by

$$y = f(x) = b_1 + b_2(x - x_n) + b_3(x - x_n)(x - x_{n-1}) + \cdots + b_{n+1}(x - x_n)(x - x_{n-1}) \ldots (x - x_1)$$

At point $x = x_n$ the value of the function is given by

$$y_n = f(x_1) = b_1$$

At point $x = x_{n-1}$ the value of the function is given by

$$y_{n-1} = f(x_{n-1}) = b_1 + b_2(x_{n-1} - x_n)$$

At point $x = x_{n-2}$ the value of the function is given by

$$y_{n-2} = f(x_{n-2}) = b_1 + b_2(x_{n-2} - x_n) + b_3(x_{n-2} - x_n)(x_{n-2} - x_{n-1})$$

And so on.

The points x_i's are equally spaced with an interval size of h, therefore, we can write

$$x_{n-1} - x_n = -h,\ x_{n-2} - x_n = x_{n-2} - x_{n-1} - h = -2h,\ ...,\ x_1 - x_n = -nh$$

Rewriting the y_i's in terms of h as

$$y_n = f(x_n) = b_1$$
$$y_{n-1} = f(x_{n-1}) = b_1 + b_2(-h)$$
$$y_{n-2} = f(x_{n-2}) = b_1 + b_2(-2h) + b_3(-2h^2)$$
$$\vdots$$
$$y_1 = f(x_1) = b_1 + b_2(x_1 - x_n) + b_3(x_1 - x_n)(x_1 - x_{n-1}) + \cdots + b_n(x_1 - x_n)(x_1 - x_{n-1}) \ldots (x_1 - x_2)$$
$$y_1 = f(x_1) = b_1 + b_2(-nh) + b_3(-nh)(-(n-1)h) + \cdots + b_n(-nh)(-(n-1)h) \ldots (-h)$$

Rearranging the above to evaluate coefficients b_i as

$$b_1 = y_n$$

$$b_2 = \frac{y_{n-1} - b_1}{-h} = \frac{y_{n-1} - y_n}{-h} = \frac{\nabla y_n}{1!h}$$

$$b_3 = \frac{y_{n-2} - (-2h)b_2 - b_1}{2h^2} = \frac{y_{n-2} - 2(y_{n-1} - y_n) - y_n}{2h^2}$$

$$= \frac{y_{n-2} - y_{n-1} - y_{n-1} - y_n}{2h^2}$$

$$= \frac{\nabla y_{n-1} - \nabla y_n}{2h^2}$$

$$= \frac{\nabla^2 y_n}{h^2 2!}$$

In general, the $(n + 1)$th coefficient is given by

$$b_{n+1} = \frac{y_1 - ny_n + y_1}{h^n n!}$$

$$= \frac{\nabla^n y_n}{h^n n!}$$

The polynomial function can be written as

$$y = f(x) = y_n + \left(\frac{\nabla y_n}{1!h}\right)(x - x_n) + \left(\frac{\nabla^2 y_n}{h^2 2!}\right)(x - x_n)(x - x_{n-1}) + \cdots + \left(\frac{\nabla^n y_n}{h^n n!}\right)(x - x_n)(x - x_{n-1}) \ldots (x - x_1)$$

Again defining a dimensionless variable z called phase, as

$$z = \frac{x - x_n}{h}$$

$$x - x_n = hz$$

$$x - x_{n-1} = x - (x_n - h) = x - x_n + h = h(z + 1)$$

$$x - x_{n-2} = x - (x_{n-1} - h) = h(z + 1) + h = h(z + 2)$$

$$\vdots$$

$$x - x_1 = x - (x_n + (n - 1)h) = h(z + (n - 1))$$

Rewriting the polynomial as

$$y = f(x) = y_n + \left(\frac{\nabla y_n z}{1!}\right) + \left(\frac{\nabla^2 y_n}{2!}\right) z(z+1) + \cdots + \left(\frac{\nabla^n y_n}{n!}\right) z(z+1)(z+2) \ldots (z + (n-1)) \tag{4.11a}$$

where y_n is the value of the function at $x = x_n$.

The above relation is true for interpolating the polynomial function at any point in the interval $[x_{n-1}, x_n]$.

In general, for interpolating the function at any point in the interval $[x_{k-1}, x_k]$ the polynomial function can be rewritten as

$$y = f(x) = y_k + \left(\frac{\nabla y_k z}{1!}\right) + \left(\frac{\nabla^2 y_k}{2!}\right) z(z + 1) + \cdots + \left(\frac{\nabla^n y_k}{n!}\right) z(z + 1)(z + 2) \ldots (z + (k - 1)) \tag{4.11b}$$

where $z = (x - x_k)/h$.

Equations (4.11a) and (4.11b) are known as **Newton's backward interpolation formulas.**

4.13 Numerical Examples (NFD and NBD Interpolation Formulas)

EXAMPLE 4.8 Interpolate the function $y = f(x)$ at point $x = 1.5$ using the following tabulated data.

x_i	1	2	3	4	5	6	7	8
$y_i = f(x_i)$	1	8	27	64	125	216	343	512

Solution

The forward difference table (Table 4.11) of the tabulated function is constructed as follows:

Table 4.11 HFDT form—Example 4.8

x_i	$y_i = f(x_i)$	Δy_i	$\Delta^2 y_i$	$\Delta^3 y_i$	$\Delta^4 y_i$
1	1	7	12	6	0
2	8	19	18	6	0
3	27	37	24	6	0
4	64	61	30	6	0
5	125	91	36	6	
6	216	127	42		
7	343	169			
8	512				

Using the Newton's forward interpolation formula [Eq. (4.9a)]

$$y = f(x) = y_1 + \left(\frac{\Delta y_1 z}{1!}\right) + \left(\frac{\Delta^2 y_1}{2!}\right) z(z-1) + \left(\frac{\Delta^3 y_1}{3!}\right) z(z-1)(z-2)$$

Using $x = 1.5$, $x_1 = 1.0$, $h = 1.0$, and the values of forward differences,

$$z = \frac{x - x_1}{h} = \frac{1.5 - 1.0}{1.0} = 0.5$$

$$y = f(1.5) = 1 + (0.5) \times (7) + (0.5) \times (-0.5) \times \left(\frac{12}{2!}\right)$$

$$+ (0.5) \times (-0.5) \times (-0.5) \times \left(\frac{6}{3!}\right)$$

$$= 3.375$$

EXAMPLE 4.9 Using the NFD formula, find the value of sin α at 25 degrees angle from the table given below:

α	10	20	30	40	50
sin α	0.1736	0.342	0.5	0.6428	0.766

Solution

We construct the following forward difference Table 4.12.

Table 4.12 HFDT form—Example 4.9

$x_i = \alpha_i$	$y_i = f(x_i)$	Δy_i	$\Delta^2 y_i$	$\Delta^3 y_i$	$\Delta^4 y_i$
10	0.1736	0.1684	−0.0104	−0.0048	0.0004
20	0.342	0.158	−0.0152	−0.0044	
30	0.5	0.1428	−0.0196		
40	0.6428	0.1232			
50	0.766				

Using the NFD formula (4.9b) with $k = 2$, we get

$$y = y_2 + \frac{\Delta y_2}{1} z + \frac{\Delta^2 y_2}{2} z(z-1) + \Delta^3 y_2 \frac{z(z-1)(z-2)}{6}$$

Substituting from Table 4.12 with $\alpha = x = 25$, $h = 10$, we get

$$y(25) = 0.422$$

EXAMPLE 4.10 Calculate $f(21)$ using the following tabulated function.

x_i	0	5	10	15	20
$y_i = f(x_i)$	1.0	1.6	3.8	8.2	15.4

Solution

As the point $x = 21$ lies at the end of the table, therefore the Newton's backward interpolation formula will give a more accurate value of the function.

We construct the following backward difference Table 4.13.

Table 4.13 HBDT form—Example 4.10

x_i	$y_i = f(x_i)$	∇y_i	$\nabla^2 y_i$	$\nabla^3 y_i$	$\nabla^4 y_i$
0	1.0				
5	1.6	0.6			
10	3.8	2.2	1.6		
15	8.2	4.4	2.2	0.6	
20	15.4	7.2	2.8	0.6	0

Using the Newton's backward interpolation formula [Eq. (4.11a)],

$$y = f(x) = y_n + \left(\frac{\nabla y_n z.}{1!}\right) + \left(\frac{\nabla^2 y_n}{2!}\right) z(z+1) + \left(\frac{\nabla^3 y_n}{3!}\right) z(z+1)(z+2)$$

Using $x = 21$, $x_n = 20$, $h = 5$ and the values of backward differences, we get

$$z = \frac{x - x_n}{h} = \frac{21 - 20}{5} = 0.2$$

$$y = f(21) = 1.54 + (0.2) \times (7.2) + (0.2) \times (1.2) \times \left(\frac{2.8}{2!}\right)$$

$$+ (0.2) \times (1.2) \times (2.2) \times \left(\frac{0.6}{3!}\right)$$

$$= 17.23$$

4.14 Algorithm (AL43) for Forward Difference Interpolation

This algorithm is transformed to a computer program written in C++ language and presented at the end of this chapter (see **p43.cpp**).

1. Declare/define the function/subprogram **fact** to calculate the factorial.
2. Declare/define function/subprogram **nfdi** to implement the method.
3. Start the (main) function.
4. Define the main function which calls the appropriate subprogram/ function according to given choice.
5. Stop (main).

Details of function/subprogram **nfdi**:

1. Start
2. Enter the number of tabulated points, n
   and the point of interpolation X
3. Enter the coordinates (x_i, y_i) using for loop
4. i=1
   While X>xi
      i=i+1
5. k=i–1
   $z=(X-x_k)/(x_{k+1}-x_k)$
6. Declare a 2-dimensional (fd) array for the forward difference operator, Δ
   compute elements of fd_{ij}
   for j=1 to n–1 do
   begin
      for i=1 to n–j do
      begin
         If (j=1) then
            $fd_{ij}=y_{i+1}-y_i$
         else
            $fd_{ij}=fd_{i+1j-1}-fd_{ij-1}$
         endif
      endfor
   write fd_{ij}
   endfor
7. Interpolated value calculation
   $sm=y_k$

```
   for i=1 to n–k
   begin
       product=1
     for j=0 to i–1
       product=product*(z–j)
     endfor
       m=fact(i) {call factorial function}
       sm=sm+fd_ki*pr/m
     endfor
   write 'interpolated value of y at X is', sm
8. Return
```

4.15 Algorithm (AL44) for Backward Difference Table Construction

This algorithm is transformed to a computer program written in C++ language and presented at the end of this chapter (see **p44.cpp**).

1. Declare/define the function/subprogram **bdt** to implement the method.
2. Start the (main) function.
3. Define the main function which calls the appropriate subprogram/ function according to given choice.
4. Stop (main).

Details of function/subprogram **bdt**:

1. Start
2. Enter the number of tabulated points, n
3. Enter the coordinates (x_i, y_i) using for loop
4. Declare a 2-dimensional (bd) array for the backward difference operator, ∇

```
   compute elements of bd_ij
   for j=1 to n–1 do
   begin
   for i=j+1 to n do
   begin
     If (j=1) then
       bd_ij=y_i–y_i-1
     else
       bd_ij=fd_ij-1–fd_i-1j-1
     endif
   endfor
   write bd_ij
   endfor
5. Return
```

4.16 Algorithm (AL45) for Backward Difference Interpolation Formula

This algorithm is transformed to a computer program written in C++ language and presented at the end of this chapter (see **p45.cpp**).

1. Declare/define the function/subprogram **fact** to calculate the factorial.
2. Declare/define the function/subprogram **nbdi** to implement the method.
3. Start the (main) function.
4. Define the main function which calls the appropriate subprogram/ function according to given choice.
5. Stop (main).

Details of function/subprogram **nbdi**:

1. Start
2. Enter the number of tabulated points, n
   and the point of interpolation X
3. Enter the coordinates (x_i, y_i) using for loop
4. i=n
   While X<x_i
   i=i–1
5. k=i
   $z=(X-x_k)/(x_k-x_{k-1})$
6. Declare a two-dimensional (bd) array for the backward difference operator, ∇
   compute elements of bd_{ij}
   for j=1 to n–1 do
   begin
   for i=j+1 to n do
   begin
      If (j=1) then
         $bd_{ij}=y_i-y_{i-1}$
      else
         $bd_{ij}=bd_{ij-1}-bd_{i-1j-1}$
      endif
   endfor
   write bd_{ij}
   endfor
7. Interpolated value calculation
   $sm=y_k$
   for i=1 to k–1
   begin
      product=1
      product=product∗(z+j)
      m=fact(i) {call factorial function}

sm=sm+bd$_{ki}$*pr/m
endfor
write 'interpolated value of y at X is', sm
8. Return

4.17 Divided Differences and the Divided Difference Table for Unequally Spaced Points

Let a function $y = f(x)$ be given in a tabulated form as in Table 4.1 such that the points x_i need not be equally spaced. The divided differences are obtained by dividing the differences between two successive values of the function y_i by that of the x_i values and represented by the symbol Δ_d (called the divided difference operator) as follows:

$$\Delta_d y_1 = \frac{y_2 - y_1}{x_2 - x_1}; \quad \Delta_d^2 y_1 = \frac{\Delta_d y_2 - \Delta_d y_1}{x_3 - x_1}; \quad \Delta_d^3 y_1 = \frac{\Delta_d^2 y_2 - \Delta_d^2 y_1}{x_4 - x_1}$$

$$\Delta_d y_2 = \frac{y_3 - y_2}{x_3 - x_2}; \quad \Delta_d^2 y_2 = \frac{\Delta_d y_3 - \Delta_d y_2}{x_4 - x_2}; \quad \Delta_d^3 y_2 = \frac{\Delta_d^2 y_3 - \Delta_d^2 y_2}{x_5 - x_2}$$

$$\Delta_d y_3 = \frac{y_4 - y_3}{x_4 - x_3}; \quad \Delta_d^2 y_3 = \frac{\Delta_d y_4 - \Delta_d y_3}{x_5 - x_3}; \quad \Delta_d^3 y_3 = \frac{\Delta_d^2 y_4 - \Delta_d^2 y_3}{x_6 - x_3}$$

and so on.

A table of divided differences can be constructed using these values of the differences in two forms: (a) Horizontal divided difference table (HDDT) and (b) Diagonal divided difference table (DDDT). In HDDT the divided differences are placed alongside the points (x_i, y_i) as shown in Table 4.14.

In general, we can write

$$\Delta_d^j y_i = \frac{\Delta_d^{j-1} y_{i+1} - \Delta_d^{j-1} y_i}{x_{i+j} - x_i}$$

Table 4.14 HDDT form

Iteration (*i*)	x_i	y_i	$\Delta_d y_i$	$\Delta_d^2 y_i$	$\Delta_d^3 y_i$	$\Delta_d^4 y_i$
1	x_1	y_1	$\frac{y_2 - y_1}{x_2 - x_1}$	$\frac{\Delta_d y_2 - \Delta_d y_1}{x_3 - x_1}$	$\frac{\Delta_d^2 y_2 - \Delta_d^2 y_1}{x_4 - x_1}$	$\frac{\Delta_d^3 y_2 - \Delta_d^3 y_1}{x_5 - x_1}$
2	x_2	y_2	$\frac{y_3 - y_2}{x_3 - x_2}$	$\frac{\Delta_d y_3 - \Delta_d y_2}{x_4 - x_2}$	$\frac{\Delta_d^2 y_3 - \Delta_d^2 y_2}{x_5 - x_2}$	
3	x_3	y_3	$\frac{y_4 - y_3}{x_4 - x_3}$	$\frac{\Delta_d y_4 - \Delta_d y_3}{x_5 - x_3}$		
4	x_4	y_4	$\frac{y_5 - y_4}{x_5 - x_4}$			
5	x_5	y_5				

In the diagonal divided difference table, the divided differences are placed diagonally across the columns as shown in Table 4.15.

Table 4.15 DDDT form

Iteration (*i*)	x_i	y_i	$\Delta_d y_i$	$\Delta_d^2 y_i$	$\Delta_d^3 y_i$	$\Delta_d^4 y_i$
1	x_1	y_1				
			$\dfrac{y_2 - y_1}{x_2 - x_1}$			
2	x_2	y_2		$\dfrac{\Delta_d y_2 - \Delta_d y_1}{x_3 - x_1}$		
			$\dfrac{y_3 - y_2}{x_3 - x_2}$		$\dfrac{\Delta_d^2 y_2 - \Delta_d^2 y_1}{x_4 - x_1}$	
3	x_3	y_3		$\dfrac{\Delta_d y_3 - \Delta_d y_2}{x_4 - x_2}$		$\dfrac{\Delta_d^3 y_2 - \Delta_d^3 y_1}{x_5 - x_2}$
			$\dfrac{y_4 - y_3}{x_4 - x_3}$		$\dfrac{\Delta_d^2 y_3 - \Delta_d^2 y_2}{x_5 - x_2}$	
4	x_4	y_4		$\dfrac{\Delta_d y_4 - \Delta_d y_3}{x_5 - x_3}$		
			$\dfrac{y_5 - y_4}{x_5 - x_4}$			
5	x_5	y_5				

4.18 Numerical Examples (Divided Differences)

EXAMPLE 4.11 Construct a table of divided differences from the following given set of points:

x_i	2.5	3.0	4.5	4.75	6.0	7.0
$y_i = f(x_i)$	8.85	11.45	20.66	22.85	38.6	55.6

Solution

Using the HDDT form, the divided difference table is obtained as shown in Table 4.16.

4.19 Newton's Divided Difference Interpolation Formula for Unequal Intervals

When a function $y = f(x)$ is tabulated at unequal intervals of x_i points we use the divided difference interpolation formula. It can also be used for equally spaced points.

Table 4.16 HDDT form

i	x_i	y_i	$\Delta_d y_i$	$\Delta_d^2 y_i$	$\Delta_d^3 y_i$	$\Delta_d^4 y_i$	$\Delta_d^5 y_i$
1	2.5	8.85	$\frac{11.45-8.85}{3-2.5}=5.2$	$\frac{6.14-5.2}{4.5-2.5}=0.47$	$\frac{1.5-0.47}{4.75-2.5}=0.46$	$\frac{0.35-0.46}{6-2.5}=-0.03$	$\frac{-0.1725}{4.5}=-0.038$
2	3.0	11.45	$\frac{20.66-11.45}{4.5-3}=6.14$	$\frac{8.76-6.14}{4.75-3}=1.5$	$\frac{2.56-1.5}{6-3}=0.35$	$\frac{-0.24-0.35}{7-3}=-0.1475$	
3	4.5	20.66	$\frac{22.85-20.66}{4.75-4.5}=8.76$	$\frac{12.6-8.76}{6-4.5}=2.56$	$\frac{1.96-2.56}{7-4.5}=-0.24$		
4	4.75	22.85	$\frac{38.6-22.85}{6-4.75}=12.6$	$\frac{17-12.6}{7\ 4.75}=1.96$			
5	6.0	38.6	$\frac{55.6-38.6}{7-6}=17.0$				
6	7.0	55.6					

Let the function be given by

$$y = f(x) = b_0 + b_1(x - x_1) + b_2(x - x_1)(x - x_2) + \cdots + b_n(x - x_1)(x - x_2) \ldots (x - x_n) \qquad (4.12)$$

where b_i's are the unknown coefficients to be determined.

At point $x = x_1$ the value of the function is given by

$$y_1 = f(x_1) = b_0$$

At point $x = x_2$ the value of the function is given by

$$y_2 = f(x_2) = b_0 + b_1(x_2 - x_1)$$

At point $x = x_3$ the value of the function is given by

$$y_3 = f(x_3) = b_0 + b_1(x_3 - x_1) + b_2(x_3 - x_1)(x_3 - x_2)$$

$$\vdots$$

$$y_n = f(x_n) = b_0 + b_1(x_n - x_1) + b_2(x_n - x_1)(x_n - x_2) + \cdots$$

and so on.

From the above, we obtain the coefficients as

$$b_0 = y_1$$

$$b_1 = \frac{y_2 - y_1}{x_2 - x_1}$$

$$b_2 = \frac{\dfrac{y_3 - y_2}{x_3 - x_2} - \dfrac{y_2 - y_1}{x_2 - x_1}}{x_3 - x_1}$$

and so on.

Using the definition of divided differences, we can write the above coefficients as

$$b_0 = y_1$$

$$b_1 = \Delta_d y_1$$

$$b_2 = \Delta_d^2 y_1$$

$$\vdots$$

$$b_n = \Delta_d^n y_1$$

Substituting the above coefficients into the polynomial Eq. (4.12), we get

$$y = f(x) = y_1 + (\Delta_d y_1)(x - x_1) + (\Delta_d^2 y_1)(x - x_1)(x - x_2) + \cdots + (\Delta_d^n y_1)(x - x_1)(x - x_2) \ldots (x - x_n) \qquad (4.13)$$

Equation (4.13) is valid for a point x lying in the interval $[x_1, x_2]$.

For any point x lying in the interval $[x_k, x_{k+1}]$, we can write

$$y = f(x) = y_k + (\Delta_d y_k)(x - x_k) + (\Delta_d^2 y_k)(x - x_k)(x - x_{k+1}) + \cdots + (\Delta_d^{n-k} y_k)(x - x_k)(x - x_{k+1}) \ldots (x - x_{n-1}) \qquad (4.14)$$

Equations (4.13) and (4.14) are called **Newton's divided difference interpolation formulas**.

4.20 Numerical Examples (Divided Differences Formula)

EXAMPLE 4.12 Using the divided difference interpolation formula and the divided difference table (Table 4.16) of Example 4.11, calculate the value of the function at $x = 2.75$.

Solution

From the difference table of Example 4.11, we infer that $x = 2.75$ lies between $x_1 = 2.5$ and $x_2 = 3.0$. Using Eq. (4.14) for $k = 1$, we obtain

$$y = f(x) = y_1 + (\Delta_d y_1)(x - x_1) + (\Delta_d^2 y_1)(x - x_1)(x - x_2) + (\Delta_d^3 y_1)(x - x_1)(x - x_2)(x - x_3) + (\Delta_d^4 y_1)(x - x_1)(x - x_2)(x - x_3)(x - x_4) + (\Delta_d^5 y_1)(x - x_1)(x - x_2)(x - x_3)(x - x_4)(x - x_5)$$

$$\begin{aligned} y = f(2.75) &= 8.85 + 5.2 \times (2.75 - 2.5) + 0.47 \times (0.25) \times (-0.25) \\ &\quad + 0.45 \times (0.25) \times (-0.25) \times (-1.75) - 0.037 \times (0.25) \\ &\quad \times (-0.25) \times (-1.75) \times (-2) - 0.04 \times (0.25)(-0.25) \\ &\quad \times (-1.75) \times (-2) \times (-3.25) \\ &= 8.85 + 1.3 - 0.029 + 0.0492 - 0.00809 - 0.028 \\ &= 10.134 \end{aligned}$$

EXAMPLE 4.13 Using the divided difference interpolation, find the values of the following tabulated function at $x = 2$, $x = 8$ and $x = 15$.

x_i	4	5	7	10	11	13
$y_i = f(x_i)$	48	100	294	900	1210	2028

Solution

First, we make the divided difference table (Table 4.17) for the given tabulated function.

Table 4.17 HDDT form—Example 4.13

i	x_i	y_i	$\Delta_d y_i$	$\Delta_d^2 y_i$	$\Delta_d^3 y_i$	$\Delta_d^4 y_i$
1	4	48	$\frac{100-48}{5-4} = 52$	$\frac{97-52}{7-4} = 15$	$\frac{21-15}{10-4} = 1$	0
2	5	100	$\frac{294-100}{7-5} = 97$	$\frac{202-97}{10-5} = 21$	$\frac{27-21}{11-5} = 1$	0
3	7	294	$\frac{900-294}{10-7} = 202$	$\frac{310-202}{11-7} = 27$	$\frac{33-27}{13-7} = 1$	
4	10	900	$\frac{1210-900}{11-10} = 310$	$\frac{409-310}{13-10} = 33$		
5	11	1210	$\frac{2028-1210}{13-11} = 409$			
6	13	2028				

Using the interpolation formula [Eq. (4.14) for $k = 1$, $x = 2$, $x_k = 4$, we get

$$y = f(x) = y_1 + (\Delta_d y_1)(x - x_1) + (\Delta_d^2 y_1)(x - x_1)(x - x_2) + (\Delta_d^3 y_1)(x - x_1)(x - x_2)(x - x_3)$$

$$y = f(2) = 48 + 52(2 - 4) + 15(2 - 4)(2 - 5) + (1)(2 - 4)(2 - 5)(2 - 7)$$

or $$f(2) = 4$$

For $x = 8$, $k = 3$, $x_k = 7$, we get

$$y = f(8) = y_3 + (\Delta_d y_3)(x - x_3) + (\Delta_d^2 y_3)(x - x_3)(x - x_4) + (\Delta_d^3 y_3)(x - x_3)(x - x_4)(x - x_5)$$

$$y = f(8) = 294 + 202(8 - 7) + 27(8 - 7)(8 - 10) + (1)(8 - 7)(8 - 10)(8 - 11)$$

or $$f(8) = 294 + 202 - 54 + 6 = 448$$

For $x = 15$, $k = 5$ and $x_k = 11$

$$y = f(15) = y_5 + (\Delta_d y_5)(x - x_5) = 1210 + (15 - 11)(409) = 2846$$

4.21 Algorithm (AL46) for Divided Difference Table Construction

This algorithm is transformed to a computer program written in C++ language and presented at the end of this chapter (see **p46.cpp**).

1. Declare/define the function/subprogram **ddt** to implement the method.
2. Start the (main) function.
3. Define the main function which calls the appropriate subprogram/ function according to given choice.
4. Stop (main).

Details of function/subprogram **ddt**:

1. Start
2. Enter the number of tabulated points, n
3. Enter the coordinates (x_i, y_i) using for loop
4. Declare a 2-dimensional (dd) array for the divided difference operator, Δ_d.

5. Compute the elements of dd_{ij}

```
for j=1 to n–1 do
begin
   for i=1 to n–j do
   begin
      If (j=1) then
         dd_ij=(y_i+1–y_i)/(x_i+j–x_i)
         write dd_ij
      else
         dd_ij=(dd_i+1j–1–dd_ij–1)/(x_i+j–x_i)
         write dd_ij
      endif
   endfor
endfor
```

6. Return

4.22 Algorithm (AL47) for Divided Difference Interpolation Formula

This algorithm is transformed to a computer program written in C++ language and presented at the end of this chapter (see **p47.cpp**).

1. Declare/define the function/subprogram **nddi** to implement the method.
2. Start the (main) function.
3. Define the main function which calls the appropriate subprogram/ function according to given choice.
4. Stop (main).

Details of function/subprogram **nddi**:

1. Start
2. Enter the number of tabulated points, n and the point of interpolation X
3. Enter the coordinates (x_i, y_i) using for loop
4. i=1

```
while X > xi
i=i+1
```

5. k=i–1
6. Declare a 2-dimensional (dd) array for the divided difference operator, Δ_d
7. Compute the elements of dd_{ij}

```
for j=1 to n–1 do
```

```
    begin
      for i=1 to n–j do
        begin
          If (j=1) then
             fd_ij=(y_i+1–y_i)/(x_i+j–x_i)
          else
          dd_ij=(dd_i+1j–1–dd_ij–1)/(x_i+j–x_i) dd_ij=(dd_i+1j–1–dd_ij–1)/(x_i+j–x_i)
          endif
        endfor
    endfor
8. Interpolated value calculation
    sm=y_k
    for i=1 to n
    begin
       product=1
       for j=0 to i–1
       product=product*(X–x_k+j)
       endfor
       sm=sm+dd_ki*pr
    endfor
    Write 'interpolated value of y at X is', sm
9. Return
```

4.23 Central Differences and the Central Difference Table

When a function $y = f(x)$ is to be interpolated at a point which is midway of a set of tabulated values (x_i, y_i), the central differences are used to obtain the value of the function more accurately than the forward and the backward differences. The central differences converge more rapidly than the other differences.

Let the coordinates (x_i, y_i) be given for equally spaced x_i's and let x_0 be the centre-point of the tabulated values at which the value of the function is $f(x_0)$. Let $x_0 + h$, $x_0 + 2h$, ... be the values of x_i for points below x_0. Similarly let $x_0 - h$, $x_0 - 2h$, ... be the values of x_i above x_0 in the tabulated set. The values of the function at these points are given by

$$y_0 = f_0 = f(x_0)$$

$$y_1 = f_1 = f(x_0 + h)$$

$$y_2 = f_2 = f(x_0 + 2h) \text{ ..., etc.}$$

$$y_{-1} = f_{-1} = f(x_0 - h)$$

$$y_{-2} = f_{-2} = f(x_0 - 2h)$$

$$y_{-3} = f_{-3} = f(x_0 - 3h) \text{ ..., etc.}$$

Defining a central difference operator δ^i with the help of the forward difference operator Δ^i and constructing the central differences table as follows, we get Table 4.18.

Table 4.18 The central difference table

x_i	y_i	$\delta^1 y_i$	$\delta^2 y_i$	$\delta^3 y_i$	$\delta^4 y_i$
$x_0 - 2h$	y_{-2}				
		$\Delta^1 y_{-2} = \delta^1 y_{-3/2}$			
$x_0 - h$	y_{-1}		$\Delta^2 y_2 = \delta^2 y_{-1}$		
		$\Delta^1 y_{-1} = \delta^1 y_{-1/2}$		$\Delta^3 y_{-2} = \delta^3 y_{-1/2}$	
$\mathbf{x_0}$	$\mathbf{y_0}$		$\boldsymbol{\Delta^2 y_{-1} = \delta^2 y_0}$		$\boldsymbol{\Delta^4 y_{-2} = \delta^4 y_0}$
		$\boldsymbol{\Delta^1 y_0 = \delta^1 y_{1/2}}$		$\boldsymbol{\Delta^3 y_{-1} = \delta^3 y_{1/2}}$	
$x_0 + h$	y_1		$\Delta^2 y_0 = \delta^2 y_1$		
		$\Delta^1 y_1 = \delta^1 y_{3/2}$			
$x_0 + 2h$	y_2				

From Table 4.18, we can see that the odd central differences Δ^1, Δ^3, etc. lie below the central line ($x = x_0$), while the even central differences Δ^2, Δ^4, etc. lie on the central line.

Also in Table 4.18, we define the central difference operator of order '1' as

$$\Delta y_{-2} = \delta^1 y_{-3/2} = y_{-1} - y_{-2}$$

$$\Delta y_{-1} = \delta^1 y_{-1/2} = y_0 - y_{-1}$$

$$\Delta y_0 = \delta^1 y_{1/2} = y_1 - y_0$$

$$\Delta y_1 = \delta^1 y_{3/2} = y_2 - y_1$$

The central difference operator of order '2' is defined as

$$\Delta^2 y_{-2} = \delta^2 y_{-1} = \Delta y_{-1} - \Delta y_{-2} = \delta^1 y_{-1/2} - \delta^1 y_{-3/2}$$

$$\Delta^2 y_{-1} = \delta^2 y_0 = \Delta y_0 - \Delta y_{-1} = \delta^1 y_{1/2} - \delta^1 y_{-1/2}$$

$$\Delta^2 y_0 = \delta^2 y_1 = \Delta y_1 - \Delta y_0 = \delta^1 y_{3/2} - \delta^1 y_{1/2}$$

The central difference operator of order '3' is defined as

$$\Delta^3 y_{-2} = \delta^3 y_{-1/2}$$

$$\Delta^3 y_{-1} = \delta^3 y_{1/2}$$

The central difference operator of order '4' is defined as

$$\Delta^4 y_{-2} = \delta^4 y_0$$

In addition to the central difference operator, we also define below some other useful operators used in numerical analysis.

(i) **Shift (or displacement or translation) operator (*E*):** This operator is defined by an operation on a function $y = f(x)$ as

$$Ey_x = Ef(x) = y_{x+h} = f(x + h)$$

With $h = 1$ and $x = 0$ in the above relation, we can write $Ey_0 = Ef(0) = y_1$
With $h = 1$ and $x = 1$ in the above relation, we can write $Ey_1 = Ef(1) = y_2$ and so on. Similarly, the higher order shift operations can be defined as follows:

$$E^2y_x = E^2f(x) = E(y_{x+h}) = y_{x+2h} = f(x + 2h)$$
$$E^ny_x = E^nf(x) = y_{x+nh} = f(x + nh)$$

(ii) **Inverse shift operator (E^{-1}):** This operator is defined by an operation on a function $y = f(x)$ as

$$E^{-1}y_x = E^{-1}f(x) = y_{x-h} = f(x - h)$$
$$E^{-n}y_x = E^{-n}f(x) = y_{x-nh} = f(x - nh)$$

(iii) **Averaging operator (μ):** This operator is defined by an operation on a function $y = f(x)$ as

$$\mu y_x = \mu f(x) = \frac{y_{x+h/2} + y_{x-h/2}}{2} = \frac{f(x + h/2) + f(x - h/2)}{2}$$

(iv) **Differential operator (*D*):** This operator is defined by an operation $D = d/dx$ which acting on a function $y = f(x)$ gives the derivative dy/dx of the given function.

(v) **Relations between different operators**

1. E and Δ: By definition, $\Delta y_x = y_{x+h} - y_x$

$$= Ey_x - y_x$$
$$= (E - 1)y_x$$

Therefore, $E = \Delta + 1$

2. E and ∇: By definition, $\nabla y_x = y_x - y_{x-h}$

$$= y_x - E^{-1}y_x$$
$$= (1 - E^{-1})y_x$$

Therefore, $E^{-1} = \nabla + 1$

3. E and δ: By definition, $\delta f(x) = \delta y_x = y_{x+h/2} - y_{x-h/2}$

$$= f(x + h/2) - f(x - h/2)$$
$$= E^{1/2}f(x) - E^{-1/2}f(x)$$

Therefore, $\delta = E^{1/2} - E^{-1/2} = (E - 1)E^{-1/2} = \Delta E^{-1/2}$

Also we can write $\delta = E^{1/2} - E^{-1/2} = (1 - E^{-1})E^{1/2} = \nabla E^{1/2}$

4. E and D: By Taylor's series we can write the expansion of the function $y = f(x)$ as follows:

$$y_{x+h} = y_x + h\left(\frac{dy_x}{dx}\right) + \left(\frac{h^2}{2!}\right)\left(\frac{d^2 y_x}{dx^2}\right) + \cdots$$

$$y_{x+h} = y_x + h\,(Dy_x) + \left(\frac{h^2}{2!}\right)(D^2 y_x) + \cdots$$

$$Ey_x = y_x + h(Dy_x) + \left(\frac{h^2}{2!}\right)(D^2 y_x) + \cdots$$

$$Ey_x = (1 + hD + \left(\frac{h^2}{2!}\right)D^2 + \cdots)y_x$$

$$Ey_x = e^{hD}y_x$$
$$E = e^{hD}$$

5. D and Δ: Since $E = 1 + \Delta = e^{hD}$

$$hD = \log_e E = \log_e (1 + \Delta) = \Delta - \left(\frac{1}{2}\right)\Delta^2 + \left(\frac{1}{3}\right)\Delta^3 - \cdots$$

$$D = \left(\frac{1}{h}\right)\left(\Delta - \left(\frac{1}{2}\right)\Delta^2 + \left(\frac{1}{3}\right)\Delta^3 - \cdots\right)$$

6. D and ∇: Since $E = (1 - \nabla)^{-1} = e^{hD}$

$$D = -\left(\frac{1}{h}\right)(\log_e (1 - \nabla)$$

$$D = \left(\frac{1}{h}\right)\left(\nabla + \left(\frac{1}{2}\right)\nabla^2 + \left(\frac{1}{3}\right)\nabla^3 + \cdots\right)$$

4.24 Gauss Central (Forward) Difference Interpolation Formula

From Newton's forward difference interpolation formula (4.9b), we have

$$y = f(x) = y_0 + \frac{\Delta y_0 z}{1!} + \frac{\Delta^2 y_0}{2!}z(z-1) + \cdots + \frac{\Delta^n y_0}{n!}z(z-1)(z-2)\ldots(z-(n-1))$$

Using $y_0 = Ey_{-1}$

$y_1 = Ey_0$

$y_2 = Ey_1$

and so on,

and also using $\Delta^2 y_0 = \Delta^2(Ey_{-1}) = \Delta^2(1 + \Delta)y_{-1} = \Delta^2 y_{-1} + \Delta^3 y_{-1}$

$$\Delta^3 y_0 = \Delta^3(Ey_{-1}) = \Delta^3(1 + \Delta)y_{-1} = \Delta^3 y_{-1} + \Delta^4 y_{-1}$$

$$\Delta^4 y_0 = \Delta^4 y_{-1} + \Delta^5 y_{-1}$$

in the Newton's interpolation formula, we obtain

$$y = f(x) = y_0 + \frac{\Delta y_0 z}{1!} + \frac{\Delta^2 y_{-1}}{2!} z(z-1) + \frac{\Delta^3 y_{-1}}{3!} z(z-1)(z+1) +$$

$$\frac{\Delta^4 y_{-1}}{4!} z(z-1)(z-2)(z+1) + \cdots +$$

$$\frac{\Delta^n y_{-1}}{n!} z(z-1)(z-2) \ldots (z-(n-1)) \tag{4.15}$$

This is called **Gauss central difference formula** in terms of the forward differences.

4.25 Numerical Examples (Central Difference and Other Operators)

EXAMPLE 4.14 Using the following table determine the values of (a) $\delta^4 y_3$ and (b) $\mu^4 y_3$.

x_i	1	2	3	4	5
$y_i = f(x_i)$	2	5	10	17	26

Solution

(a) Using the relation $\delta = \Delta E^{-1/2}$

$$\delta^4 y_3 = (\Delta E^{-1/2})^4 y_3 = \Delta^4 E^{-2} y_3$$

Using $E^{-r} y_x = y_{x-rh}$

Let $h = 1,\ x = 3,\ r = 2,\ x - rh = 3 - 2 = 1$

So $E^{-2} y_3 = y_1$ and $\delta^4 y_3 = \Delta^4 y_1$

Using $\Delta = E + 1$, $\Delta^4 y_1 = (E + 1)^4 y_1 = (E^4 + 1 - 4E^3 - 6E^2 - 4E)y_1$

Therefore $\delta^4 y_3 = (E^4 + 1 - 4E^3 - 6E^2 - 4E)y_1$

Using $E^r y_x = y_{x+rh}$ in the above expression,

$\delta^4 y_3 = y_5 + y_1 - 4y_4 + 6y_3 - 4y_2$

$\delta^4 y_3 = 26 + 2 - 4(17) + 6(10) - 4(5) = 0$

(b) $$\mu^4 y_3 = \left[\frac{(E^{1/2} - E^{-1/2})}{2}\right]^4 y_3$$

$$= \frac{1}{16}(E^2 y_3 + 4Ey_3 + 6y_3 + 4E^{-1} y_3 + E^{-2} y_3)$$

$$= \frac{1}{16}(y_5 + 4y_4 + 6y_3 + 4y_2 + y_1)$$

$$= \frac{1}{16}[26 + 4(17) + 6(10) + 4(5) + 2]$$

$$= 11$$

EXAMPLE 4.15 Find the value of $f(x)$ at $x = 32$ using the Gauss formula and the following tabulated values.

x_i	25	30	35	40
$y_i = f(x_i)$	0.2707	0.3027	0.3386	0.3794

Solution

Given $x = 32$, $h = 5$, $x_0 = 30$, $z = (32 - 30)/5 = 0.4$, we construct the forward difference Table 4.19.

Table 4.19 Forward difference table—Example 4.15

x_i	y_i	$\delta^1 y_i$	$\delta^2 y_i$	$\delta^3 y_i$
25	0.2707			
		$\Delta y_{-1} = \delta^1 y_{-1/2} = 0.032$		
30	0.3027		$\Delta^2 y_{-1} = \delta^2 y_0 = 0.0039$	
		$\Delta y_0 = \delta^1 y_{-1/2} = 0.0359$		$\Delta^3 y_{-1} = \delta^3 y_{1/2} = 0.0010$
35	0.3386		$\Delta^2 y_{-1} = \delta^2 y_1 = 0.0049$	
		$\Delta y_1 = \delta^1 y_{3/2} = 0.0408$		
40	0.3794			

Using the Gauss formula,

$$y = f(x) = y_0 + \frac{\Delta y_0 z}{1!} + \frac{\Delta^2 y_{-1}}{2!} z(z-1) + \frac{\Delta^3 y_{-1}}{3!} z(z-1)(z+1)$$

At $x = 32$, $x_0 = 30$, we get

$$y = f(32) = 0.3027 + (0.4)(0.0359) + \frac{(0.0039)(0.4)(0.4-1)}{2}$$

$$+ \frac{(0.001)(0.4)(0.4-1)(0.4+1)}{6} = 0.3165$$

EXAMPLE 4.16 Find the value of $f(x)$ at $x = 3.5$ using the Gauss formula and the following tabulated values.

x_i	2	3	4	5
$y_i = f(x_i)$	2.626	3.454	4.784	6.986

Solution

Given $x = 3.5$, $h = 1$, $x_0 = 3$, $z = \dfrac{3.5-3}{1} = 0.5$, we construct the forward difference Table 4.20.

Table 4.20 Forward difference table—Example 4.16

x_i	y_i	$\delta^1 y_i$	$\delta^2 y_i$	$\delta^3 y_i$
2	2.626			
		$\Delta y_{-1} = \delta^1 y_{-1/2} = 0.828$		
3	3.454		$\Delta^2 y_{-1} = \delta^2 y_0 = 0.502$	
		$\Delta y_0 = \delta^1 y_{-1/2} = 1.33$		$\Delta^3 y_{-1} = \delta^3 y_{1/2} = 0.37$
4	4.784		$\Delta^2 y_{-1} = \delta^2 y_1 = 0.872$	
		$\Delta y_1 = \delta^1 y_{3/2} = 2.202$		
5	6.986			

Using the Gauss formula, we obtain

$$y = f(x) = y_0 + \frac{\Delta y_0 z}{1!} + \frac{\Delta^2 y_{-1}}{2!} z(z-1) + \frac{\Delta^3 y_{-1}}{3!} z(z-1)(z+1)$$

At $x = 3.5$, $x_0 = 3$, we get

$$y = f(3.5) = 3.454 + (0.5)(1.33) + \frac{(0.0039)(0.5)(0.5-1)}{2}$$

$$+ \frac{(0.37)(0.5)(0.5-1)(0.5+1)}{6} = 4.033$$

Exercises

1. From the following given tabulated values, find y at $x = 21$ and $x = 28$.

x	20	23	26	29
$f(x)$	0.342	0.3907	0.4384	0.4848

[**Ans.** 0.358, 0.469]

2. From the following given tabulated values, estimate the value of tan (45° 15′)

$x°$	45	46	47	48	49	50
$y = \tan x°$	1.0	1.03	1.07	1.11	1.15	1.92

[Ans. 1.009]

3. Find the pressure at temperatures 142°C and 175°C from the following tabulated values.

t (°C)	140	150	160	170	180
p (kg/cm^2)	3.7	4.9	6.3	8.1	10.2

[Ans. 3.9, 9.1]

4. The population (in thousands) of a town in the decennial census is given as in the following tabulated values.

x (year)	1891	1901	1911	1921	1931
y (population)	46	66	81	93	101

[Ans. 96.84]

Find the population for the year 1925 correct to two decimal places.

5. From the table given below estimate the order of the interpolating polynomial.

x	2.0	2.1	2.2	2.3	2.4	2.5
y	13.0	14.261	15.648	17.167	18.824	20.625

[Ans. 13.62]

Find the value of y at $x = 2.05$.

6. Obtain an interpolating polynomial for the function $f(x)$ from the following tabulated values.

x	1	2	4	7
$f(x)$	1	16	256	2401

7. Derive the Newton's forward difference formula. Estimate the population (in thousands) for the year 1965 from the following tabulated values.

x (year)	1961	1971	1981	1991	2001
y (population)	46	66	81	93	101

[Ans. 54.85]

8. Find $f(0.23)$ from the following tabulated values.

x	0.2	0.22	0.24	0.26	0.28	0.3
y	1.6596	1.6698	1.6804	1.6912	1.7024	1.7139

[**Ans.** 1.675]

9. Find a cubic polynomial which takes the following values: $y(0) = 1$, $y(1) = 0$, $y(2) = 1$, $y(3) = 10$. Also find $y(4)$.

10. Derive the Newton's backward difference formula of interpolation.

11. From the tabulated values given below, find the value of y at $x = 3.75$.

x	2.5	3	3.5	4	4.5	5
y	24.145	22.043	20.225	18.644	17.262	16.047

[**Ans.** 19.407]

C++ Programs

The C++ programs can be implemented on any O/S, namely

1. Windows O/S using Turbo C++, Dev C++ and Visual C++ compilers.
2. Linux-based Ubuntu/Knoppix/Redhat O/S using GNU C++ compiler.

These compilers have been discussed in Chapter 0. No change is required if Ubuntu is used.

While using Turbo C++, Dev C++ and Visual C++ compilers, note the following points for every program.

- Use header file `#include <iostream.h>` (for Turbo C++ only)
- Use header file `#include <math.h>`
- Use header file `#include <conio.h>`
- Use `getch()` function before the closing bracket '}' of the `main()` function.

```
Program: p41.cpp
//Lagrange Interpolation method
#include <iostream>
#include <cmath>
#include <iomanip>
using namespace std;
void li()
{
   int i,j,n;
   char option;
   float x[10],y[10],sm,pr,X;
cout<<"enter y for default values of x[i],y[i] & interpolating
point x, else enter n\n";
   cin>>option;
   if (option=='y')
   {
     n=4;X=2.0;
     x[1]=0; y[1]=5;
     x[2]=1; y[2]=6;
     x[3]=3; y[3]=50;
     x[4]=4; y[4]=105;
   }
   else
     {
       cout<<"enter the number of tabulated points\n";
       cin>>n;
       cout<<"enter the point of interpolation\n";
       cin>>X;
       for (i=1; i<=n;i++)
```

```
          {
           cout<<"x["<<i<<"]=  ";
             cin>>x[i];
           cout<<"y["<<i<<"]=  ";
             cin>>y[i];
          }
        }
       sm=0;  //initialization
     for  (i=1;  i<=n;++i)
       {
         pr=1;
         for  (j=1;  j<=n;++j)
         {
         if  (i != j)
          pr=pr*((X-x[j])/(x[i]-x[j]));
         }
         sm  =sm+y[i]*pr;
       }
      cout<<"value  of  y  at  X="<<X<<"  is  "<<sm<<endl;
     }
       main()
     {
       li();
     }
```

```
Program:  p42.cpp
//Forward  difference  table  construction
#include  <iostream>
using  namespace  std;
void  fdt()
{
   int  i,j,n;
   char  option;
   float  x[10],y[10],fd[10][10];
cout<<"enter  y  for  default  values  of  x[i],y[i]  &  interpolating
point  x,  else  enter  n\n";
   cin>>option;
   if  (option=='y')
   {
     n=5;
     x[1]=0;  y[1]=2;
     x[2]=1;  y[2]=3;
     x[3]=2;  y[3]=12;
```

```
      x[4]=3;  y[4]=35;
      x[5]=4;  y[5]=78;
   }
else
   {
      cout<<"enter  the  number  of  tabulated  points\n";
      cin>>n;
      for  (i=1;  i<=n;i++)
        {
          cout<<"x["<<i<<"]=  ";
            cin>>x[i];
          cout<<"y["<<i<<"]=  ";
            cin>>y[i];
        }
   }
   //forward  differences
   for  (j=1;  j<=(n-1);++j)
      for  (i=1;  i<=(n-j);++i)
      {
          if  (j==1)
          {
         fd[i][j]=y[i+1]-y[i];
         cout<<"fd["<<i<<j<<"]="<<fd[i][j]<<endl;
      }
      else
      {
         fd[i][j]=fd[i+1][j-1]-fd[i][j-1];
         cout<<"fd["<<i<<j<<"]="<<fd[i][j]<<endl;
      }
   }
}
   main()
{
   fdt();
}
```

Program: p43.cpp

```
//Newton's  Forward  difference  interpolation  formula
#include  <iostream>
using  namespace  std;
inline  int  fact(int  p)
{
   return  (p<1?1:p*fact(p-1));
   }
```

```
void nfdi()
{
   int i,j,k,n,m;
   char option;
   float X,z,pr,sm,x[15],y[15],fd[15][15];
cout<<"enter y for default values of x[i],y[i] & interpolating
point x, else enter n\n";
   cin>>option;
   if (option=='y')
   {
     n=8; X=1.5;
     x[1]=1; y[1]=1;
     x[2]=2; y[2]=8;
     x[3]=3; y[3]=27;
     x[4]=4; y[4]=64;
     x[5]=5; y[5]=125;
     x[6]=6; y[6]=216;
     x[7]=7; y[7]=343;
     x[8]=8; y[8]=512;
   }
 else
   {
     cout<<"enter the number of tabulated points\n";
     cin>>n;
     cout<<"enter the point of interpolation\n";
       cin>>X;
       for (i=1; i<=n;i++)
         {
           cout<<"x["<<i<<"]=  ";
             cin>>x[i];
           cout<<"y["<<i<<"]=  ";
             cin>>y[i];
         }
       }
     i=1;
     while (X>x[i])
       i=i+1;
       k=i-1;
     z=(X-x[k])/(x[k+1]-x[k]);
     //forward differences
     for (j=1; j<=(n-1);++j)
         {
         for (i=1; i<=(n-j);++i)
```

```
            {
              if (j==1)
              {
                fd[i][j]=y[i+1]-y[i];
                }
             else
                {
                fd[i][j]=fd[i+1][j-1]-fd[i][j-1];
              }
          }
        }
        //Interpolated value
          sm=y[k];
        for (i=1;i<=(n-k);i++)
          {
             pr=1;
             for (j=0;j<=(i-1);j++)
                 pr=pr*(z-j);
                 m=fact(i);
                 sm=sm+(fd[k][i]*pr)/m;
          }
    cout<<"interpolated value of y at X is "<<sm<<endl;
}
    main()
{
    nfdi();
}
```

```
Program: p44.cpp
//Backward difference table construction
#include <iostream>
using namespace std;
void bdt()
{
    int i,j,n;
    char option;
    float x[10],y[10],bd[10][10];
cout<<"enter y for default values of x[i],y[i] else enter n\n";
    cin>>option;
    if (option=='y')
    {
      n=5;
      x[1]=0; y[1]=2;
      x[2]=1; y[2]=3;
```

```
    x[3]=2;  y[3]=12;
    x[4]=3;  y[4]=35;
    x[5]=4;  y[5]=78;
    }
  else
    {
      cout<<"enter the number of tabulated points\n";
      cin>>n;
      for (i=1; i<=n;i++)
        {
          cout<<"x["<<i<<"]=  ";
            cin>>x[i];
          cout<<"y["<<i<<"]=  ";
            cin>>y[i];
        }
    }
    //backward differences
    //output format: ith row, jth column of BD table
  for (j=1; j<=(n-1);++j)
    for (i=j+1; i<=n;++i)
      {
        if (j==1)
          {
          bd[i][j]=y[i]-y[i-1];
          cout<<"bd["<<i<<j<<"]="<<bd[i][j]<<endl;
          }
        else
          {
          bd[i][j]=bd[i][j-1]-bd[i-1][j-1];
          cout<<"bd["<<i<<j<<"]="<<bd[i][j]<<endl;
          }
      }
}
  main()
{
  bdt();
}
```

```
Program: p45.cpp
//Newton's backward difference interpolation formula
#include <iostream>
using namespace std;
inline int fact(int p)
```

```
{
   return (p<1?1:p*fact(p-1));
   }
void nbdi()
{
   int i,j,k,n,m;
   char option;
   float X,z,pr,sm,x[15],y[15],bd[15][15];
cout<<"enter y for default values of x[i],y[i] & interpolating
point X, else enter n\n";
   cin>>option;
   if (option=='y')
   {
     n=5; X=21;
     x[1]=0; y[1]=1.0;
     x[2]=5; y[2]=1.6;
     x[3]=10; y[3]=3.8;
     x[4]=15; y[4]=8.2;
     x[5]=20; y[5]=15.4;
   }
else
   {
     cout<<"enter the number of tabulated points\n";
       cin>>n;
     cout<<"enter the point of interpolation\n";
       cin>>X;
     for (i=1; i<=n;i++)
       {
         cout<<"x["<<i<<"]= ";
           cin>>x[i];
         cout<<"y["<<i<<"]= ";
           cin>>y[i];
       }
   }
   i=n;
   while (X<x[i])
     i=i-1;
     k=i;
   z=(X-x[k])/(x[k]-x[k-1]);
   //backward differences
   //output format: ith row, jth column of BD table
   for (j=1; j<=(n-1);++j)
     for (i=j+1; i<=n;++i)
```

```
        {
          if (j==1)
          {
            bd[i][j]=y[i]-y[i-1];
          }
          else
          {
            bd[i][j]=bd[i][j-1]-bd[i-1][j-1];
          }
    }
    //Interpolated value
      sm=y[k];
    for (i=1;i<=(k-1);i++)
      {
        pr=1;
        for (j=0;j<=(i-1);j++)
          pr=pr*(z+j);
          m=fact(i);
          sm=sm+(bd[k][i]*pr)/m;
      }
    cout<<"interpolated value of y at X is "<<sm<<endl;
}
    main()
{
    nbdi();
}
```

```
Program: p46.cpp
//Divided difference table construction
#include <iostream>
using namespace std;
void ddt()
{
    int i,j,n;
    char option;
    float x[10],y[10],dd[10][10];
cout<<"enter y for default values of x[i],y[i] & interpolating
point x, else enter n\n";
    cin>>option;
    if (option=='y')
    {
      n=6;
      x[1]=2.5;  y[1]=8.85;
      x[2]=3.0;  y[2]=11.45;
```

```
      x[3]=4.5;  y[3]=20.66;
      x[4]=4.75;  y[4]=22.85;
      x[5]=6.0;  y[5]=38.6;
      x[6]=7.0;  y[6]=55.6;
    }
    else
      {
        cout<<"enter the number of tabulated points\n";
        cin>>n;
        for (i=1; i<=n;i++)
          {
            cout<<"x["<<i<<"]=  ";
              cin>>x[i];
            cout<<"y["<<i<<"]=  ";
              cin>>y[i];
          }
      }
      //divided differences
      for (j=1; j<=(n-1);++j)
        for (i=1; i<=(n-j);++i)
        {
            if (j==1)
              {
              dd[i][j]=(y[i+1]-y[i])/(x[i+j]-x[i]);
              cout<<"dd["<<i<<j<<"]="<<dd[i][j]<<endl;
              }
            else
            {
          dd[i][j]=(dd[i+1][j-1]-dd[i][j-1])/(x[i+j]-x[i]);
            cout<<"dd["<<i<<j<<"]="<<dd[i][j]<<endl;
            }
        }
}
    main()
{
    ddt();
}
```

Program: p47.cpp

```
//Newton's Divided difference interpolation formula
//for equal or unequal spaced x's
#include <iostream>
#include<iomanip>
```

```
using namespace std;
void nddi()
{
   int i,j,n,k;
   char option;
   float X,sm,pr,x[10],y[10],dd[10][10];
cout<<"enter y for default values of x[i],y[i] & interpolating
point X, else enter n\n";
   cin>>option;
   if (option=='y')
   {
     n=6; X=8;
     x[1]=4; y[1]=48;
     x[2]=5; y[2]=100;
     x[3]=7; y[3]=294;
     x[4]=10; y[4]=900;
     x[5]=11; y[5]=1210;
     x[6]=13; y[6]=2028;
   }
else
   {
     cout<<"enter the number of tabulated points,n= ";
     cin>>n;
     cout<<"enter the value of interpoation point, X= ";
     cin>>X;
     for (i=1; i<=n;i++)
       {
         cout<<"x["<<i<<"]= ";
           cin>>x[i];
         cout<<"y["<<i<<"]= ";
           cin>>y[i];
       }
   }
   //initialization
     i=2;
     while (X>x[i])
       i=i+1;
       k=i-1;
   //divided differences
 for (j=1; j<=(n-1);++j)
   for (i=1; i<=(n-j);++i)
     {
       if (j==1)
```

```
         {
         dd[i][j]=(y[i+1]-y[i])/(x[i+j]-x[i]);
         }
       else
      {
   dd[i][j]=(dd[i+1][j-1]-dd[i][j-1])/(x[i+j]-x[i]);
      }
}
//interpolated  value
   sm=y[k];
   for  (i=1;i<=n;i++)
   {
      pr=1;
      for  (j=0;j<=i-1;j++)
        pr  *=(X-x[k+j]);
        sm  +=pr*dd[k][i];
   }
   cout<<"Interpolated  value  at  X  is=  "<<sm<<endl;
}
   main()
{
   nddi();
}
```

5

Numerical Differentiation

5.1 Introduction

The procedure of evaluating the derivative of a function from a given set of values of a function is known as **numerical differentiation**. When a function $y = f(x)$ is represented by a set of tabulated values, its derivative at a given point, which cannot be evaluated analytically, can be found by the methods of numerical differentiation. In this technique the tabulated function is represented by one of the interpolation formulas which is then differentiated any number of times as required to give the approximate value of the derivative. If the function is tabulated at equal intervals, then the interpolation formulas of Newton, Stirling or Bessels are applicable. The Lagrange's interpolation formula or divided interpolation formula is applicable when the function is tabulated at unequal intervals.

If the derivative of a tabulated function is required at a point near the beginning of the table, then the Newton's forward difference interpolation formula is applicable, and for a point near the end of the table the Newton's backward interpolation formula is useful and gives better results. For finding the derivative near the centre of the table, the formulas based on central differences may be used.

Numerical differentiation methods provide only approximations to the values of derivatives because in numerical differentiation round-off and truncation errors cannot be avoided. Such errors originate within the methods themselves and they also increase at each step of differentiating the polynomial function.

5.2 Derivative of a Function Using Newton's Forward Difference Interpolation

Let a function $y = f(x)$ be tabulated $x = x_1, x_2, x_3, ..., x_n$, such that $x_2 = x_1 + h$, $x_3 = x_1 + 2h$, $x_4 = x_1 + 3h$, ..., $x_n = x_1 + nh$.

The Newton's forward interpolation formula for the approximating polynomial is given by

$$y = f(x) = y_1 + \frac{\Delta y_1}{1!} z + \frac{\Delta^2 y_1}{2!} z(z-1) + \frac{\Delta^3 y_1}{3!} z(z-1)(z-2)$$

$$+ \frac{\Delta^4 y_1}{4!} z(z-1)(z-2)(z-3)$$

$$+ \frac{\Delta^5 y_1}{5!} z(z-1)(z-2)(z-3)(z-4) + \ldots$$

where $\Delta^i y_1$ is the forward difference of ith order whose value is determined from Table 5.1.

The preceding formula is valid for any point x lying in the interval $[x_1, x_2]$. Rewriting this formula gives

$$y = f(x) = f(x_1) + \frac{\Delta f(x_1)}{1!} z + \frac{\Delta^2 f(x_1)}{2!} (z^2 - z)$$

$$+ \frac{\Delta^3 f(x_1)}{3!} (z^3 - 3z^2 + 2z)$$

$$+ \frac{\Delta^4 f(x_1)}{4!} (z^4 - 6z^3 + 11z^2 - 6z)$$

$$+ \frac{\Delta^5 f(x_1)}{5!} (z^5 - 10z^4 + 35z^3 - 50z^2 + 24z) + \cdots$$

where $z = \dfrac{x - x_1}{h}$

Using the chain rule $\dfrac{d}{dx} = \dfrac{d}{dz} * \dfrac{dz}{dx} = \dfrac{1}{h} * \dfrac{d}{dz}$

we get $\dfrac{dy}{dx} = \dfrac{df(x)}{dx} = \dfrac{1}{h} * \dfrac{df(x)}{dz}$

The derivative dy/dx at any general point $x = x$ is given by

$$\frac{dy}{dx} = f'(x) = \frac{df(x)}{dx}$$

$$= \frac{1}{h}\left[\frac{\Delta f(x_1)}{1!} + \frac{\Delta^2 f(x_1)}{2!}(2z-1) + \frac{\Delta^3 f(x_1)}{3!}(3z^2 - 6z + 2) + \frac{\Delta^4 f(x_1)}{4!}(4z^3 - 18z^2 + 22z - 6) + \frac{\Delta^5 f(x_1)}{5!}(5z^4 - 40z^3 + 105z^2 - 100z + 24) + \cdots\right] \quad (5.1a)$$

Table 5.1 Forward difference table

i	x_i	y_i	Δy_i	$\Delta^2 y_i$	$\Delta^3 y_i$	$\Delta^4 y_i$	$\Delta^5 y_i$
1	x_1	y_1	$\Delta y_1 = y_2 - y_1$	$\Delta^2 y_1 = \Delta y_2 - \Delta y_1$	$\Delta^3 y_1 = \Delta^2 y_2 - \Delta^2 y_1$	$\Delta^4 y_1 = \Delta^3 y_2 - \Delta^3 y_1$	$\Delta^5 y_1 = \Delta^4 y_2 - \Delta^4 y_1$
2	x_2	y_2	$\Delta y_2 = y_3 - y_2$	$\Delta^2 y_2 = \Delta y_3 - \Delta y_2$	$\Delta^3 y_2 = \Delta^2 y_3 - \Delta^2 y_2$	$\Delta^4 y_2 = \Delta^3 y_3 - \Delta^3 y_2$	
3	x_3	y_3	$\Delta y_3 = y_4 - y_3$	$\Delta^2 y_3 = \Delta y_4 - \Delta y_3$	$\Delta^3 y_3 = \Delta^2 y_4 - \Delta^2 y_3$		
4	x_4	y_4	$\Delta y_4 = y_5 - y_4$	$\Delta^2 y_4 = \Delta y_5 - \Delta y_4$			
5	x_5	y_5	$\Delta y_5 = y_6 - y_5$				
6	x_6	y_6					

Rewriting Eq. (5.1a) in terms of variable y, we have

$$\frac{dy}{dx}=\frac{1}{h}\left[\Delta y_1+\frac{\Delta^2 y_1}{2!}(2z-1)+\frac{\Delta^3 y_1}{3!}(3z^2-6z+2)\right.$$
$$+\frac{\Delta^4 y_1}{4!}(4z_3-18z_2+22z-6)$$
$$\left.+\frac{\Delta 5 y_1}{5!}(5z^4-40z^3+105z^2-100z+24)+\cdots\right] \quad (5.1b)$$

The value of the derivative at $x = x_1$ is obtained by using $z = 0$ in Formula (5.1a),

$$\frac{dy}{dx}=f'(x_1)=\frac{1}{h}\left[\frac{\Delta f(x_1)}{1!}-\frac{\Delta^2 f(x_1)}{2!}+2\frac{\Delta^3 f(x_1)}{3!}\right.$$
$$\left.-6\frac{\Delta^4 f(x_1)}{4!}+24\frac{\Delta^5 f(x_1)}{5!}+\cdots\right] \quad (5.2a)$$

or

$$\frac{dy}{dx}=f'(x_1)=\frac{1}{h}\left[\frac{\Delta y_1}{1!}-\frac{\Delta^2 y_1}{2!}+\frac{2\Delta^3 y_1}{3!}\right.$$
$$\left.-6\frac{\Delta^4 y_1}{4!}+24\frac{\Delta^5 y_1}{5!}+\cdots\right] \quad (5.2b)$$

The second order derivative of the function at any general point $x = x$ is given by using the chain rule again as follows.

$$\frac{d^2 f(x)}{dx^2}=\frac{df'(x)}{dz}\frac{dz}{dx}=\frac{1}{h}\frac{df'(x)}{dz}$$

Differentiating Eq. (5.1a) w.r.t. z and substituting in the preceding chain rule expression gives

$$\frac{d^2 f(x)}{dx^2}=f''(x)=\frac{df'(x)}{dx}$$
$$=\frac{1}{h^2}\left[\Delta^2 f(x_1)+\frac{\Delta^3 f(x_1)}{3!}(6z-6)\right.$$
$$+\frac{\Delta^4 f(x_1)}{4!}(12z^2-36z+22)$$
$$\left.+\frac{\Delta^5 f(x_1)}{5!}(20z^3-120z^2+210z-100)+\cdots\right] \quad (5.3a)$$

In terms of variable y, we can rewrite Eq. (5.3a) as

$$\frac{d^2 f(x)}{dx^2}=f''(x)=\frac{df'(x)}{dx}$$
$$=\frac{1}{h^2}\left[\Delta^2 y_1+\frac{\Delta^3 y_1}{3!}(6z-6)+\frac{\Delta^4 y_1}{4!}(12z^2-36z+22)\right.$$
$$\left.+\frac{\Delta^5 y_1}{5!}(20z^3-120z^2+210z-100)+\cdots\right] \quad (5.3b)$$

The value of the derivative at $x = x_1$ is obtained by using $z = 0$ in Eq. (5.3a)

$$\frac{d^2 f(x)}{dx^2} = f''(x) = \frac{df'(x)}{dx}$$

$$= \frac{1}{h^2}\left[\Delta^2 f(x_1) - \Delta^3 f(x_1) + \frac{11}{12}\Delta^4 f(x_1) - \frac{5}{6}\Delta^5 f(x_1) + \cdots\right] \tag{5.4a}$$

or
$$\frac{d^2 y}{dx^2} = f''(x_1) = \frac{1}{h^2}\left[\Delta^2 y_1 - \Delta^3 y_1 + \frac{11}{12}\Delta^4 y_1 - \frac{5}{6}\Delta^5 y_1 + \cdots\right] \tag{5.4b}$$

In a similar way, more higher order derivatives can be calculated.

Using the differential operator $D = d/dx$, we can rewrite Eq. (5.2b) as

$$Dy_1 = \frac{1}{h}\left[\Delta - \frac{\Delta^2}{2} + \frac{\Delta^3}{3} - \frac{\Delta^4}{4} + \frac{\Delta^5}{5} + \cdots\right]y_1 \tag{5.2b}$$

Similarly, the second order derivative is obtained from Eq. (5.4b) as

$$D^2 y_1 = \frac{1}{h^2}\left[\Delta^2 - \Delta^3 + \frac{11}{12}\Delta^4 - \frac{5}{6}\Delta^5 + \cdots\right]y_1 \tag{5.4b}$$

5.3 Numerical Examples (Derivative Using Forward Differences)

EXAMPLE 5.1 A function $y = f(x)$ is tabulated below. Find the value of dy/dx at $x = 1$.

x_i	1	2	3	4	5	6
$y_i = f(x_i)$	2.7183	3.3210	4.0552	4.9530	6.0496	7.3891

Solution

Constructing the forward difference table (Table 5.2) from the above tabulated values of the function.

Table 5.2 Forward difference table—Example 5.1

x_i	$y_i = f(x_i)$	Δy_i	$\Delta^2 y_i$	$\Delta^3 y_i$	$\Delta^4 y_i$	$\Delta^5 y_i$
1	2.7183	0.6027	0.1315	0.0321	0.0031	0.0058
2	3.3210	0.7342	0.1636	0.0352	0.0089	
3	4.0552	0.8978	0.1988	0.0441		
4	4.9530	1.0966	0.2429			
5	6.0496	1.3395				
6	7.3891					

Using Eq. (5.2b) for $x = x_1 = 1$, $h = 1$, $z = 0$

$$\left.\frac{dy}{dx}\right|_{x=1} = f'(x_1) = 1\left[\Delta y_1 - \frac{1}{2}\Delta^2 y_1 + \frac{1}{3}\Delta^3 y_1 - \frac{1}{4}\Delta^4 y_1 + \frac{1}{5}\Delta^5 y_1\right]$$

$$= \left[0.6027 - \frac{1}{2}(0.1315) + \frac{1}{3}(0.0321) - \frac{1}{4}(0.0031) + \frac{1}{5}(0.0058)\right]$$

$$= 0.5480$$

EXAMPLE 5.2 A function $y = f(x)$ is tabulated below. Find the value of $\frac{dy}{dx}$ and $\frac{d^2y}{dx^2}$ at $x = 3$.

x_i	0	5	10	15	20
$y_i = f(x_i)$	1.5708	1.5738	1.5828	1.5981	1.62

Solution

Constructing the forward difference table (Table 5.3) from the above tabulated values of the function.

Table 5.3 Forward difference table—Example 5.3

x_i	$y_i = f(x_i)$	Δy_i	$\Delta^2 y_i$	$\Delta^3 y_i$	$\Delta^4 y_i$
0	1.5708	0.0030	0.0060	0.0003	0.0
5	1.5738	0.0090	0.0063	0.0003	0.0
10	1.5828	0.0153	0.0066		
15	1.5981	0.0219			
20	1.62				

Using Eqs. (5.1b) and (5.3b) for $x = 3$, $h = 5$, $x_1 = 0$, $z = 3/5 = 0.6$, we get, respectively,

$$\left.\frac{dy}{dx}\right|_{x=3} = f'(3) = \frac{1}{5}\left(\Delta y_1 - \left(\frac{0.1}{2}\right)\Delta^2 y_1 - \left(\frac{0.52}{6}\right)\Delta^3 y_1\right)$$

$$= \frac{1}{5}\left[0.0030 + (0.1)(0.006) - \left(\frac{0.52}{6}\right)(0.0003)\right]$$

$$= 0.0007$$

and
$$\left.\frac{d^2y}{dx^2}\right|_{x=3} = f''(3) = \frac{1}{5^2}\left[\Delta^2 y_1 + \frac{\Delta^3 y_1}{6}(6\times 0.6 - 6)\right]$$

$$= 0.00023$$

5.4 Algorithm (AL51) for the Derivative at the Tabulated Point Using Forward Differences

This algorithm is transformed to a computer program written in C++ language and presented at the end of this chapter (see **p51.cpp**).

1. Declare/define the function/subprogram **dernfdi** to implement the method.
2. Start the (main) function.
3. Define the main function which calls the appropriate subprogram/ function according to given choice.
4. Stop (main).

Details of function/subprogram **dernfdi**:

1. Start
2. Enter the number of tabulated points (n) and the point of differentiation (X)
3. Enter the coordinates (x_i, y_i) using for loop
4. i=1
   while X>x_i
   i=i+1
5. k=i
   h=$x_{k+1}-x_k$
6. Declare a 2-dimensional (fd) array for the forward difference operator, Δ
   compute the elements of forward differences fd_{ij}
   for j=1 to n–1 do
   begin
      for i=1 to n–j do
      begin
         If (j=1) then
            $fd_{ij}=y_{i+1}-y_i$
         else
            $fd_{ij}=fd_{i+1j-1}-fd_{ij-1}$
         endif
      endfor
   write fd_{ij}
   endfor
7. Derivative formula
   sum=0
   for j=1 to n–k
   sm=sm+$fd_{kj}*(-1)^{j+1}/j$
   dy/dx=sum/h
8. Return

5.5 Algorithm (AL52) for Derivative at any Point Using Forward Differences

This algorithm is transformed to a computer program written in C++ language and presented at the end of this chapter (see **p52.cpp**).

1. Declare/define the function/subprogram **fact** to calculate the factorial.
2. Declare/define the function/subprogram **dernfdi** to implement the method.
3. Start the (main) function.
4. Define the main function which calls the appropriate subprogram/function according to given choice.
5. Stop (main).

Details of function/subprogram **dernfdi**:

1. Start
2. Enter the number of tabulated points (n) and the point of differentiation (X)
3. Enter the coordinates (x_i, y_i) using for loop
4. i=1

   while X>x_i

   i=i+1
5. k=i

   h=$x_{k+1}-x_k$

   z=$(X-x_k)/(x_{k+1}-x_k)$
6. Declare a 2-dimensional (fd) array for the forward difference operator, Δ

   compute the elements of forward differences fd_{ij}

   for j=1 to n–1 do

   begin

       for i=1 to n–j do

       begin

           If (j=1) then

               $fd_{ij}=y_{i+1}-y_i$

           else

               $fd_{ij}=fd_{i+1j-1}-fd_{ij-1}$

           endif

       endfor

   endfor
7. Derivative formula

       sum=fd_{k1}

   for j=2 to n–k

       sum1=0

```
for p=0 to j–1
        pr=1
        for m=0 to j–1
        if m≠p
        pr=(pr)(z–m)
        endfor
        sm1=sm1+pr
        endfor
    sum=sum+fd_kj*sum1/j!
  endfor
  dy/dx=sum/h
8. Return
```

5.6 Derivative of a Function Using Newton's Backward Difference Interpolation

Let a function $y = f(x)$ be tabulated $x = x_1, x_2, x_3, ..., x_n$ such that $x_2 = x_1 + h$, $x_3 = x_1 + 2h$, $x_4 = x_1 + 3h$, ..., $x_n = x_1 + nh$.

Defining $z = (x - x_n)/h$, we can write the backward difference interpolation formula (see Chapter 4) as

$$y = f(x) = y_n + \frac{\nabla y_n}{1!} z + \frac{\nabla^2 y_n}{2!} z(z+1) + \cdots + \frac{\nabla^n y_n}{n!} z(z+1)(z+2) \ldots (z+(n-1)) \tag{5.5}$$

where y_n is the value of the function at $x = x_n$ and ∇^i is the backward difference of ith order. The backward differences are calculated using Table 5.4.

Table 5.4 Backward difference table

i	x_i	$y_i = f(x_i)$	∇y_i	$\nabla^2 y_i$	$\nabla^3 y_i$	$\nabla^4 y_i$
1	x_1	y_1				
2	x_2	y_2	$\nabla y_2 = y_2 - y_1$			
3	x_3	y_3	$\nabla y_3 = y_3 - y_2$	$\nabla^2 y_3 = \nabla y_3 - \nabla y_2$		
4	x_4	y_4	$\nabla y_4 = y_4 - y_3$	$\nabla^2 y_4 = \nabla y_4 - \nabla y_3$	$\nabla^3 y_4 = \nabla^2 y_4 - \nabla^2 y_3$	
5	x_5	y_5	$\nabla y_5 = y_5 - y_4$	$\nabla^2 y_5 = \nabla y_5 - \nabla y_4$	$\nabla^3 y_5 = \nabla^2 y_5 - \nabla^2 y_4$	$\nabla^4 y_5 = \nabla^3 y_5 - \nabla^3 y_4$

Differentiating Eq. (5.5) with respect to x and using the chain rule,

$$\frac{d}{dx} = \frac{d}{dz}\frac{dz}{dx} = \frac{1}{h}\frac{d}{dz} \qquad \left(\because \quad z = \frac{x - x_n}{h}\right)$$

we get

$$\frac{dy}{dx} = \frac{1}{h}\frac{dy}{dz}$$

The derivative dy/dx at any general point $x = x$ is given by

$$\frac{dy}{dx} = \frac{1}{h}\left[\nabla y_n + \frac{\nabla^2 y_n}{2!}(2z+1) + \frac{\nabla^3 y_n}{3!}(3z^2+6z+2) + \frac{\nabla^4 y_n}{4!}(4z^3+18z^2+22z+6) + \frac{\nabla^5 y_n}{5!}(5z^4+40z^3+105z^2+100z+24)+\cdots\right] \tag{5.6}$$

At $x = x_n$ the derivative is obtained by putting $z = 0$ in Eq. (5.6), i.e.

$$\frac{dy}{dx} = \frac{1}{h}\left[\nabla y_n + \frac{\nabla^2 y_n}{2} + \frac{\nabla^3 y_n}{3} + \frac{\nabla^4 y_n}{4} + \frac{\nabla^5 y_n}{5} + \cdots\right] \tag{5.7}$$

The second order derivative is obtained by differentiating Eq. (5.6) as

$$\frac{d^2 y}{dx^2} = f''(x) = \frac{df'(x)}{dx}$$

$$= \frac{1}{h^2}\left[\nabla^2 y_n + \nabla^3 y_n(z+1) + \frac{\nabla^4 y_n}{12}(6z^2+18z+11)+\cdots\right] \tag{5.8}$$

At $x = x_n$ the derivative is obtained by putting $z = 0$ in (Eq. 5.8), i.e.

$$\frac{d^2 y}{dx^2} = \frac{1}{h}\left[\nabla^2 y_n + \nabla^3 y_n + \frac{11}{12}\nabla^4 y_n + \cdots\right] \tag{5.9}$$

Using the relation between the differential operator D with the shift operator E and the backward difference operator ∇, we have

$$E = e^{hD} = \frac{1}{1-\nabla}$$

From this, we get $D = -\frac{1}{h}\log_e(1-\nabla)$

Therefore, we can rewrite Eqs. (5.7) and (5.9) as

$$\frac{dy}{dx} = Dy_n$$

$$\frac{d^2 y}{dx^2} = D^2 y_n$$

5.7 Numerical Examples (Derivative Using Backward Differences)

EXAMPLE 5.3 For a rotating body the following values of the angles of rotation are recorded as a function of time. Calculate the angular velocity and the angular acceleration at $t = 0.6$ s.

t(s)	0	0.2	0.4	0.6	0.8	1.0
α (rad)	0	0.12	0.49	1.12	2.02	3.2

Solution

Constructing the backward difference table (Table 5.5) from the above tabulated values of the given function, we have

Table 5.5 Backward difference table—Example 5.3

t(s)	α(rad)	$\nabla\alpha$	$\nabla^2\alpha$	$\nabla^3\alpha$	$\nabla^4\alpha$
0	0				
0.2	0.12	0.12			
0.4	0.49	0.37	0.25		
0.6	1.12	0.63	0.26	0.01	
0.8	2.02	0.9	0.27	0.01	0
1.0	3.2	1.18	0.28	0.01	0

Using Eq. (5.6) for $x_n = 1.0$, $h = 0.2$, $x = 0.6$, $z = (x - x_n)/h = -2$ for angular velocity, we get

$$\frac{dy}{dx} = \frac{d\alpha}{dt} = \frac{1}{h}\left[\nabla y_n + \frac{\nabla^2 y_n}{2!}(2z+1) + \frac{\nabla^3 y_n}{3!}(3z^2 + 6z + 2)\right]$$

$$= \frac{1}{0.2}\left[1.18 - \frac{3}{2}(0.28) + \frac{1}{3}(0.01)\right]$$

$$= 3.82 \text{ rad/s}$$

Using Eq. (5.8) for angular acceleration, we get

$$\frac{d^2\alpha}{dt^2} = \frac{1}{h^2}[\nabla^2 y_n + \nabla^3 y_n(z+1) + \cdots]$$

$$= \frac{1}{0.04}(0.28 - 0.01)$$

$$= 6.75 \text{ rad/s}^2$$

EXAMPLE 5.4 Using the backward differences, calculate the derivative of the tabulated function given below at $x = 0.4$.

x	0.1	0.2	0.3	0.4
$y = f(x)$	1.10517	1.22140	1.34986	1.49182

Solution

Constructing the backward difference table (Table 5.6) from the above tabulated values of the given function, we have

Table 5.6 Backward difference table—Example 5.4

x	y	∇y	$\nabla^2 y$	$\nabla^3 y$
0.1	1.10517			
0.2	1.22140	0.11623		
0.3	1.34986	0.12846	0.01223	
0.4	1.49182	0.14196	0.01350	0.00127

Using Eq. (5.7) for $x_n = 0.4$, $h = 0.1$, $x = 0.4$, $z = (x - x_n)/h = 0$, we get

$$\frac{dy}{dx} = \frac{1}{h}\left[\nabla y_n + \frac{\nabla^2 y_n}{2} + \frac{\nabla^3 y_n}{3}\right]$$

$$= 0.14196 + \frac{0.0135}{2} + \frac{0.00127}{3}$$

$$= 1.4913$$

5.8 Algorithm (AL53) for Derivative at any Point Using the Backward Differences

This algorithm is transformed to a computer program written in C++ language and presented at the end of this chapter (see **p53.cpp**).

1. Declare/define the function/subprogram **fact** to calculate the factorial.
2. Declare/define the function/subprogram **dernbdi** to implement the method.
3. Start the (main) function.
4. Define the main function which calls the appropriate subprogram/ function according to given choice.
5. Stop (main).

Details of function/subprogram **dernbdi**:

1. Start
2. Enter the number of tabulated points (n) and the point of differentiation (X)
3. Enter the coordinates (x_i, y_i) using for loop
4. i=n
while X<x_i
i=i-1
5. k=i
$h=x_{k+1}-x_k$
$z=(X-x_k)/(x_k-x_{k-1})$
6. Declare a 2-dimensional (bd) array for the forward difference operator, Δ
compute the elements of forward differences bd_{ij}

```
      for j=1 to n–1 do
      begin
         for i=j+1 to n do
         begin
            If (j=1) then
               bd_ij=y_i–y_i-1
            else
               bd_ij=bd_ij-1–bd_i-1j-1
            endif
         endfor
      endfor
   7. Derivative formula
      sum=bd_k1
      for j=2 to k–1
         sum1=0
       for m=0 to j–1
               pr=1
               for m=0 to j–1
               if m≠p
               pr=(pr)(z+m)
               endfor
            sm1=sm1+pr
            endfor
         sum=sum+bd_kj*sum1/j!
      endfor
      dy/dx=sum/h
   8. Return
```

5.9 Algorithm (AL54) for Derivative at the Tabulated Point Using Backward Differences

This algorithm is transformed to a computer program written in C++ language and presented at the end of this chapter (see **p54.cpp**).

1. Declare/define the function/subprogram **dernbdi** to implement the method.
2. Start the (main) function.
3. Define the main function which calls the appropriate subprogram/function according to given choice.
4. Stop (main).

Details of function/subprogram **dernbdi**:

1. Start
2. Enter the number of tabulated points (n) and the point of differentiation (X)

3. Enter the coordinates (x_i, y_i) using for loop
4. i=n
   while $X<x_i$
   i=i–1
5. k=i
   $h=x_{k+1}-x_k$
6. Declare a 2-dimensional (bd) array for the backward difference operator, ∇
   compute the elements of forward differences bd_{ij}
```
for j=1 to n–1 do
begin
    for i=j+1 to n do
    begin
        If (j=1) then
            bd_ij=y_i–y_i–1
        else
            bd_ij=bd_ij–1–bd_i–1j–1
        endif
    endfor
    write bd_ij
endfor
```
7. Derivative formula
```
sum=0
for j=1 to k–1
sm=sm+bd_kj/j
dy/dx=sum/h
```
8. Return

5.10 Derivative of a Function at a Point Using Divided Differences

Consider a function $y = f(x)$ which is tabulated at unequally spaced values of x. We know that such a function can be approximated by the divided difference formula given in Chapter 4 by Eqs. (4.13) and (4.14) as follows.

$$y = f(x) = y_1 + (\Delta_d y_1)(x - x_1) + (\Delta_d^2 y_1)(x - x_1)(x - x_2) + \cdots + (\Delta_d^n y_1)(x - x_1)(x - x_2) \ldots (x - x_n)$$

The above equation is valid for a point x lying in the interval $[x_1, x_2]$.

For any point x lying in the interval $[x_k, x_{k+1}]$, we can write

$$y = f(x) = y_k + (\Delta_d y_k)(x - x_k) + (\Delta_d^2 y_k)(x - x_k)(x - x_{k+1}) + \cdots + (\Delta_d^{n-k} y_k)(x - x_k)(x - x_{k+1}) \ldots (x - x_{n-1})$$

We differentiate the above equation to obtain the derivative as

$$\frac{dy}{dx} = \Delta_d y_k + \Delta_d^2 y_k[(x - x_k) + (x - x_{k+1})] + \Delta_d^3 y_k[(x - x_{k+2})(x - x_{k+1}) + (x - x_{k+2})(x - x_k) + (x - x_k)(x - x_{k+1})] + \cdots \quad (5.10)$$

The values of divided differences can be obtained by constructing the difference table (Table 5.7) from the given values of the function.

Table 5.7 Divided difference table

i	x_i	y_i	$\Delta_d y_i$	$\Delta_d^2 y_i$	$\Delta_d^3 y_i$	$\Delta_d^4 y_i$
1	x_1	y_1	$\dfrac{y_2 - y_1}{x_2 - x_1}$	$\dfrac{\Delta_d y_2 - \Delta_d y_1}{x_3 - x_1}$	$\dfrac{\Delta_d^2 y_2 - \Delta_d^2 y_1}{x_4 - x_1}$	$\dfrac{\Delta_d^3 y_2 - \Delta_d^3 y_1}{x_5 - x_1}$
2	x_2	y_2	$\dfrac{y_3 - y_2}{x_3 - x_2}$	$\dfrac{\Delta_d y_3 - \Delta_d y_2}{x_4 - x_2}$	$\dfrac{\Delta_d^2 y_3 - \Delta_d^2 y_2}{x_5 - x_2}$	
3	x_3	y_3	$\dfrac{y_4 - y_3}{x_4 - x_3}$	$\dfrac{\Delta_d y_4 - \Delta_d y_3}{x_5 - x_3}$		
4	x_4	y_4	$\dfrac{y_5 - y_4}{x_5 - x_4}$			
5	x_5	y_5				

5.11 Numerical Examples (Derivative Using the Divided Differences)

EXAMPLE 5.5 From the following table, calculate the derivative at $x = 5$.

x	0	2	3	4	7	9
$y = f(x)$	4	26	58	112	466	922

Solution

We first construct the divided difference table (Table 5.8) to apply the divided difference formula [Eq. (5.10)] for the calculation of the derivative.

Table 5.8 Divided difference table—Example 5.5

i	x_i	y_i	$\Delta_d y_i$	$\Delta_d^2 y_i$	$\Delta_d^3 y_i$	$\Delta_d^4 y_i$
1	0	4	11	7	1	0
2	2	26	32	11	1	0
3	3	58	54	16	1	
4	4	112	118	22		
5	7	466	228			
6	9	922				

Using the above tabulated values in Eq. (5.10) with $x = 5$, $k = 1$. So $x_1 = 0$, $x_2 = 2$, $x_3 = 3$, $x_4 = 4$

$$\frac{dy}{dx} = \Delta_d y_1 + \Delta_d^2 y_1[(x - x_1) + (x - x_2)]$$
$$+ \Delta_d^3 y_1[(x - x_3)(x - x_2) + (x - x_3)(x - x_1) + (x - x_1)(x - x_2)]$$

or $$\frac{dy}{dx} = 11 + 56 + 31 = 98$$

5.12 Algorithm (AL55) for Derivative at Any Point Using the Divided Differences

This algorithm is transformed to a computer program written in C++ language and presented at the end of this chapter (see **p55.cpp**).

1. Declare/define the function/subprogram **dernddi** to implement the method.
2. Start the (main) function.
3. Define the main function which calls the appropriate subprogram/function according to given choice.
4. Stop (main).

Details of function/subprogram **dernddi**:

1. Start
2. Enter the number of tabulated points (n) and point of differentiation (X)
3. Enter the coordinates (x_i, y_i) using for loop
4. i=2
   while X>x_i
   i=i+1
5. k=i–2
6. Declare a 2-dimensional (dd) array for the divided difference operator, Δ
   compute the elements of divided differences dd_{ij}
   for j=1 to n–1 do
   begin
      for i=1 to n–j do
   begin
      If (j=1) then
         $dd_{ij}=(y_{i+1}-y_i)/(x_{i+j}-x_i)$
      else
         $dd_{ij}=dd_{i+1j-1}-dd_{ij-1}$
      endif
   endfor
   endfor

7. Derivative formula

```
    sum=dd_k1
for j=2 to n–k
    sum1=0
for m=0 to j–1
        product=1
        for p=0 to j–1
        if m≠p
        product=(product)*(X–x_k+p)
        endfor
      sm1=sm1+product
      endfor
   sum=sum+dd_kj*sum1
 endfor
 dy/dx=sum
```

8. Return

5.13 Maximum/Minimum of a Function

For a given set of data points we can derive an expression of the interpolating polynomial in terms of the forward/backward/divided differences. A smooth curve can then be drawn to represent the function. Further, we can also find the value of x at which the function $y = f(x)$ has the maximum/minimum values. Let us consider the interpolating polynomial of forward differences from which the derivative is given by

$$\frac{dy}{dx} = \frac{1}{h}\left[\Delta y_1 + \frac{\Delta^2 y_1}{2!}(2z-1) + \frac{\Delta^3 y_1}{3!}(3z^2 - 6z + 2) + \frac{\Delta^4 y_1}{4!}(4z^3 - 18z^2 + 22z - 6) + \frac{\Delta^5 y_1}{5!}(5z^4 - 40z^3 + 105z^2 - 100z + 24) + \cdots\right]$$

The condition for maximum/minimum is $dy/dx = 0$, which gives

$$\Delta y_1 + \frac{\Delta^2 y_1}{2!}(2z-1) + \frac{\Delta^3 y_1}{3!}(3z^2 - 6z + 2) + \frac{\Delta^4 y_1}{4!}(4z^3 - 18z^2 + 22z - 6) + \frac{\Delta^5 y_1}{5!}(5z^4 - 40z^3 + 105z^2 - 100z + 24) + \cdots = 0 \tag{5.11}$$

By solving Eq. (5.11) for the variable z, we can get the value of x at which the function has an extremum.

We can use other formulas based on backward/divided differences that are discussed in this chapter, as well as obtain the points of extrema of the function.

5.14 Numerical Examples (Maximum/Minimum)

EXAMPLE 5.6 Determine the value of x at which the following tabulated function has a minimum.

x_i	0.6	0.65	0.7	0.75
$y_i = f(x_i)$	0.6221	0.6155	0.6138	0.6170

Solution

Constructing the forward difference table (Table 5.9) from the given tabulated values,

Table 5.9 Forward difference table—Example 5.6

x_i	$y_i = f(x_i)$	Δy_i	$\Delta^2 y_i$	$\Delta^3 y_i$
0.6	0.6221	–0.0066	0.0049	0
0.65	0.6155	–0.0017	0.0049	
0.7	0.6138	0.0032		
0.75	0.6170			

Since the minimum value appears to be near $x = 0.65$, therefore, taking $x_1 = 0.65$ in Eq. (5.11), we get

$$\Delta y_1 + \frac{\Delta^2 y_1}{2!}(2z-1) = 0$$

or

$$-0.0017 + \frac{0.0049}{2}(2z - 1) = 0$$

Solving for z gives $z = 0.8469$

With $h = 0.05$, $z = \dfrac{x - x_1}{h} = 0.8469$

This gives $x = 0.6923$. At this value of x, the given function will have a minimum value.

Exercises

1. Find the first and second order derivatives of the tabulated function given below at $x = 1.2$.

x	1	2	3	4	5
$y = f(x)$	0	1	5	6	8

[**Ans.** –1.5, 1.416]

2. Find the first and second order derivatives of the tabulated function given below at $x = 500$.

x	500	510	520	530	540	550
$y = \log_e x$	6.21	6.23	6.25	6.27	6.29	6.31

[**Ans.** 0.002, –0.000004]

3. Using the divided differences, find the first order derivative at $x = 4$ from the given table:

x	1	2	4	8	10
$y = f(x)$	0	1	5	21	27

[**Ans.** 2.83]

4. Using the backward differences, calculate the value of derivative at $x = 56$ from the given table:

x	50	51	52	53	54	55	56
$y = f(x)$	3.68	3.71	3.73	3.76	3.78	3.8	3.83

[**Ans.** –0.023]

5. Find the value of x at which the tabulated function y is a maximum. Also, find the maximum value of the function.

x	60	75	90	105	120
$y = f(x)$	28.2	38.2	43.2	40.9	37.7

[**Ans.** 92.11, 43.27]

C++ PROGRAMS

The C++ programs can be implemented on any O/S, namely

1. Windows O/S using Turbo C++, Dev C++ and Visual C++ compilers.
2. Linux-based Ubuntu/Knoppix/Redhat O/S using GNU C++ compiler.

These compilers have been discussed in Chapter 0. No change is required if Ubuntu is used.

While using Turbo C++, Dev C++ and Visual C++ compilers, note the following points for every program.

- Use header file `#include <iostream.h>` (for Turbo C++ only)
- Use header file `#include <math.h>`
- Use header file `#include <conio.h>`
- Use `getch()` function before the closing bracket '}' of the `main()` function.

Program: p51.cpp

```
//Derivative at a tabulated point using the NFDI formula
#include <iostream>
#include <cmath>
using namespace std;
void dernfdi()
{
   int i,j,k,n,m;
   char option;
   float z,X,h,pr,sm,x[15],y[15],fd[15][15],dery;
cout<<"enter y for default values of x[i],y[i] & tabulated
point x, else enter n\n";
   cin>>option;
   if (option=='y')
   {
     n=6; X=1.0;
     x[1]=1; y[1]=2.7183;
     x[2]=2; y[2]=3.3210;
     x[3]=3; y[3]=4.0552;
     x[4]=4; y[4]=4.9530;
     x[5]=5; y[5]=6.0496;
     x[6]=6; y[6]=7.3891;
   }
   else
   {
       cout<<"enter the number of tabulated points\n";
       cin>>n;
```

```
    cout<<"enter the tabulated point of differentiation\n";
      cin>>X;
    for (i=1; i<=n;i++)
      {
        cout<<"x["<<i<<"]= ";
          cin>>x[i];
        cout<<"y["<<i<<"]= ";
          cin>>y[i];
        }
      }
    i=1;
    while (X>x[i])
      i=i+1;
      k=i;
    h=(x[k+1]-x[k]);
    //forward differences
    for (j=1; j<=(n-1);++j)
      {
        for (i=1; i<=(n-j);++i)
          {
            if (j==1)
            {
            fd[i][j]=y[i+1]-y[i];
            cout<<"fd["<<i<<j<<"]="<<fd[i][j]<<endl;
            }
          else
            {
              fd[i][j]=fd[i+1][j-1]-fd[i][j-1];
        cout<<"fd["<<i<<j<<"]="<<fd[i][j]<<endl;
        }
      }
    }
  //derivative value
    sm=0;
  for (j=1;j<=n-k;j++)
      sm=sm+(fd[k][j]*pow(-1,j+1))/j;
    dery=sm/h;
  cout<<"derivative of y at X is "<<dery<<endl;
}
  main()
{
  dernfdi();
}
```

Program: p52.cpp

```
//Derivative of a function at any point using the NFDI
formula
#include <iostream>
#include <cmath>
using namespace std;
inline int fact(int p)
{
   return (p<1?1:p*fact(p-1));
   }
void dernfdi()
{
   int i,j,k,n,m,p;
   char option;
   float z,X,h,pr,sm,sm1,x[15],y[15],fd[15][15],dery;
cout<<"enter y for default values of x[i],y[i] & tabulated
point x, else enter n\n";
   cin>>option;
   if (option=='y')
   {
     n=5; X=3;
     x[1]=0; y[1]=1.5708;
     x[2]=5; y[2]=1.5738;
     x[3]=10; y[3]=1.5828;
     x[4]=15; y[4]=1.5981;
     x[5]=20; y[5]=1.62;
     }
   else
     {
       cout<<"enter the number of tabulated points\n";
       cin>>n;
     cout<<"enter the tabulated point of differentiation\n";
       cin>>X;
       for (i=1; i<=n;i++)
         {
           cout<<"x["<<i<<"]= ";
             cin>>x[i];
           cout<<"y["<<i<<"]= ";
             cin>>y[i];
           }
         }
       i=1;
```

```
        while (X>x[i])
          i=i+1;
          k=i;
        h=(x[k+1]-x[k]);
        z=(X-x[k])/(x[k+1]-x[k]);
     //forward differences
     for (j=1; j<=(n-1);++j)
        {
          for (i=1; i<=(n-j);++i)
            {
              if (j==1)
               {
               fd[i][j]=y[i+1]-y[i];
               cout<<"fd["<<i<<j<<"]="<<fd[i][j]<<endl;
               }
              else
               {
                 fd[i][j]=fd[i+1][j-1]-fd[i][j-1];
            cout<<"fd["<<i<<j<<"]="<<fd[i][j]<<endl;
            }
          }
        }
     //derivative value
       sm=fd[k][1];
     for (j=2;j<=n-k;j++)
       {
         sm1=0;
         for (p=0;p<=j-1;p++)
         { pr=1;
           for (m=0;m<=j-1;m++)
             if (m != p)
               pr *=(z-m);
             sm1 += pr;
             }
           sm=sm+(fd[k][j]*sm1)/fact(j);
         }
       dery=sm/h;
   cout<<"derivative of y at X is "<<dery<<endl;
}
   main()
{
   dernfdi();
}
```

Program: p53.cpp

```
//Derivative of a function at any point using the NBDI formula
#include <iostream>
#include <cmath>
using namespace std;
inline int fact(int p)
{
   return (p<1?1:p*fact(p-1));
   }
void dernbdi()
{
   int i,j,k,n,m,p;
   char option;
   float z,X,h,pr,sm,sm1,x[15],y[15],bd[15][15],dery;
cout<<"enter y for default values of x[i],y[i] & any point X,
else enter n\n";
   cin>>option;
   if (option=='y')
   {
     n=6; X=5;
     x[1]=1; y[1]=2.7183;
     x[2]=2; y[2]=3.3210;
     x[3]=3; y[3]=4.0552;
     x[4]=4; y[4]=4.9530;
     x[5]=5; y[5]=6.0496;
     x[6]=6; y[6]=7.3891;
     }
   else
     {
       cout<<"enter the number of tabulated points\n";
       cin>>n;
    cout<<"enter the point of differentiation\n";
     cin>>X;
     for (i=1; i<=n;i++)
       {
         cout<<"x["<<i<<"]= ";
           cin>>x[i];
         cout<<"y["<<i<<"]= ";
           cin>>y[i];
         }
       }
    i=n;
```

```
    while (X<x[i])
    i=i-1;
      k=i;
    h=(x[k+1]-x[k]);
    z=(X-x[k])/(x[k]-x[k-1]);
  //backward differences
    //output format: ith row, jth column of BD table
    for (j=1; j<=(n-1);++j)
      for (i=j+1; i<=n;++i)
        {
        if (j==1)
          {
          bd[i][j]=y[i]-y[i-1];
          cout<<"bd["<<i<<j<<"]="<<bd[i][j]<<endl;
          }
        else
        {
          bd[i][j]=bd[i][j-1]-bd[i-1][j-1];
          cout<<"bd["<<i<<j<<"]="<<bd[i][j]<<endl;
        }
      }
  //derivative value
    sm=bd[k][1];
  for (j=2;j<=k-1;j++)
    {
      sm1=0;
      for (p=0;p<=j-1;p++)
      { pr=1;
        for (m=0;m<=j-1;m++)
          if (m != p)
            pr *=(z+m);
          sm1 += pr;
          }
        sm=sm+(bd[k][j]*sm1)/fact(j);
      }
    dery=sm/h;
  cout<<"derivative of y at X is "<<dery<<endl;
}
  main()
{
  dernbdi();
}
```

Program: p54.cpp

```
//Derivative of a function at the tabulated point using the
NBDI formula
#include <iostream>
#include <cmath>
using namespace std;
void dernbdi()
{
   int i,j,k,n,m,p;
   char option;
   float z,X,h,pr,sm,sm1,x[15],y[15],bd[15][15],dery;
cout<<"enter y for default values of x[i],y[i] & any point X,
else enter n\n";
   cin>>option;
   if (option=='y')
   {
     n=6; X=5;
     x[1]=1; y[1]=2.7183;
     x[2]=2; y[2]=3.3210;
     x[3]=3; y[3]=4.0552;
     x[4]=4; y[4]=4.9530;
     x[5]=5; y[5]=6.0496;
     x[6]=6; y[6]=7.3891;
     }
   else
     {
       cout<<"enter the number of tabulated points\n";
       cin>>n;
     cout<<"enter the tabulated point of differentiation\n";
       cin>>X;
     for (i=1; i<=n;i++)
       {
         cout<<"x["<<i<<"]= ";
           cin>>x[i];
         cout<<"y["<<i<<"]= ";
           cin>>y[i];
         }
     }
   i=n;
   while (X<x[i])
     i=i-1;
     k=i;
   h=(x[k+1]-x[k]);
```

```
//backward differences
   //output format: ith row, jth column of BD table
   for (j=1; j<=(n-1);++j)
     for (i=j+1; i<=n;++i)
       {
         if (j==1)
           {
           bd[i][j]=y[i]-y[i-1];
           cout<<"bd["<<i<<j<<"]="<<bd[i][j]<<endl;
           }
         else
         {
           bd[i][j]=bd[i][j-1]-bd[i-1][j-1];
           cout<<"bd["<<i<<j<<"]="<<bd[i][j]<<endl;
         }
       }
   //derivative value
     sm=0;
   for (j=1;j<=k-1;j++)
       sm=sm+bd[k][j]/j;
     dery=sm/h;
   cout<<"derivative of y at X is "<<dery<<endl;
}
   main()
{
   dernbdi();
}
```

Program: p55.cpp

```
//Derivative of a function at a any point using divided
difference formula
#include <iostream>
#include <cmath>
using namespace std;
void dernddi()
{
   int i,j,k,n,m,p;
   char option;
   float X,pr,sm,sm1,x[15],y[15],dd[15][15],dery;
cout<<"enter y for default values of x[i],y[i] & tabulated
point X, else enter n\n";
   cin>>option;
   if (option=='y')
```

```
{
  n=6;  X=6;
  x[1]=0;  y[1]=4;
  x[2]=2;  y[2]=26;
  x[3]=3;  y[3]=58;
  x[4]=4;  y[4]=112;
  x[5]=7;  y[5]=466;
  x[6]=9;  y[6]=922;
  }
else
  {
    cout<<"enter the number of tabulated points,n\n";
      cin>>n;
    cout<<"enter the tabulated point of differentiation,
    X\n";
      cin>>X;
      for (i=1; i<=n;i++)
      {
      cout<<"x["<<i<<"]=  ";
        cin>>x[i];
      cout<<"y["<<i<<"]=  ";
        cin>>y[i];
      }
  }
  //initialization
    i=2;
    while (X>x[i])
      i=i+1;
      k=i-2;
  //divided differences
 for (j=1; j<=(n-1);++j)
   for (i=1; i<=(n-j);++i)
     {
       if (j==1)
         {
       dd[i][j]=(y[i+1]-y[i])/(x[i+j]-x[i]);
         }
     else
     {
 dd[i][j]=(dd[i+1][j-1]-dd[i][j-1])/(x[i+j]-x[i]);
     }
   }
```

```
    //derivative value
      sm=dd[k][1];
    for (j=2;j<=n-k;j++)
      {
        sm1=0;
        for (m=0;m<=j-1;m++)
        { pr=1;
          for (p=0;p<=j-1;p++)
            if (m != p)
              pr *=(X-x[k+p]);
          sm1 += pr;
        }
        sm=sm+(dd[k][j]*sm1);
      }
      dery=sm;
    cout<<"derivative of y at X is "<<dery<<endl;
}
    main()
{
    dernddi();
}
```

6

Numerical Integration

6.1 Introduction

The analytical methods of finding the value of a definite integral of some functions like $f(x) = e^{-x^3}$ either do not exist or are very difficult to solve. Also, when a function is presented in a tabulated form, the analytical methods of integration cannot be used. Under these circumstances, the numerical methods of integration are used to find the numerical value of an integral. These methods give an approximate value of the integral of $f(x)$ as given by

$$I = \int_a^b f(x)dx \tag{6.1}$$

The basic idea of numerical integration is very similar to that of numerical differentiation, in which a polynomial function $p(x)$ of a suitable degree is assumed to approximate the function $f(x)$. The integral can therefore be approximated as

$$I = \int_a^b f(x)dx = \int_a^b p(x)dx \tag{6.2}$$

The polynomial function $p(x)$ can be any one of the interpolation polynomials discussed in Chapter 4. The degree of accuracy attained by numerical methods of integration depends on the order of the polynomial used in approximating the given function. If the fitted polynomial is exact, the error will be zero and result will be exact. The method of integrating an appropriate polynomial $p(x)$ in place of the function $f(x)$ is known as **quadrature**.

Graphically the integral of the function $f(x)$ over the given limits represents the area under the curve $f(x)$ vs x as shown in Figure 6.1.

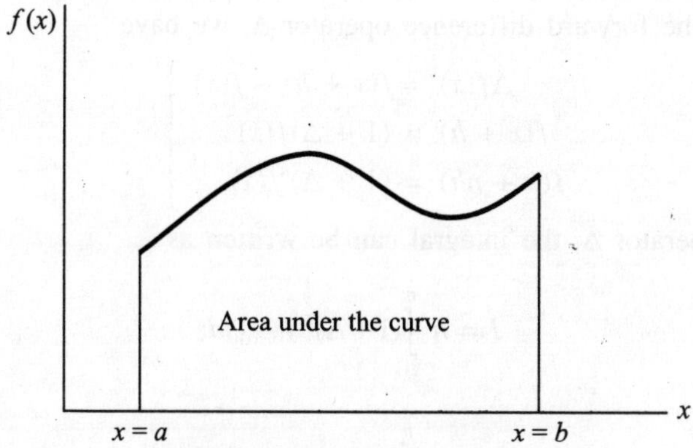

Figure 6.1 Area as integral.

6.2 General Quadrature Formula (GQF)

Consider the integral given in Eq. (6.1) wherein the range of integration $[a, b]$ can be assumed to be divided into equal intervals of size h such that

$$x = x_0 = a, \quad x_1 = x_0 + h, \quad x_2 = x_0 + 2h, \ \ldots, \quad x_n = x_0 + nh = b$$

The value of the function at different points is

$$y_0 = f(x_0) = f(a), \qquad y_1 = f(x_1), \qquad y_2 = f(x_2), \ \ldots, \qquad y_n = f(x_n) = f(b)$$

and so the above integral can be rewritten as

$$I = \int_{x_0}^{x_0 + nh} f(x)dx \tag{6.3}$$

Transforming to a dimensionless new variable, we get

$$z = \frac{x - x_0}{h}$$

$$x = x_0 + hz$$

$$dx = h(dz)$$

At $\quad x = x_0, \ z = 0$

At $\quad x = x_0 + nh, \ z = n$

Rewriting the integral as

$$I = h\int_0^n f(x_0 + hz)dz$$

In terms of the forward difference operator Δ, we have

$$\left.\begin{aligned} \Delta f(x) &= f(x+h) - f(x) \\ f(x+h) &= (1+\Delta)f(x) \\ f(x+nh) &= (1+\Delta)^n f(x) \end{aligned}\right\} \tag{6.4}$$

Using the operator Δ, the integral can be written as

$$I = h\int_0^n (1+\Delta)^z f(x_0)dz$$

or

$$I = h\int_0^n (1+\Delta)^z y_0 dz$$

Using the binomial series expansion

$$I = h\int_0^n \left[1 + z\Delta + \frac{(z^2 - z)\Delta^2 y_0}{2!} + \frac{(z^3 - 3z^2 + 2z)\Delta^3 y_0}{3!}\right]dz$$

On integration, this gives

$$I = h\left[ny_0 + \frac{n^2\Delta y_0}{2} + \frac{(2n^3 - 3n^2)\Delta^2 y_0}{12} + \frac{(n^4 - 4n^3 + 4n^2)\Delta^3 y_0}{24} + \cdots\right] \tag{6.5}$$

Equation (6.5) is called the **general quadrature formula** (GQF).

6.3 Trapezoidal Rule

From the general quadrature formula, we can derive a number of integration formulas by taking different values of n. For $n = 1$, there can be only two function values, $y_0 = f(x_0) = f(a)$ and $y_1 = f(x_0 + h) = f(b)$ as evident from Eqs. (6.4) and (6.5). Therefore, neglecting the forward difference terms from the second order onwards, we get

$$I = h\left(y_0 + \frac{\Delta y_0}{2}\right) = h\left(\frac{y_0 + y_1}{2}\right) = \frac{h}{2}[f(a) + f(b)] \tag{6.6}$$

Let the interval $[a, b]$ be divided into n-equal intervals such that $x_0 = a$, $x_1 = a + h$, $x_2 = a + 2h$, ..., $x_n = a + nh = b$.

Applying Eq. (6.6) to each of the above intervals, we get

$$I_0 = \int_{x_0}^{x_0+h} f(x)dx = \left(\frac{h}{2}\right)[f(x_0) + f(x_0 + h)] = \left(\frac{h}{2}\right)(y_0 + y_1)$$

$$I_1 = \int_{x_0+h}^{x_0+2h} f(x)dx = \left(\frac{h}{2}\right)[f(x_0+h) + f(x_0+2h)] = \left(\frac{h}{2}\right)(y_1 + y_2)$$

$$I_2 = \int_{x_0+2h}^{x_0+3h} f(x)dx = \left(\frac{h}{2}\right)[f(x_0+2h) + f(x_0+3h)] = \left(\frac{h}{2}\right)(y_2 + y_3)$$

$$\vdots$$

$$I_n = \int_{x_0+(n-1)h}^{x_0+nh} f(x)dx = \left(\frac{h}{2}\right)[f(x_0+(n-1)h) + f(x_0+nh)] = \left(\frac{h}{2}\right)(y_{n-1} + y_n)$$

Adding $I_0 + I_1 + I_2 + \ldots + I_n$, we get

$$I = \left(\frac{h}{2}\right)[(y_0 + y_n) + 2(y_1 + y_2 + \ldots + y_{n-1})]$$

or $$I = \left(\frac{h}{2}\right)[f(a) + f(b) + 2(f(x_1) + f(x_2) + \ldots + f(x_{n-1}))] \tag{6.7}$$

Equation (6.7) is called the **trapezoidal rule**. It gives the accurate values of the integral without error when $f(x)$ is a linear function of x.

6.4 Geometrical Interpretation of Trapezoidal Rule

The trapezoidal rule is so called because geometrically it approximates a small curved part of the function by a straight line and interprets the area under the curved part as the area of the trapezoid as shown in Figure 6.2.

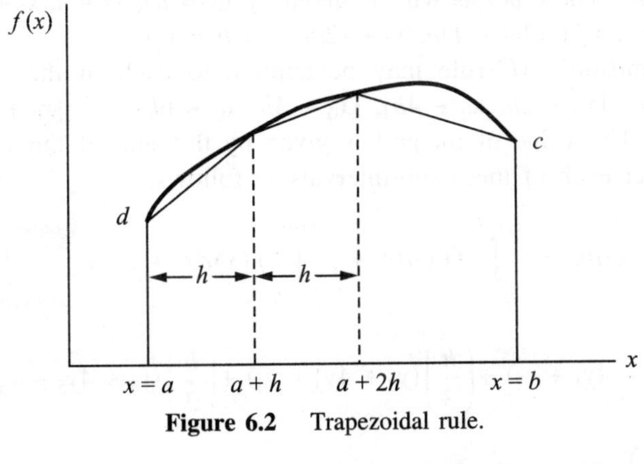

Figure 6.2 Trapezoidal rule.

The entire area under the curve representing the function can be approximated by the sum of small areas of the trapezoids. Each small area of a trapezoid consists of x-coordinates separated by the h interval and has a value which equals the sum of values of the integrals such as I_0, I_1, etc. given in the trapezoidal rule. The trapezoidal rule gives the exact value of the integral for a linear integrand function because the function is approximated by a straight line in calculating the area.

6.5 Simpson's 1/3 Rule

For integrating nonlinear functions of degree $n \leq 3$, the Simpson's 1/3 rule can be used. To obtain the formula for this rule, put $n = 2$ in Eq. (6.4) and in the GQF (6.5) (by neglecting the terms of order greater than three) and then the integral becomes

$$I = \int_a^b f(x)\,dx = h\left[2y_0 + 2\Delta y_0 + \frac{16-12}{12}\Delta^2 y_0\right]$$

$$= h[2y_0 + 2(y_1 - y_0) + \left(\frac{1}{3}\right)(y_2 - 2y_1 + y_0)]$$

$$= \left(\frac{h}{3}\right)(y_0 + 4y_1 + y_2)$$

$$= \left(\frac{h}{3}\right)[f(a) + 4y_1 + f(b)] \tag{6.8}$$

where $y_0 = f(a) = f(x_0)$, $y_1 = f(x_1) = f(x_0 + h)$, $y_1 = f(b) = f(x_0 + 2h)$

Equation (6.8) is known as **Simpson's 1/3 rule.**

If the integration interval $[a, b]$ is divided into an even number of sub-intervals n (= $2m$), there will be ($2m$ + 1) number of points contained in the interval $[a, b]$. These points will be given by x_0 (= a), $x_0 + h$, $x_0 + 2h$, ..., $(x_0 + (2m - 2)h)$, $x_0 + (2m - 1)h$, $x_0 + (2m)h$ (= $b = x_n$).

The Simpson's 1/3-rule may be applied to each of the sub-intervals $[x_0, x_0 + 2h]$, $[x_0 + 2h, x_0 + 4h]$, $[x_0 + 4h, x_0 + 6h]$, ..., $[x_0 + (2m - 2)h, x_0 + (2m)h]$. The value of integral is given by the sum of the values of the integrals over each of these sub-intervals as follows:

$$I = \int_{x_0}^{x_0+nh} f(x)\,dx = \int_{x_0}^{x_0+2h} f(x)\,dx + \int_{x_0+2h}^{x_0+4h} f(x)\,dx + \ldots + \int_{x_0+(2m-2)h}^{x_0+(2m)h} f(x)\,dx$$

$$= \frac{h}{3}(y_0 + 4y_1 + y_2) + \left(\frac{h}{3}\right)(y_2 + 4y_3 + y_4) + \left(\frac{h}{3}\right)(y_4 + 4y_5 + y_6) + \ldots$$

$$+ \left(\frac{h}{3}\right)(y_{(2m-2)} + 4y_{(2m-1)} + y_{2m})$$

$$= \frac{h}{3}[y_0 + y_{2m} + 4(y_1 + y_3 + y_5 + \dots + y_{2m-1}) + 2(y_2 + y_4 + y_6 + \dots + y_{2m-2})]$$

$$= \frac{h}{3}[y_0 + y_{2m} + 4(y_1 + y_3 + y_5 + \dots + y_{2m-1}) + 2(y_2 + y_4 + y_6 + \dots + y_{2m-2})]$$

$$= \frac{h}{3}[y_0 + y_n + 4(y_1 + y_3 + y_5 + \dots + y_{n-1}) + 2(y_2 + y_4 + y_6 + \dots + y_{n-2})]$$

$$= \frac{h}{3}[f(a) + f(b) + 4(f(x_1) + f(x_3) + \dots + f(x_{n-1})) + 2(f(x_2) + f(x_4) + \dots + f(x_{n-2}))] \quad (6.9)$$

Equation (6.9) is known as Simpson's 1/3 rule for n-intervals.

6.6 Geometrical Interpretation of Simpson's 1/3 Rule

In deriving the Simpson's rule, forward differences of order 3 and above have been neglected and the order of the polynomial to be integrated is quadratic. Therefore, the function $y = f(x)$ can be assumed to be a parabola passing through the points lying in the interval $[x_0, x_n]$ as shown in Figure 6.3. The area under the parabola is divided into n-intervals of size h. The sum of the areas under all these sub-intervals gives the value of the integral. The exact error-free value of the integral is obtained if the form of the function $f(x)$ is $ax^2 + bx + c$.

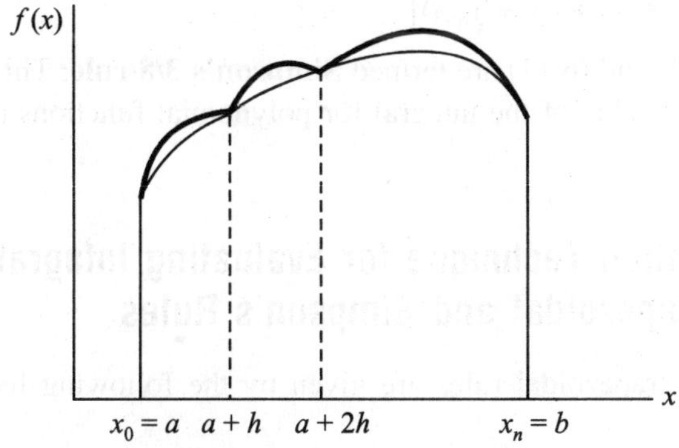

Figure 6.3 Simpson's 1/3 rule.

6.7 Simpson's 3/8 Rule

For polynomial functions of degree three or more, better results can be obtained using this rule which is an improvement over the 1/3 rule. Substituting $n = 3$ in the GQF (6.5) gives (by neglecting forward differences of order 4 and above).

$$I = \int_a^b f(x)dx = h\left[3y_0 + \frac{9}{2}\Delta y_0 + \frac{54-27}{12}\Delta^2 y_0 + \frac{81-108+36}{24}\Delta^3 y_0\right]$$

$$= h[3y_0 + \frac{9}{2}(y_1 - y_0) + \frac{9}{4}(y_2 - 2y_1 + y_0) + \frac{3}{8}(y_3 - 3y_2 + 3y_1 - y_0)]$$

$$= \frac{3}{8}h[y_0 + 3y_1 + 3y_2 + y_3] \qquad (6.10)$$

Now assuming that the interval $[a, b]$ is divided into an odd number of sub-intervals n $(= 2m + 1)$ given by $[x_0, x_0 + 3h]$, $[x_0 + 3h, x_0 + 6h]$, $[x_0 + 6h, x_0 + 9h]$, …, $[x_0 + (2m - 2)h, x_0 + (2m + 1)h]$. The value of integral is given by the sum of the values of the integrals over each of these sub-intervals as follows.

$$I = \int_{x_0}^{x_0+3h} f(x)dx + \int_{x_0+3h}^{x_0+6h} f(x)dx + \ldots + \int_{x_0+(2m-2)h}^{x_0+(2m+1)h} f(x)dx$$

$$= \frac{3h}{8}[y_0 + 3y_1 + 3y_2 + y_3] + \frac{3h}{8}[y_3 + 3y_4 + 3y_5 + y_6] + \ldots$$

$$+ \frac{3h}{8}[y_{2m-2} + 3y_{2m-1} + 3y_{2m} + y_{2m+1}]$$

$$= \frac{3h}{8}[(y_0 + y_n) + 3(y_1 + y_2 + y_4 + y_5 + \ldots + y_{n-1})$$

$$+ 2(y_3 + y_6 + \cdots + y_{n-3})] \qquad (6.11)$$

Equations (6.10) and (6.11) are termed **Simpson's 3/8 rule**. This rule gives the exact, error-free value of the integral for polynomial functions of the form $ax^3 + bx^2 + cx + d$.

6.8 Tabulation Technique for Evaluating Integrals Using the Trapezoidal and Simpson's Rules

Simpson's and trapezoidal rules are given by the following formulas.

$$Y_t = \frac{h}{2}[(y_0 + y_n) + 2(y_1 + y_2 + y_3 + \ldots + y_{n-1})]$$

$$Y_S = \frac{h}{3}[(y_0 + y_n) + 4(y_1 + y_3 + y_5 + \ldots + y_{n-1})$$

$$+ 2(y_2 + y_4 + y_6 + \ldots + y_{n-2})]$$

Now construct Table 6.1 as follows.

Table 6.1

x_i	$y_i = f(x_i)$	y_i $i = 1, 3, 5, ..., (n-1)$	y_i $i = 1, n$	y_i $i = 2, 4, 6, ..., (n-2)$
x_0	y_0	–	y_0	–
x_1	y_1	y_1	–	–
x_2	y_2	–	–	y_2
x_3	y_3	y_3	–	–
x_4	y_4	–	–	y_4
$\vdots$	$\vdots$	$\vdots$	$\vdots$	$\vdots$
x_{n-3}	y_{n-3}	y_{n-3}	–	–
x_{n-2}	y_{n-2}	–	–	y_{n-2}
x_{n-1}	y_{n-1}	y_{n-1}	–	–
x_n	y_n	–	y_n	–
		$\Sigma y_i = Y_1$	$\Sigma y_i = Y_0$	$\Sigma y_i = Y_2$

The formulas for the trapezoidal and Simpson's rules can now be rewritten as

$$I_t = \frac{h}{2}[Y_0 + 2(Y_1 + Y_2)] \tag{6.12}$$

$$I_{S(1/3)} = \frac{h}{3}(Y_0 + 4Y_1 + 2Y_2) \tag{6.13}$$

6.9 Weddle's Rule

In order to obtain an even more accurate value of the integral, we can make use of the Weddle's rule. In this case we need to have at least six sub-intervals between the lower and upper limits of the integral and thus a total of at least seven data points. To get the Weddle's formula, we substitute $n = 6$ in Eq. (6.5). This gives

$$I = \int_{x_0}^{x_0+6h} f(x)\,dx$$

$$= h[6y_0 + 18\Delta y_0 + 27\Delta^2 y_0 + 24\Delta^3 y_0 + \frac{123}{10}\Delta^4 y_0 + \frac{33}{10}\Delta^5 y_0 + \frac{41}{140}\Delta^6 y_0]$$

Approximating 41/140 as 3/10, we can rewrite the above equation as

$$I = \int_{x_0}^{x_0+6h} f(x)dx = \frac{3h}{10}(y_0 + 5y_1 + y_2 + 6y_3 + y_4 + 5y_5 + y_6)$$

Similarly, we can write

$$I = \int_{x_0+6h}^{x_0+12h} f(x)dx = \frac{3h}{10}(y_6 + 5y_7 + y_8 + 6y_9 + y_{10} + 5y_{11} + y_{12})$$

$$\vdots$$

$$I = \int_{x_0+(n-6)h}^{x_0+nh} f(x)dx = \frac{3h}{10}(y_{n-6} + 5y_{n-5} + y_{n-4} + 6y_{n-3} + y_{n-2} + 5y_{n-1} + y_n)$$

On adding the above integrals, we get

$$I = \int_{x_0}^{x_0+nh} f(x)dx = \frac{3h}{10}(y_0 + 5y_1 + y_2 + 6y_3 + y_4$$

$$+ 5y_5 + 2y_6 + 5y_7 + y_8 + \cdots) \tag{6.14}$$

Equation (6.14) is called the **Weddle's rule**. It gives accurate and error-free result, if the polynomial is of degree 6.

6.10 Numerical Examples (Trapezoidal, Simpson's and Weddle's Rules)

EXAMPLE 6.1 Find the value of the integral $I = \int_0^5 \frac{dx}{1+x}$ using the trapezoidal rule with $h = 1$.

Solution

Here $f(x) = 1/(1 + x)$, $a = 0$, $b = 5$, $n = (b - a)/h = 5$, construct Table 6.2.

Table 6.2 Example 6.1

x_i	$y_i = f(x_i)$	y_i ($i = 1, 5$)	y_i ($i = 1, 3$)	y_i ($i = 2, 4$)
0	1.0	1.0	–	–
1	0.5	–	0.5	–
2	0.33	–	–	0.33
3	0.25	–	0.25	–
4	0.2	–	–	0.2
5	0.17	0.17	–	–

From the above table, we obtain, $Y_0 = 1.17$, $Y_1 = 0.75$, $Y_2 = 0.53$

From trapezoidal rule (6.12) we get, $I_t = \frac{1}{2}[1.17 + 2(0.7 + 0.53)] = 1.87$

or directly using Eq. (6.7)

$$I_t = \frac{h}{2}[y_0 + y_5 + 2(y_1 + y_2 + y_3 + y_4)]$$

$$= \frac{1}{2}[1.0 + 0.17 + 2(0.5 + 0.33 + 0.25 + 0.2)] = 1.87$$

EXAMPLE 6.2 Find the value of the integral $I = \int_0^1 dx\, x^{-3/2} \tan^{-1} x$ using the Simpson's 1/3 rule with $h = 0.1$.

Solution

Here $f(x) = x^{-3/2} \tan^{-1} x$, $a = 0$, $b = 1$, $n = (b - a)/h = 10$. Construct Table 6.3, using $x_0 = 0$, $x_1 = 0.1$, $x_2 = 0.2$, ..., $x_n = 1.0$.

Table 6.3 Example 6.2

x_i	$y_i = f(x_i)$	y_i $(i = 0, 10)$	y_i $(i = 1, 3, 5)$	y_i $(i = 2, 4, 6)$
0	–	0	–	–
0.1	3.15211	–	3.15211	–
0.2	2.20707	–	–	2.20707
0.3	1.77373	–	1.77373	–
0.4	1.50411	–	–	1.50411
0.5	1.31141	–	1.31141	–
0.6	0.54042	–	–	0.54042
0.7	0.61073	–	0.61073	–
0.8	0.67474	–	–	0.67474
0.9	0.73282	–	0.73282	–
1.0	0.78540	0.78540	–	–

From the above table, we obtain, $Y_0 = 0.78540$, $Y_1 = 7.5808$, $Y_2 = 4.92634$.

From Simpson's rule, we get

$$I_S = \frac{1}{3}h(Y_0 + 4Y_1 + 2Y_2)(30.3232, 9.85268)$$

$$= \frac{0.1}{3}[0.78540 + 4(8.5808) + 2(4.92634)]$$

$$= 1.365376$$

or directly using Eq. (6.9)

$$I_S = \frac{h}{3}[y_0 + y_{10} + 4(y_1 + y_3 + y_5 + y_7 + y_9) + 2(y_2 + y_4 + y_6 + y_8)]$$

$$= \frac{0.1}{3}[0 + 0.7854 + 4(3.15211 + 1.77373 + 1.31141 + 0.61073 + 0.73282) + 2(2.20707 + 1.50411 + 0.54042 + 0.67474 + 0.78540)]$$

$$= 1.365376$$

EXAMPLE 6.3 Find the value of the integral $I = \int_0^1 f(x)dx$ using the trapezoidal rule for the following tabulated function with $h = 0.1$ (Table 6.4).

TABLE 6.4 Example 6.3

x_i	$y_i = f(x_i)$
0	1.0
0.1	1.2
0.2	1.4
0.3	1.6
0.4	1.8
0.5	2.0
0.6	2.2
0.7	2.4
0.8	2.6
0.9	2.8
1.0	3.0

Solution

Here $h = 0.1$, $x_0 = 0$, $x_{10} = 1$, $y_0 = 1$, $y_{10} = 3.0$

Using the trapezoidal rule (6.7),

$$I_t = \frac{h}{2}[y_0 + y_{10} + 2(y_1 + y_2 + y_3 + y_4 + y_5 + y_6 + y_7 + y_8 + y_9)]$$

$$= 2.0$$

EXAMPLE 6.4 Find the value of the integral $I = \int_0^6 f(x)dx$ using the Simpson's 3/8 rule for the following tabulated function with $h = 1$ (Table 6.5).

Table 6.5 Example 6.4

x_i	$y_i = f(x_i)$
0	0.146
1	0.161
2	0.176
3	0.19
4	0.204
5	0.217
6	0.23

Solution

Here $h = 1$, number of intervals, $n = 6$, $n - 1 = 5$, $n - 3 = 3$

$$x_0 = 0,\ x_n = x_6 = 6,\ y_0 = 0.146,\ y_6 = 0.23$$

Using the Simpson's 3/8 rule,

$$I_t = \frac{3h}{8}[y_0 + y_n + 3(y_1 + y_2 + y_4 + y_5 + \ldots + y_{n-1}) + 2(y_3 + y_6 + \ldots + y_{n-3})]$$

$$= \frac{3h}{8}[y_0 + y_6 + 3(y_1 + y_2 + y_4 + y_5) + 2y_3]$$

$$= \frac{3}{8}[0.146 + 0.23 + 3(0.161 + 0.176 + 0.204 + 0.217) + 2(0.19)]$$

$$= 1.13625$$

EXAMPLE 6.5 Find the value of the integral $I = \int_{0.5}^{0.7} dx\, x^{1/2} e^{-x}$ using the Simpson's 1/3 rule with $n = 4$ intervals.

Solution

Here $y = f(x) = x^{1/2}e^{-x}$, $n = 4$, $n - 1 = 3$, $n - 2 = 2$,

$a = 0.5$, $b = 0.7$, $h = (b - a)/n = 0.05$

Construct Table 6.6, using $x_0 = 0.5$, $x_n = 0.7$.

Table 6.6 Example 6.5

x_i	$y_i = f(x_i)$
0.5	0.429
0.55	0.428
0.6	0.425
0.65	0.421
0.7	0.415

Using Simpson's 1/3 rule [Eq. (6.13)],

$$I = \frac{h}{3}[(y_0 + y_n) + 4(y_1 + y_3 + y_5 + \cdots + y_{n-1}) + 2(y_2 + y_4 + y_6 + \cdots + y_{n-2})]$$

$$= \frac{h}{3}[(y_0 + y_4) + 4(y_1 + y_3) + 2y_2]$$

$$= \frac{0.05}{3}[0.429 + 0.415 + 4(0.428 + 0.421) + 2(0.425)]$$

$$= 0.085$$

EXAMPLE 6.6 Find the value of the integral $I = \int_0^6 \frac{dx}{1+x^3}$ using the Weddle's rule with $h = 1$.

Solution

Here $f(x) = 1/(1 + x^3)$, $a = 0$, $b = 6$, $n = (b - a)/h = 6$. Construct Table 6.7.

Table 6.7 Example 6.6

x_i	$y_i = f(x_i)$
0	1
1	0.5
2	0.111
3	0.036
4	0.015
5	0.008
6	0.005

Using Weddle's rule [Eq. (6.14)] for $n = 6$ intervals

$$I = \int_0^6 \frac{dx}{1+x^3} = \frac{3h}{10}[y_0 + 5y_1 + y_2 + 6y_3 + y_4 + 5y_5 + y_6]$$

$$= \frac{3}{10}[1 + 2.5 + 0.111 + 6(0.036) + 0.015 + 5(0.008) + 0.005]$$

$$= 1.166$$

6.11 Algorithm (AL61) for the Integration by Trapezoidal Rule

This algorithm is transformed to a computer program written in C++ language and presented at the end of this chapter (see **p61.cpp**).

1. Declare/define the function/subprogram **func**.
2. Declare/define the function/subprogram **traptab** for tabulated data points.
3. Declare/define the function/subprogram **trapfun** for a given function.
4. Start the (main) function.
5. Define the main function which calls the appropriate subprogram/function according to given choice.
6. Stop (main).

Details of function/subprogram **func()**:

1. Start
2. Define the inline function 1/(1+*x*)
3. Return (value of the function)

Details of function/subprogram **traptab()**:

1. Start
2. Enter choice for default tabulated points and limits or for new values
3. For new values, enter the number of tabulated points (*k*) and the limits of integration (*a*, *b*)
4. Number of intervals, n=k–1
5. Enter the co-ordinates (x_i, y_i) using 'for' loop
6. h=(b–a)/n

   sum=(y_1+y_{n+1})/2

   for i=2 to n

   sum=sum+y_i
7. itrap=h*sum
8. 'value of integral=', itrap
9. Return

Details of function/subprogram **trapfun()**:

1. Start
2. Enter the number of tabulated points (k) and the limits of integration (a, b)
3. Number of intervals, n=k–1
4. sum=(func(a)+func(b))/2
5. h=(b–a)/n
6. for i=1 to n–1 do
   sum=sum+func(a+ih)
7. itrap=h*sum
8. 'value of integral=',itrap
9. Return

6.12 Algorithm (AL62) for the Integration by Simpson's 1/3 Rule

This algorithm is transformed to a computer program written in C++ language and presented at the end of this chapter (see **p62.cpp**).

1. Declare/define the function/subprogram **func**.
2. Declare/define the function/subprogram **simptab** for tabulated data points.
3. Declare/define the function/subprogram **simpfun** for a given function.
4. Start the (main) function.
5. Define the main function which calls the appropriate subprogram/ function according to given choice.
6. Stop (main).

Details of function/subprogram **func()**:

1. Start
2. Define the inline function x^2
3. Return (value of the function)

Details of function/subprogram **simptab()**:

1. Start
2. Enter choice for default tabulated points and limits or for new values
3. For new values, enter the number of tabulated points (k) and the limits of integration (a, b)
4. Number of intervals, n=k–1
5. Enter the coordinates (x_i,y_i) using 'for' loop
6. h=(b–a)/n
   sum=(y_1 + y_{n+1})/2
   sum2=0

for i=2 to n in steps of 2
sum2=sum2+y_i
7. sum4=0
for i=3 to <n in steps of 2
sum4=sum4+y_i
8. isimp=(h/3)∗(sum+2∗sum2+4∗sum4)
9. 'value of integral=', isimp
10. Return

Details of function/subprogram **simpfun()**:

1. Start
2. Enter the number of intervals (n) and the limits of integration (a, b)
3. sum=func(a)+func(b)
4. h=(b–a)/n
sum2=0
for i=1 to n–2 in steps of 2
sum4=sum4+func(a+ih)
5. sum4=0
for i=2 to n–2 in steps of 2
sum2=sum2+func(a+ih)
6. isimp=(h/3)∗(sum+2∗sum2+4∗sum4)
7. 'value of integral=', isimp
8. Return

6.13 Algorithm (AL63) for the Integration by Simpson's 3/8 Rule

This algorithm is transformed to a computer program written in C++ language and presented at the end of this chapter (see **p63.cpp**).

1. Declare/define the function/subprogram **func**.
2. Declare/define the function/subprogram **simptab** for tabulated data points.
3. Declare/define the function/subprogram **simpfun** for a given function.
4. Start the (main) function.
5. Define the main function which calls the appropriate subprogram/function according to given choice.
6. Stop (main).

Details of function/subprogram **func()**:

1. Start
2. Define the inline function x^3
3. Return (value of the function)

Details of function/subprogram **simptab()**:

1. Start
2. Enter choice for default tabulated points and limits or for new values
3. For new values, enter number of tabulated points (k) and the limits of integration (a, b)
4. Number of intervals, n=k–1
5. Enter the co-ordinates (x_i,y_i) using 'for' loop
6. h=(b–a)/n
   $sum=(y_1+ y_{n+1})/2$
   sum3=0
   for i=2 to <n in steps of 3
   $sum3=sum3+y_i+y_{i+1}$
7. sum2=0
   for i=4 to n in steps of 3
   $sum2=sum2+y_i$
8. isimp=(3h/8)∗(sum+2∗sum2+3∗sum3)
9. 'value of integral=', isimp
10. Return

Details of function/subprogram **simpfun()**:

1. Start
2. Enter number of intervals (n) and the limits of integration (a, b)
3. sum=func(a)+func(b)
4. h=(b–a)/n
   sum3=0
   for i=1 to <n in steps of 3
   sum3=sum3+func(a+ih)+ func(a+ih+h)
5. sum2=0
   for i=3 to <n in steps of 3
   sum2=sum2+func(a+ih)
6. isimp=(3h/8)∗(sum+2∗sum2+3∗sum3)
7. 'value of integral=', isimp
8. Return

6.14 Algorithm (AL64) for Integration by Weddle's Rule

This algorithm is transformed into a computer program written in the C++ language and presented at the end of this chapter (see **p64.cpp**).

1. Declare/define the function/subprogram **wedtab** for tabulated data points.
2. Start the (main) function.

3. Define the main function which calls the appropriate subprogram/ function according to given choice.
4. Stop (main).

Details of function/subprogram **wedtab()**:

1. Start
2. Enter choice for default tabulated points and limits or for new values
3. For new values, enter number of tabulated points (k) and the limits of integration (a, b)
4. Number of intervals, n=k–1
5. Enter the co-ordinates (x_i,y_i) using 'for' loop
6. h=(b–a)/n
   sum1=y_1+5*y_2+y_3+6*y_4+y_5+5*y_6+y_7
   sum2=y_7+5*y_8+y_9+6*y_{10}+y_{11}+5*y_{12}+y_{13}
   if (k=7)
   iwed=sum1*((3*h)/10);
   if (k=13)
   iwed=sum2*((3*h)/10);
7. 'value of integral=', iwed
8. Return

6.15 Gauss Quadrature Formula

Integration formulas using the Simpson and Trapezoidal rules involve computing the function $f(x)$ over fixed intervals. It was found by Gauss that the estimate of the integral can be improved by computing the values of the function at unequal intervals of the variable x.

Consider a function $f(x)$, whose integral is given by

$$I = \int_a^b f(x)\,dx \tag{6.15}$$

Using a change of variable, we convert the above integral to the following form

$$I = \left(\frac{b-a}{2}\right)\int_a^b g(y)\,dy \tag{6.16}$$

where $g(y)$ is transformed function obtained from the given function $f(x)$ using the following relation

$$x = py + q$$

where p and q are unknowns to be determined such that at $x = a$, $y = -1$ and at $x = b$, $y = 1$.

Now, $$y = \frac{x-q}{p}$$

Therefore at $x = a$, $y = \dfrac{a-q}{p}$ implies $-p + q = a$

and at $x = b$, $y = \dfrac{b-q}{p}$ implies $p + q = b$

this gives
$$p = \frac{b-a}{2} \tag{6.17}$$

$$q = \frac{b+a}{2} \tag{6.18}$$

Therefore,
$$x = \frac{b-a}{2}y + \frac{b+a}{2}$$

$$dx = \frac{b-a}{2}dy$$

The integral becomes

$$I = \frac{b-a}{2}\int_{-1}^{1} g(y)dy$$

Rewriting as
$$I = \frac{b-a}{2}\Sigma R_i g(y_i) \tag{6.19}$$

Equation (6.19) is called **Gauss quadrature formula**, where

$$\int_{-1}^{1} g(y)dy = \Sigma R_i g(y_i) = R_1 g(y_1) + R_2 g(y_2) + \cdots + R_n g(y_n) \tag{6.20}$$

where R_i's are called weights and $g(y_i)$ is the transformed function at the given y_i and the Σ is from $i = 1$ to n; n is the number of quadrature points selected.

The values of weights are determined in the following way and are tabulated for reference in Table 6.8.

In Eq. (6.20), there are $2n$ parameters that can be chosen to determine the weights by a proper choice of the polynomial function $g(y)$ of degree not exceeding $(2n - 1)$.

For example, let $n = 2$, therefore, $2n - 1 = 3$, which means that $g(y)$ can be 1, y, y^2, y^3. From Eq. (6.20), we can write

$$\int_{-1}^{1} g(y)dy = \Sigma R_i g(y_i) = R_1 g(y_1) + R_2 g(y_2)$$

For $g(y) = 1$, this gives $R_1 + R_2 = 2$
For $g(y) = y$, this gives $R_1 y_1 + R_2 y_2 = 0$
For $g(y) = y^2$, this gives $R_1 y_1^2 + R_2 y_2^2 = 2/3$
For $g(y) = y^3$, this gives $R_1 y_1^2 + R_2 y_2^3 = 0$

The above four equations have four unknowns that are determined as

$R_1 = R_2 = 1$

$$y_1 = -\frac{1}{\sqrt{3}} = -0.5773503$$

$$y_2 = \frac{1}{\sqrt{3}} = 0.5773503$$

$$\int_{-1}^{1} g(y)dy = R_1 g(y_1) + R_2 g(y_2) = g(-0.5773503) + g(0.5773503)$$

Therefore,

$$I = \int_a^b f(x)dx = \left(\frac{b-a}{2}\right)\int_{-1}^{1} g(y)dy$$
$$= g(-0.5773503) + g(0.5773503) \tag{6.21}$$

Equation (6.21) is valid for $n = 2$ and is called the **Gauss–Legendre formula**.

This formula will give the exact value of integral for any function of up to degree 3. Integral formulas for other values of n can be derived using Legendre polynomials and the corresponding weights can be determined. Table 6.8 gives the values of weights and abscissa.

Table 6.8 Values of weights and abscissa in Gauss quadrature formula

n	i	y_i	R_i
2	1	–0.57735 02692	1
	2	0.57735 02692	1
3	1	–0.7745967	0.5555556
	2	0	0.8888889
	3	0.7745967	0.5555556
4	1	–0.8611363	0.3478549
	2	–0.3399810	0.6521452
	3	0.3399810	0.6521452
	4	0.8611363	0.3478549
5	1	–0.9061799	0.2369269
	2	–0.5384693	0.4786287
	3	0	0.5688889
	4	0.5384693	0.4786287
	5	0.9061799	0.2369269

6.16 Numerical Examples (GQF)

EXAMPLE 6.7 Find the value of the integral using the Gauss quadrature formula.

$$I = \int_{-1}^{1} e^x dx$$

Solution

Let $n = 2$ and using the Gauss–Legendre formula, we get

$$I = \left(\frac{b-a}{2}\right)[R_1 g(y_1) + R_2 g(y_2)]$$

With $a = -1$, $b = 1$, $R_1 = 1 = R_2$, $g(y_1) = e^{-0.5773502}$, $g(y_2) = e^{0.5773502}$

$$I = 2.34269$$

For a better result, we can take a higher value of n and use Table 6.8.

EXAMPLE 6.8 Find the value of the integral using the Gauss–Legendre formula.

$$I = \int_2^4 (x^2 + 2x)dx$$

Solution

Since $f(x)$ is a polynomial of degree 2, we can use the Gauss–Legendre formula (6.21) directly to obtain the exact value of the integral.

Let
$$x = \frac{b-a}{2}y + \frac{a+b}{2}$$

$$= \frac{4-2}{2}y + \frac{2+4}{2}$$

$$= y + 3$$

$$g(y) = (y + 3)^2 + 2(y + 3) = y^2 + 8y + 15$$

$$I = \left(\frac{b-a}{2}\right)[R_1 g(y_1) + R_2 g(y_2)]$$

$$= \left(\frac{b-a}{2}\right)[R_1((y_1)^2 + 8y_1 + 15) + R_2((y_2)^2 + 8y_2 + 15)]$$

$$= \left(\frac{4-2}{2}\right)[1.0((-0.5773505)^2 + 8(-0.5773505) + 15)$$
$$+ 1.0((0.5773505)^2 + 8(0.5773505) + 15)]$$

$$= 30.67$$

Example 6.9 Find the value of the integral using the Gauss quadrature/ Legendre formula.

$$I = \int_0^1 x\,dx$$

Solution

Let $n = 2$ and using the Gauss–Legendre formula, we get

$$I = \left(\frac{b-a}{2}\right)[R_1 g(y_1) + R_2 g(y_2)]$$

With $a = 0$, $b = 1$, $R_1 = 1 = R_2$, $y_1 = -0.5773505$, $y_2 = 0.5773505$

$$g(y) = \frac{y+1}{2}$$

Substituting the values of $g(y_1)$ and $g(y_2)$, we obtain

$$I = 0.5$$

6.17 Algorithm (AL65) for Integration by Gauss Quadrature

This algorithm is transformed to a computer program written in C++ language and presented at the end of this chapter (see **p65.cpp**).

1. Declare/define the function/subprogram **func**.
2. Declare/define the function/subprogram **gqf** for tabulated data points.
3. Start the (main) function.
4. Define the main function which calls the appropriate subprogram/ function.
5. Stop (main).

Details of function/subprogram **func()**:

1. Start
2. Define inline the function $y^2+8y+15$
3. Return (value of the function)

Details of function/subprogram **gqf()**:

1. Start
2. Enter the number of quadrature points n and limits of the integration (a, b)
3. Enter the co-ordinates (w_i, y_i) using 'for' loop
4. h=b-a
   sum=0
   for i=1 to n
   sum=sum+w_i∗func(y_i)
   igq=h∗(sum/2)
5. 'value of integral=', igq
6. Return

6.18 Errors in Numerical Integration Methods

We have used four numerical methods: trapezoidal rule, Simpson's 1/3 rule, Simpson's 1/8 rule, and Weddle's rule for integration by General Quadrature formula in which truncation of a series is necessary. The errors due to truncations arise in each of these numerical methods. In the trapezoidal method, where there is only single strip, the truncation error is

$$E_t \propto h^2$$

where $h = (b - a)/n$ is the step-size for n sub-intervals.

The above equation implies that the truncation error will decrease if the number n of intervals increases so as to decrease the strip size h.

In Simpson's 1/3 and 3/8 rules there are two strips, and four strips respectively, of areas between the limits of integration. The truncation errors in these methods are

$$E_{S1/3} \propto h^4$$

$$E_{S3/8} \propto h^5$$

These expressions show that as the number of strips is increased, the error decreases because the step-size h is a fraction.

In Weddle's rule too, the minimum number of sub-intervals required is six, therefore the truncation error is minimum which is given by

$$E_W \propto h^6$$

By increasing the number of intervals n, the truncation error decreases but this also increases the number of calculations involving arithmetic operations. This results in an increase in the round-off error, which is caused due to limited number of significant digits used in a calculation. Therefore, we conclude that there are always an optimum number of intervals into which the limit interval should be divided to get the correct result in any method. Table 6.9 summarizes a comparison of the different methods.

Table 6.9 Comparison of different methods

Method	*Degree (polynomial)*	*No. of intervals*	*Order of error*	*Error magnitude*
Trapezoidal method	1	Arbitrary	h^2	$\sim(b - a)\cdot h^2/12$
Simpson's 1/3 rule	2	Even (2, 4,...)	h^4	$\sim(b - a)\cdot h^4/180$
Simpson's 3/8 rule	3	Multiple of 3	h^5	$\sim(b - a)\cdot h^5/80$
Weddle rule	6	Multiple of 6	h^6	$\sim(b - a)\cdot h^6/840$

Exercises

1. Find the value of the integral $I = \int_1^2 f \dfrac{dx}{x}$ using (i) Simpson's rules and (ii) Weddle's rule.

   [**Ans.** 0.6932]

2. Find the value of the integral of the function

   $$f(x) = (1 - 0.162 \sin^2(x))^{1/2}$$

   over the limits $x = 0$ to 90° with $h = 15°$ using trapezoidal and Weddle's rule.

   [**Ans.** 1.5057, 1.5062]

3. If $f(x) = 1/(1 + x)^2$, prove that $I = \int_0^6 f(x)\,dx = 0.2311$.

4. Using the Gauss quadrature formula, find the value the integral $I = \int_{-2}^{2} e^{-\frac{x}{2}} dx$. **[Ans.** 4.685]

5. Using the Gauss quadrature formula, find the value the integral $I = \int_{2}^{4} (x^4 + 1) dx$. **[Ans.** 200.401]

C++ PROGRAMS

The C++ programs can be implemented on any O/S, namely

1. Windows O/S using Turbo C++, Dev C++ and Visual C++ compilers.
2. Linux based Ubuntu/Knoppix/Redhat O/S using GNU C++ compiler.

These compilers have been discussed in Chapter 0. No change is required if Ubuntu is used.

While using Turbo C++, Dev C++ and Visual C++ compilers, note the following points for every program.

- Use header file `#include <iostream.h>` (for Turbo C++ only)
- Use header file `#include <math.h>`
- Use header file `#include <conio.h>`
- Use `getch()` function before the closing bracket '}' of the `main()` function.

Program: p61.cpp

```
//Integral of a function by trapezoidal rule
#include <iostream>
#include <cmath>
using namespace std;
inline float func(float x)
{
   return (1/(1+x));
   }
void traptab()
{
   char option;
   int i,n,k;
   float x[15],y[15],a,b,h,sm,itrap;
cout<<"enter y for default values of x[i],y[i] & limits a,b
of integral else enter n\n";
   cin>>option;
   if (option=='y')
   {
   //n is the number of intervals
   //k is the number of tabulated points
     k=6; n=k-1; a=0; b=5;
     x[1]=0; y[1]=1.0;
     x[2]=1; y[2]=0.5;
     x[3]=2; y[3]=0.33;
     x[4]=3; y[4]=0.25;
     x[5]=4; y[5]=0.2;
     x[6]=5; y[6]=0.17;
     }
```

```
   else
      {
        cout<<"enter the number of tabulated points,k\n";
        cin>>k;
        n=k-1;
        cout<<"enter the limit points of integration, a b\n";
        cin>>a>>b;
        for (i=1; i<=n+1;i++)
          {
            cout<<"x["<<i<<"]= ";
              cin>>x[i];
            cout<<"y["<<i<<"]= ";
              cin>>y[i];
            }
        }
      h=(b-a)/n;
      sm =(y[1]+y[n+1])/2;
      for (i=2;i<=n;i++)
      sm += y[i];
      itrap=h*sm;
    cout<<"value of integral is "<<itrap<<endl;
    }
void trapfun()
    {
      int n,i,k;
      float h,a,b,sm,itrap;
    cout<<"input the no. of tabulated points, k\n";
    cin>>k;
    n=k-1;
    cout<<"input integration limits, a b\n";
    cin>>a>>b;
    h=(b-a)/n;
    sm=(func(a)+func(b))/2;
    for (i=1;i<=n-1;i++)
      sm +=func(a+(i*h));
    itrap=h*sm;
    cout<<"value of integral is "<<itrap<<endl;
    }
main()
{
    char ch;
    cout<<"enter choice '1' for tabulated function or choice '2'
for known function\n";
    cin>>ch;
```

```
    if (ch=='1')
      traptab();
    else
      trapfun();
}
```

Program: p62.cpp

```
//Integral of a function by Simpson's 1/3 rule
#include <iostream>
#include <cmath>
using namespace std;
inline float func(float x)
{
    return (x*x);
    }
void simptab()
{
    char option;
    int i,n,k;
    float x[15],y[15],a,b,h,sm,isimp,sm2,sm4;
cout<<"enter y for default values of x[i],y[i] & limits a,b
of integral else enter n\n";
    cin>>option;
    if (option=='y')
    {
    //n is the number of intervals
    //k is the number of tabulated points
      k=11; n=k-1; a=0; b=1;
      x[1]=0; y[1]=1.0;
      x[2]=0.1; y[2]=1.01;
      x[3]=0.2; y[3]=1.04;
      x[4]=0.3; y[4]=1.09;
      x[5]=0.4; y[5]=1.16;
      x[6]=0.5; y[6]=1.25;
      x[7]=0.6; y[7]=1.36;
      x[8]=0.7; y[8]=1.49;
      x[9]=0.8; y[9]=1.64;
      x[10]=0.9; y[10]=1.81;
      x[11]=1.0; y[11]=2.0;
      }
    else
      {
        cout<<"enter the number of tabulated points,k\n";
        cin>>k;
```

```
    n=k-1;
    cout<<"enter the limit points of integration, a b\n";
    cin>>a>>b;
    for (i=1; i<=n+1;i++)
      {
        cout<<"x["<<i<<"]= ";
          cin>>x[i];
        cout<<"y["<<i<<"]= ";
          cin>>y[i];
        }
      }
    h=(b-a)/n;
    sm =y[1]+y[n+1];
    sm2=0;
    sm4=0;
    for (i=2;i<=n;i+=2)
    sm4 += y[i];
    for (i=3;i<=n-1;i+=2)
    sm2 += y[i];
    isimp=(h/3)*(sm+2*sm2+4*sm4);
  cout<<"value of integral is "<<isimp<<endl;
  }
  void simpfun()
  {
    int n,i;
    float h,a,b,sm,isimp,sm2,sm4;
  cout<<"input the no. of intervals,(even no.), n\n";
  cin>>n;
  cout<<"input integration limits, a b\n";
  cin>>a>>b;
  h=(b-a)/n;
  sm=func(a)+func(b);
  sm2=0;
  sm4=0;
  for (i=1;i<n;i+=2)
  sm4 +=func(a+(i*h));
  for (i=2;i<n;i+=2)
  sm2 +=func(a+(i*h));
  isimp=(h/3)*(sm+2*sm2+4*sm4);
  cout<<"value of integral is "<<isimp<<endl;
  }
main()
```

```
{
   char ch;
   cout<<"enter choice '1' for tabulated function or choice '2'
for known function\n";
   cin>>ch;
   if (ch=='1')
     simptab();
   else
   simpfun();
}
```

Program: p63.cpp

```
//Integral of a function by Simpson's 3/8 rule
#include <iostream>
#include <cmath>
using namespace std;
inline float func(float x)
{
   return (x*x*x);
   }
void simptab()
{
   char option;
   int i,n,k;
   float x[15],y[15],a,b,h,sm,isimp,sm2,sm3;
cout<<"enter y for default values of x[i],y[i] & limits a,b
of integral else enter n\n";
   cin>>option;
   if (option=='y')
   {
   //n is the number of intervals
   //k is the number of tabulated points
     k=10; n=k-1; a=0.1; b=1;
     x[1]=0.1; y[1]=1.001;
     x[2]=0.2; y[2]=1.008;
     x[3]=0.3; y[3]=1.027;
     x[4]=0.4; y[4]=1.064;
     x[5]=0.5; y[5]=1.125;
     x[6]=0.6; y[6]=1.216;
     x[7]=0.7; y[7]=1.343;
     x[8]=0.8; y[8]=1.512;
     x[9]=0.9; y[9]=1.729;
     x[10]=1.0; y[10]=2.0;
   // x[11]=1.0; y[11]=2.0;
     }
```

```
else
  {
    cout<<"enter the number of tabulated points,k\n";
    cin>>k;
    n=k-1;
    cout<<"enter the limit points of integration, a b\n";
    cin>>a>>b;
    for (i=1; i<=n+1;i++)
      {
        cout<<"x["<<i<<"]= ";
          cin>>x[i];
        cout<<"y["<<i<<"]= ";
          cin>>y[i];
      }
    }
  h=(b-a)/n;
  sm =y[1]+y[n+1];
  sm2=0;
  sm3=0;
  for (i=2;i<n;i+=3)
  sm3 += y[i]+y[i+1];
  for (i=4;i<=n;i+=3)
  sm2 += y[i];
  isimp=(3*h/8)*(sm+2*sm2+3*sm3);
 cout<<"value of integral is "<<isimp<<endl;
 }
 void simpfun()
 {
  int n,i;
  float h,a,b,sm,isimp,sm2,sm3;
 cout<<"input the no. of intervals,(6,12, 18,etc), n\n";
 cin>>n;
 cout<<"input integration limits, a b\n";
 cin>>a>>b;
 h=(b-a)/n;
 sm=func(a)+func(b);
 sm2=0;
 sm3=0;
 for (i=1;i<n;i+=3)
 sm3 +=func(a+(i*h))+func(a+(i*h)+h);
 for (i=3;i<n;i+=3)
 sm2 +=func(a+(i*h));
 isimp=(3*h/8)*(sm+2*sm2+3*sm3);
 cout<<"value of integral is "<<isimp<<endl;
 }
```

```
main()
{
   char ch;
   cout<<"enter choice '1' for tabulated function or choice '2'
for known function\n";
   cin>>ch;
   if (ch=='1')
     simptab();
   else
     simpfun();
}
```

Program: p64.cpp

```
//Integral of a function by Weddle's rule
#include <iostream>
#include <cmath>
using namespace std;
void wedtab()
{
   char option;
   int i,n,k;
   float x[15],y[15],a,b,sm1,sm2,iwed,h;
   cout<<"enter y for default values of x[i],y[i] & limits a,b
of integral else enter n\n";
   cin>>option;
   if (option=='y')
   {
   //n is the number of intervals
   //k is the number of tabulated points
     k=7; n=k-1; a=0; b=6;
     x[1]=0; y[1]=1.0;
     x[2]=1; y[2]=0.5;
     x[3]=2; y[3]=0.111;
     x[4]=3; y[4]=0.036;
     x[5]=4; y[5]=0.015;
     x[6]=5; y[6]=0.008;
     x[7]=6; y[7]=0.005;
     }
   else
     {
       cout<<"enter the number of tabulated points, k\n";
       cin>>k;
       n=k-1;
       cout<<"enter the limit points of integration, a b\n";
```

```
        cin>>a>>b;
          for (i=1;i<=n+1;i++)
          {
            cout<<"x["<<i<<"]= ";
              cin>>x[i];
            cout<<"y["<<i<<"]= ";
              cin>>y[i];
            }
          }
        h=(b-a)/n;
        sm1=y[1]+5*y[2]+y[3]+6*y[4]+y[5]+5*y[6]+y[7];
        sm2=y[7]+5*y[8]+y[9]+6*y[10]+y[11]+5*y[12]+y[13];
        if (k==7)
        iwed=sm1*((3*h)/10);
        if (k==13)
        iwed=sm2*((3*h)/10);
      cout<<"value of integral is "<<iwed<<endl;
      }
main()
{
   wedtab();
}
```

Program: p65.cpp

```
//Integral of a function by Gauss quadrature formula
#include <iostream>
#include <cmath>
using namespace std;
inline float func(float y)
{
   return (y*y+8*y+15);
   }
   void gqf()
   {
     int i,n;
     float w[15],y[15],a,b,sm,igq,h;
       cout<<"enter the number of points of quadrature, n\n";
       cin>>n;
       cout<<"enter the limit points of integration, a b\n";
       cin>>a>>b;
       for (i=1;i<=n;i++)
         {
           cout<<"w["<<i<<"]= ";
             cin>>w[i];
```

```
            cout<<"y["<<i<<"]=  ";
              cin>>y[i];
            }
          h=b-a;
          sm=0;
          for  (i=1;i<=n;i++)
          sm  +=  w[i]*func(y[i]);
        igq=h*(sm/2);
    cout<<"value  of  integral  is  "<<igq<<endl;
    }
main()
{
    gqf();
}
```

7

Numerical Solution of Ordinary Differential Equations

7.1 Introduction

A differential equation is an equation which contains independent and dependent variables in addition to one or more derivatives of the dependent variables, which can be both partial and ordinary. An **ordinary differential equation** is one that only involves ordinary derivatives along with dependent and independent variables. For example,

$$\frac{dy}{dx} = -\frac{x}{y}$$

$$\frac{dy}{dx} = x^2 + y^2$$

$$\left(\frac{d^2y}{dx^2}\right) + y = 0$$

In science and engineering, differential equations are used to represent physical phenomena or practical applications. For instance, physical phenomena such as simple harmonic motion, radioactivity, and rate of cooling, etc. can be represented by differential equations. Similarly, in engineering applications such as the rate of heat flow in a medium, bending of beams, distribution of temperature in a medium, etc. are represented by differential equations. Recently bio-physical phenomena such as spread of medicine in bloodstream, simulation of nerve cell functioning, etc. have also been investigated through differential equations. Needless to say that the study of numerical methods is incomplete without differential equations.

The numerical solution of a differential equation is an approximate solution of the equation which is obtained with the help of some numerical method. The numerical method is required because sometimes the exact solution is not possible by analytical methods and numerical solution is reliable to the desired degree of accuracy. In this chapter, we will study the solution of ordinary differential equations (ODEs) of first order and second order by different numerical methods.

In solving a differential equation of the first order such as

$$\frac{dy}{dx} = f(x, y) \tag{7.1}$$

we need to find the values y_i (i = 2, 3, 4, ...) of the dependent variable corresponding to the values x_i (i = 2, 3, 4, ...) of the independent variable. The value of the dependent variable, y_1, at an initial point x_1 should be known in order to solve the given equation by any numerical method. This is termed **initial condition for the given differential equation.**

7.2 Euler's Method for the Solution of ODE

The Euler's method is based on the technique of developing a piecewise linear approximation to the solution by extrapolating the solution from the initial point using the value of the slope at this point.

Let us consider the differential equation (7.1), namely

$$\frac{dy}{dx} = f(x, y)$$

with an initial condition that at $x = x_1$, $y = y_1$.

We develop the solution of the above differential equation using the mean value theorem which states that,

"If a function is continuous and differentiable between two points $A(x_1, y_1)$ and $B(x_2, y_2)$, then the slope of the line joining these points is equal to the derivative of the function at least at one other point c between these two points" such that

$$y'(c) = \left.\frac{dy}{dx}\right|_{x=c} = \frac{y(x_2) - y(x_1)}{x_2 - x_1}$$

Substituting $c = x_1$ and $h = x_2 - x_1$, we get

$$\frac{y(x_2) - y(x_1)}{x_2 - x_1} = hy'(x_1)$$

where $$y'(x_1) = f(x_1, y_1)$$

Therefore, $$y(x_2) - y(x_1) = hf(x_1, y_1)$$

$$y(x_2) = y(x_1) + hf(x_1, y_1)$$

$$y_2 = y_1 + hf(x_1, y_1)$$

This gives the first point of approximation to the solution curve $y = f(x, y)$. The second point of approximation is given by

$$y_3 = y_2 + hf(x_2, y_2)$$

In general, the $(i + 1)$th approximation to the solution curve from the ith point is given by

$$y_{i+1} = y_i + hf(x_i, y_i) \tag{7.2}$$

Equation (7.2) is known as **Euler's formula.**

7.3 Geometrical Interpretation of Euler's Method

The Euler's method basically is a technique of developing a piecewise linear approximation of the function $f(x)$ as illustrated in Figure 7.1. As shown in this figure, from the initial point (x_1, y_1), a straight line with a slope $dy/dx = f(x_1, y_1)$ at point '1' is drawn. The point where this line intersects the vertical line at point $(x_2 = x_1 + h)$ gives the next approximation y_2 to the solution curve and the differential equation. Similarly the successive solutions y_3, y_4 are obtained by drawing straight lines of respective slopes from points '2' and '3' as shown.

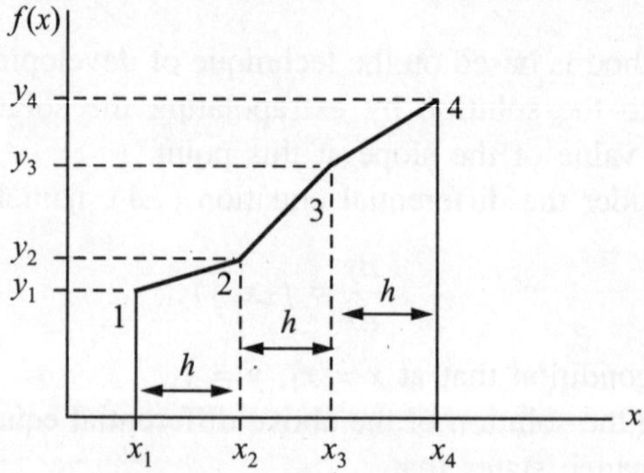

Figure 7.1 Euler's method.

The error in Euler's method is proportional to h^2 at each step. The drawback of this method is that it becomes unstable as the number of iterations increases.

7.4 Numerical Examples (Euler's Method)

EXAMPLE 7.1 Find the solution in the interval [0, 1] of the following differential equation

$$\frac{dy}{dx} = x + y$$

given $h = 0.2$ and $y_1 = 0$ at $x_1 = 0$.

Solution

Using the Euler's formula, $y_{i+1} = y_i + hf(x_i, y_i)$
and using $f(x, y) = x + y$ and $h = 0.2$, $x_1 = 0$, $y_1 = 0$, we get

For $i = 1$, $\quad y_2 = y_1 + (0.2)(x_1 + y_1)$

or $$y_2 = y_1 + (0.2)(0 + 0)$$
$$= 0$$

Thus the first approximation to the solution is $\mathbf{y_2 = 0}$ at $x_2 = 0.2$.

For $i = 2$, $$y_3 = y_2 + (0.2)(x_2 + y_2)$$

or $$y_3 = 0 + (0.2)(0.2 + 0)$$
$$= 0.04$$

Thus the second approximation to the solution is $\mathbf{y_3 = 0.04}$ at $x_3 = 0.4$.

For $i = 3$, $$y_4 = y_3 + (0.2)(x_3 + y_3)$$

or $$y_4 = 0.04 + (0.2)(0.4 + 0.04)$$
$$= 0.128$$

Thus the third approximation to the solution is $\mathbf{y_4 = 0.128}$ at $x_4 = 0.6$.

For $i = 4$, $$y_5 = y_4 + (0.2)(x_4 + y_4)$$
$$y_5 = 0.128 + (0.2)(0.6 + 0.128)$$
$$= 0.274$$

Thus the fourth approximation to the solution is $\mathbf{y_5 = 0.274}$ at $x_5 = 0.8$.

For $i = 5$, $$y_6 = y_5 + (0.2)(x_5 + y_5)$$
$$y_6 = 0.274 + (0.2)(0.8 + 0.274)$$
$$= 0.488$$

Thus the fifth approximation to the solution is $\mathbf{y_6 = 0.488}$ at $x_6 = 1.0$.

Now we can tabulate all the above results and also construct a solution curve through the coordinates.

i	x_i	y_i
1	0	0
2	0.2	0
3	0.4	0.04
4	0.6	0.128
5	0.8	0.274
6	1.0	0.488

EXAMPLE 7.2 Given the differential equation

$$\frac{dy}{dx} = xy \quad \text{with } y(1) = 5$$

Find the solution of the differential equation at each point in the interval [1, 1.5] using the step-size $h = 0.1$.

Solution

Using the Euler's formula, $y_{i+1} = y_i + hf(x_i, y_i)$

and using $f(x, y) = xy$ with $h = 0.1$, $x_1 = 1$, $y_1 = 5$, we get

For $i = 1$, $y_2 = y_1 + (0.1)(x_1\ y_1)$

or $y_2 = y_1 + (0.1)(1 \times 5)$

$= 5.5$

Thus, the second approximation to the solution is $y_2 = 5.5$ at $x_2 = 1.1$.

For $i = 2$, $y_3 = y_2 + (0.1)(x_2\ y_2)$

or $y_3 = 5.5 + (0.1)(1.1 \times 5.5)$

$= 6.105$

The third approximation is given by (1.2, 6.105).

For $i = 3$, $y_4 = y_3 + (0.1)(x_3\ y_3)$

or $y_4 = 6.105 + (0.1)(1.2 \times 6.105)$

$= 6.838$

The fourth approximation is given by (1.3, 6.838).

For $i = 4$, $y_5 = y_4 + (0.1)(x_4\ y_4)$

or $y_4 = 6.838 + (0.1)(1.3 \times 6.838)$

$= 7.727$

The fifth approximation is given by (1.4, 7.727).

For $i = 5$, $y_6 = y_5 + (0.1)(x_5\ y_5)$

or $y_6 = 7.727 + (0.1)(1.4 \times 7.727)$

$= 8.809$

The fifth approximation is given by (1.5, 8.809).
We can obtain the solution curve by plotting y_i vs x_i.

7.5 Algorithm (AL71) for the Euler's Method

This algorithm is transformed to a computer program written in C++ language and presented at the end of this chapter (see **p71.cpp**).

1. Declare/define the function/subprogram **func**.
2. Declare/define the function/subprogram **elrde** for Euler method.
3. Start the (main) function.
4. Define the main function which calls the appropriate subprogram/ function according to given choice.
5. Stop (main).

Details of the function/subprogram **func()**:

1. Start
2. Define the inline function a*b
3. Return (value of the function)

Details of the function/subprogram **elrde()**:

1. Start
2. Enter the interval points x1, xf
3. Enter the initial value y1 at x1
4. Enter the step-size, h, of x-values
5. Initialize i=1, x=x1, y=y1
6. Repeat
```
y=y+h*func(x,y)
x=x+h
i=i+1
output x, y
until x>xf
```
7. Return

7.6 Runge-Kutta (R-K) Methods

In these methods the slopes at some intermediate points are computed and then the weighted average of the slopes is used to extrapolate the next solution point.

7.6.1 R-K Second Order Method (or Heun's Method)

Consider the differential equation,

$$\frac{dy}{dx} = f(x, y)$$

with initial condition at $x = x_1$, $y = y_1$.

Let the slope at the starting point be $s_1 = f(x_1, y_1)$.

Let the second point be at $x_2 = x_1 + h$ at which $y_2 = y_1 + s_1h$ and let the slope at this point be $s_2 = f(x_2, y_2)$.

Now let the average of these two slopes be $s = (s_1 + s_2)/2$. An improved value of the solution at the second point is calculated using this average value of slope as

$$y_2 = y_1 + sh$$

Continuing like this for the third, fourth points, etc., we can write the value of y at the $(i + 1)$th point as

$$y_{i+1} = y_i + sh \tag{7.3}$$

where
$$s = \frac{s_i + s_{i+1}}{2}$$
$$s_i = f(x_i, y_i)$$
$$s_{i+1} = f(x_i + h, y_i + s_ih)$$

Equation (7.13) is called **R-K second order formula**. From the above relations we note that the slope s in this formula depends on the values of the slopes in ith and $(i + 1)$th iterations.

7.7 Geometrical Interpretation of the Second Order R-K Method

In Figure 7.2 shown below, from point '1', we draw a straight line with slope s_1. Let this line cut the vertical line at point '2'. We draw another straight line of slope s_2 from point '1' which cuts the vertical line at point '3'. Let the average of these slopes be s. Now to locate the next solution point y_2 we draw a straight line of slope s from point '1' that cuts the vertical line drawn at $x_2 = x_1 + h$ at point '4'. The value at point '4' is $y_2 = y_1 + sh$ which represents a better approximation than the value y_2 at point '2'. Note that this value y_2 at point '2' is the same as predicted by Euler's method.

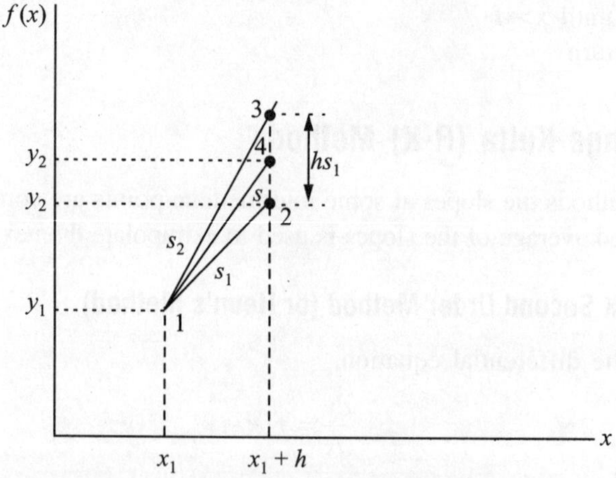

Figure 7.2 R-K second order method.

The straight line between points '1' and '4' gives the piecewise linear approximation to the actual curve.

7.8 Numerical Examples (R-K Methods)

EXAMPLE 7.3 Solve the following differential equation using the R-K second order method.

$$\frac{dy}{dx} + xy = 0 \quad \text{with } y(0) = 1$$

in the interval [0, 0.2] with step-size $h = 0.05$ up to three decimal places.

Solution

Using Eq. (7.3), $y_{i+1} = y_i + sh$

where
$$s = \frac{s_i + s_{i+1}}{2}$$
$$s_i = f(x_i, y_i)$$

$$s_{i+1} = f(x_i + h,\ y_i + s_i h)$$

$$y_{i+1} = y_i + (0.05)s$$

$$s_i = f(x_i,\ y_i) = -x_i y_i$$

$$s_{i+1} = f(x_i + 0.05,\ y_i + 0.05s_1) = -(x_i + h)(y_i + s_i h)$$

For $i = 1$, $\quad y_2 = y_1 + (0.05)s$

$$s_1 = f(x_1,\ y_1) = -x_1 y_1 = 0$$

$$s_2 = f(x_1 + 0.05,\ y_1 + 0.05s_1) = -(0.05)(1) = -0.05$$

$$s = \frac{0 - 0.05}{2} = -0.025$$

$$y_2 = y_1 + (0.05)s = 1 + (0.05)(-0.025) = 0.999$$

Thus, $\quad (x_2,\ y_2) = (0.05,\ 0.999)$

For $i = 2$, $\quad y_3 = y_2 + (0.05)s$

$$s_2 = f(x_2,\ y_2) = -x_2 y_2 = -0.0499$$

$$s_3 = f(x_2 + 0.05,\ y_2 + 0.05s_2) = -0.149$$

$$s = -0.0997$$

$$y_3 = y_2 + (0.05)s = 0.994$$

Thus, $\quad (x_3,\ y_3) = (0.1,\ 0.994)$

For $i = 3$, $\quad y_4 = y_3 + (0.05)s$

$$s_3 = f(x_3,\ y_3) = -x_3 y_3$$

$$s_4 = f(x_3 + 0.05,\ y_3 + 0.05s_3) = -(x_3 + 0.05)(y_3 + 0.05s_3)$$

$$s = -0.0.121$$

$$y_4 = y_3 + (0.05)s = 0.988$$

Thus, $\quad (x_4,\ y_4) = (0.15,\ 0.988)$

Similarly for $i = 4$, $(x_5,\ y_5) = (0.2,\ 0.979)$

for $i = 5$, $\quad (x_6,\ y_6) = (0.2,\ 0.979)$

The tabulated values of the solution are given below.

i	x_i	y_i
1	0	1
2	0.05	0.999
3	0.1	0.994
4	0.15	0.988
5	0.2	0.979

EXAMPLE 7.4 Solve the following differential equation using the R-K second order method.

$$\frac{dy}{dx} = xy \quad \text{with } y(1) = 5$$

in the interval [1, 1.5] with step-size $h = 0.1$ up to three decimal places.

Solution

Using Eq. (7.3), we can write $y_{i+1} = y_i + (0.1)s$

For $i = 1$, $\quad y_2 = y_1 + (0.1)s$

$$s_1 = f(x_1, y_1) = x_1y_1 = 1 \times 5 = 5$$

$$s_2 = f(x_1 + 0.1, y_1 + 0.1s_1) = 1.1 \times 5.5 = 6.05$$

$$s = \frac{5 + 6.05}{2} = 5.525$$

$$y_2 = y_1 + (0.1)s = 5 + 0.1 \times 5.525 = 5.553$$

The second solution point for (x_2, y_2) is (1.1, 5.553).

For $i = 2$, $\quad y_3 = y_2 + (0.1)s$

$$s_1 = f(x_2, y_2) = x_2y_2 = 1.1 \times 5.553 = 6.108$$

$$s_2 = f(x_2 + 0.1, y_2 + 0.1s_1) = 1.2 \times (5.553 + 0.1 \times 6.108)$$

$$= 1.2 \times 6.164 = 7.397$$

$$s = \frac{6.108 + 7.397}{2} = 6.752$$

$$y_2 = y_1 + (0.1)s = 5.553 + 0.1 \times 6.752 = 6.228$$

The third solution point for (x_3, y_3) is (1.2, 6.228).

For $i = 3$, $\quad y_4 = y_3 + (0.1)s$

$$s_1 = f(x_3, y_3) = x_3y_3 = 1.2 \times 6.228 = 7.474$$

$$s_2 = f(x_3 + 0.1, y_3 + 0.1s_1) = 1.3 \times (6.228 + 0.1 \times 7.474)$$

$$= 1.3 \times 6.975 = 9.068$$

$$s = \frac{7.474 + 9.068}{2} = 8.271$$

$$y_4 = y_3 + (0.1)s = 6.228 + 0.1 \times 8.271 = 7.055$$

The fourth solution point for (x_4, y_4) is (1.3, 7.055).

For $i = 4$, $\quad y_5 = y_4 + (0.1)s$

$$s_1 = f(x_4, y_4) = x_4y_4 = 1.3 \times 7.055 = 9.172$$

$$s_2 = f(x_4 + 0.1, y_4 + 0.1s_1) = 1.4 \times (7.055 + 0.1 \times 9.172)$$

$$= 1.4 \times 7.972 = 11.161$$

$$s = \frac{9.172 + 11.161}{2} = 10.166$$

$$y_5 = y_4 + (0.1)s = 7.055 + 0.1 \times 10.166 = 8.072$$

The fifth solution point for (x_5, y_5) is (1.4, 8.072).

For $i = 5$, $y_6 = y_5 + (0.1)s$

$$s_1 = f(x_5, y_5) = x_5 y_5 = 1.4 \times 8.072 = 11.301$$

$$s_2 = f(x_5 + 0.1, y_5 + 0.1s_1) = 1.5 \times (8.072 + 0.1 \times 11.301)$$

$$= 1.5 \times 9.202 = 13.803$$

$$s = \frac{11.301 + 13.803}{2} = 12.552$$

$$y_6 = y_5 + (0.1)s = 8.072 + 0.1 \times 12.552 = 9.327$$

The sixth solution point for (x_6, y_6) is (1.5, 9.327).

7.9 Algorithm (AL72) for the Second Order R-K Method

This algorithm is transformed to a computer program written in C++ language and presented at the end of this chapter (see **p72.cpp**)

1. Declare/define the function/subprogram **func**.
2. Declare/define the function/subprogram **rk2de** for R-K method.
3. Start the (main) function.
4. Define the main function which calls the appropriate subprogram/ function according to given choice.
5. Stop (main).

Details of function/subprogram **func()**:

1. Start
2. Define the inline function a*b
3. Return (value of the function)

Details of function/subprogram **rk2de()**:

1. Start
2. Enter the interval points x1, xf
3. Enter the initial value y1 at x1
4. Enter the step-size, h, of x-values
5. Initialize i=1, x=x1, y=y1
6. Repeat
   s1=func(x,y)
   s2=func(x+h,y+h*s1)
   s=(s1+s2)/2
   y=y+h*s
   x=x+h
   i=i+1
   output x, y
   until x>xf
7. Return

7.10 Runge-Kutta Fourth Order Method

Consider the differential equation,

$$\frac{dy}{dx} = f(x, y)$$

with initial conditions at $x = x_1$, $y = y_1$.

Let the slope at the starting point be $s_1 = f(x_1, y_1)$.

Let the second point be at $x_2 = x_1 + (h/2)$ at which $y_2 = y_1 + s_1(h/2)$ and let the slope be $s_2 = f(x_2, y_2)$.

Let the third point be at $x_3 = x_1 + (h/2)$ at which $y_3 = y_1 + s_2(h/2)$ and let the slope be $s_3 = f(x_3, y_3)$.

Let the fourth point be at $x_4 = x_1 + h$ at which $y_4 = y_1 + s_3h$ and let the slope be $s_4 = f(x_4, y_4)$.

Let the weighted average of these four slopes be given by $s = (s_1 + 2s_2 + 2s_3 + s_4)/6$.

An improved value of the solution at the second point is calculated using this weighted average value of slope s as

$$y_2 = y_1 + sh$$

Continuing like this for the third, fourth points, etc., we can write the value of y at the $(i + 1)$th point as

$$y_{i+1} = y_i + sh \tag{7.4}$$

where

$$s = \frac{s_1 + 2s_2 + 2s_3 + s_4}{6}$$

and

$$s_1 = f(x_i, y_i)$$

$$s_2 = f\left(x_i + \frac{h}{2}, y_i + s_1\frac{h}{2}\right)$$

$$s_3 = f\left(x_i + \frac{h}{2}, y_i + s_2\frac{h}{2}\right)$$

$$s_4 = f(x_i + h, y_i + s_3h)$$

The above relations constitute the R-K fourth order formula.

7.11 Geometrical Interpretation of R-K Fourth Order Method

As shown in Figure 7.3 starting from point '1' with coordinates (x_1, y_1), a straight line with slope s_1 is drawn. The point where this line intersects the vertical line at $x_1 + (h/2)$ gives the second point '2' with coordinates $(x_1 + (h/2), y_1 + s_1(h/2))$.

From point '1' a straight line with slope s_2 is drawn. The point where this line intersects the vertical line at $x_1 + (h/2)$ gives the third point '3' with coordinates $(x_1 + (h/2), y_1 + s_1(h/2))$.

Now from point '1' a straight line with slope s_3 is drawn. The point where this line intersects the vertical line at $x_1 + (h/2)$ gives the fourth point '4' with coordinates $(x_1 + (h/2), y_1 + s_2(h/2))$. From point '1' a straight line with slope s_4 is drawn. The point where this line intersects the vertical line at $x_1 + h$ gives the fifth point '5' with coordinates $(x_1 + h, y_1 + s_3h)$.

The weighted average of the slopes is computed as

$$s = \frac{s_1 + 2s_2 + 2s_3 + s_4}{6}$$

From point '1' a straight line with slope s is drawn that intersects the vertical line drawn at point '6' with coordinates $(x_1 + h, y_1 + sh)$. Thc point '6' is the second solution point of the differential equation. Continuing in the same way we can compute the third, fourth solution points, etc. of the differential equation.

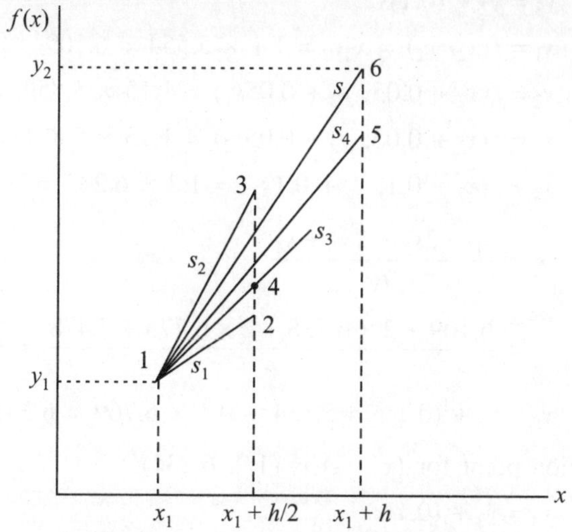

Figure 7.3 R-K fourth order method.

Thus using the R-K fourth order method a piecewise linear approximation to the actual curve can be obtained.

7.12 Numerical Examples (R-K Fourth Order Method)

EXAMPLE 7.5 Solve the following differential equation using the R-K fourth order method.

$$\frac{dy}{dx} = xy \quad \text{with } y(1) = 5$$

in the interval [1, 1.5] with step-size $h = 0.1$ up to three decimal places.

Solution

Using Eq. (7.2), we can write $y_{i+1} = y_i + (0.1)s$

For $i = 1$, $\quad y_2 = y_1 + (0.1)s$

$$s_1 = f(x_1, y_1) = x_1y_1 = 1 \times 5 = 5$$
$$s_2 = f(x_1 + 0.05,\ y_1 + 0.05s_1) = 1.05 \times 5.25 = 5.513$$
$$s_3 = f(x_1 + 0.05,\ y_1 + 0.05s_2) = 1.05 \times 5.276 = 5.540$$
$$s_4 = f(x_1 + 0.1,\ y_1 + 0.1s_3) = 1.1 \times 5.554 = 6.109$$
$$s = \frac{s_1 + 2s_2 + 2s_3 + s_4}{6}$$
$$= \frac{5 + 2 \times 5.513 + 2 \times 5.540 + 6.109}{6} = 5.536$$
$$y_2 = y_1 + (0.1)s = 5 + 0.1 \times 5.536 = 5.554$$

The second solution point (x_2, y_2) is (1.1, 5.554).

For $i = 2$, $\quad y_3 = y_2 + (0.1)s$

$$s_1 = f(x_2, y_2) = x_2y_2 = 1.1 \times 5.554 = 6.109$$
$$s_2 = f(x_2 + 0.05,\ y_2 + 0.05s_1) = 1.15 \times 5.859 = 6.738$$
$$s_3 = f(x_2 + 0.05,\ y_2 + 0.05s_2) = 1.15 \times 5.891 = 6.775$$
$$s_4 = f(x_2 + 0.1,\ y_2 + 0.1s_3) = 1.2 \times 6.232 = 7.478$$
$$s = \frac{s_1 + 2s_2 + 2s_3 + s_4}{6}$$
$$= \frac{6.109 + 2 \times 6.738 + 2 \times 6.775 + 7.478}{6} = 6.769$$
$$y_3 = y_2 + (0.1)s = 5.554 + 0.1 \times 6.769 = 6.231$$

The third solution point for (x_3, y_3) is (1.2, 6.231).

For $i = 3$, $\quad y_4 = y_3 + (0.1)s$

$$s_1 = f(x_3, y_3) = x_3y_3 = 1.2 \times 6.231 = 7.477$$
$$s_2 = f(x_3 + 0.05,\ y_3 + 0.05s_1) = 1.25 \times 6.604 = 8.256$$
$$s_3 = f(x_3 + 0.05,\ y_3 + 0.05s_2) = 1.25 \times 6.644 = 8.305$$
$$s_4 = f(x_3 + 0.1,\ y_3 + 0.1s_3) = 1.3 \times 7.062 = 9.181$$
$$s = \frac{s_1 + 2s_2 + 2s_3 + s_4}{6}$$
$$= \frac{7.477 + 2 \times 8.256 + 2 \times 8.305 + 9.181}{6} = 8.297$$
$$y_4 = y_3 + (0.1)s = 6.231 + 0.1 \times 8.297 = 7.061$$

The fourth solution point for (x_4, y_4) is (1.3, 7.061).

For $i = 4$, $\quad y_5 = y_4 + (0.1)s$

$$s_1 = f(x_4, y_4) = x_4y_4 = 1.3 \times 7.061 = 9.179$$

$$s_2 = f(x_4 + 0.05,\ y_4 + 0.05s_1) = 1.35 \times 7.520 = 10.152$$

$$s_3 = f(x_4 + 0.05,\ y_4 + 0.05s_2) = 1.35 \times 7.569 = 10.218$$

$$s_4 = f(x_4 + 0.1,\ y_4 + 0.1s_3) = 1.4 \times 9.402 = 13.163$$

$$s = \frac{s_1 + 2s_2 + 2s_3 + s_4}{6}$$

$$= \frac{9.179 + 2 \times 10.152 + 2 \times 10.218 + 13.163}{6} = 10.514$$

$$y_4 = y_3 + (0.1)s = 7.061 + 0.1 \times 10.514 = 8.112$$

The fifth solution point for (x_5, y_5) is (1.4, 8.112).

For $i = 5$, $y_6 = y_5 + (0.1)s$

$$s_1 = f(x_5, y_5) = x_5 y_5 = 1.4 \times 8.112 = 11.357$$

$$s_2 = f(x_5 + 0.05,\ y_5 + 0.05s_1) = 1.45 \times 8.680 = 12.586$$

$$s_3 = f(x_5 + 0.05,\ y_5 + 0.05s_2) = 1.45 \times 8.741 = 12.675$$

$$s_4 = f(x_5 + 0.1,\ y_5 + 0.1s_3) = 1.5 \times 9.380 = 14.07$$

$$s = \frac{s_1 + 2s_2 + 2s_3 + s_4}{6}$$

$$= \frac{11.357 + 2 \times 12.586 + 2 \times 12.675 + 14.07}{6} = 12.658$$

$$y_4 = y_3 + (0.1)s = 8.112 + 0.1 \times 12.658 = 9.378$$

The sixth solution point for (x_6, y_6) is (1.5, 9.378).

7.13 Algorithm (AL73) for the Fourth Order R-K Method

This algorithm is transformed to a computer program written in C++ language and presented at the end of this chapter (see **p73.cpp**)

1. Declare/define the function/subprogram **func**.
2. Declare/define the function/subprogram **rk4de** for the R-K method.
3. Start the (main) function.
4. Define the main function which calls the appropriate subprogram/function according to given choice.
5. Stop (main).

Details of function/subprogram **func()**:

1. Start
2. Define the inline function a*b
3. Return (value of the function)

Details of function/subprogram **rk4de()**:

1. Start
2. Enter the interval points x1, xf
3. Enter the initial value y1 at x1
4. Enter the step-size, h, of x-values
5. Initialize i=1, x=x1, y=y1
6. Repeat

```
    s1=func(x,y)
    s2=func(x+h/2,y+(h/2)*s1)
    s3=func(x+h/2,y+(h/2)*s2)
    s4=func(x+h,y+h*s3)
    s=(s1+2*s2+2*s3+s4)/6
    y=y+h*s
    x=x+h
    i=i+1
    output x,y
until x>xf
```

7. Return

7.14 Euler's Predictor-Corrector Method

In the methods discussed so far, information at a previous solution point is made use of in determining the next solution point of the differential equation. Due to this reason the previous methods can be termed single-step methods.

The Predictor-Corrector methods are multi-step methods because in these methods an initial (predicted) value of the solution is calculated and used to give a more accurate approximation of the solution point within the same iteration.

Consider the differential equation

$$y' = \frac{dy}{dx} = f(x, y)$$

with initial conditions at $x = x_i$, $y = y_i$. The solution of the equation is desired in the interval $[x_i, x_{i+1}]$.

Let the average slope be given by

$$s_{av} = \frac{1}{2}[y'(x_i) + y'(x_{i+1})]$$

By Euler's method, the solution at x_{i+1} is given by

$$y_{i+1} = y_i + \frac{h}{2}[y'(x_i) + y'(x_{i+1})]$$

or

$$y_{i+1} = y_i + \frac{h}{2}[f(x_i, y_i) + f(x_{i+1}, y_{i+1})] \tag{7.5}$$

This equation contains an unknown $f(x_{i+1}, y_{i+1})$. Therefore we cannot find y_{i+1}. But the value of y_{i+1} can be *predicted* (p) using the basic Euler's method as

$$y_{i+1}^p = y_i + hf(x_i, y_i) \tag{7.6}$$

By using this predicted value of y_{i+1}, a more accurate value of the solution point can be calculated using the following equation

$$y_{i+1}^c = y_i + \frac{h}{2}[f(x_i, y_i) + f(x_{i+1}, y_{i+1}^p)] \tag{7.7}$$

Equations (7.6) and (7.7) are called predictor and corrector formulas respectively.

The method can be implemented using the following two steps:

1. Predict a value of y_{i+1} using formula (7.6).
2. Correct the value of y_{i+1} using formula (7.7).

7.15 Numerical Examples (Predictor-Corrector Methods)

EXAMPLE 7.6 Solve the differential equation using the Predictor-Corrector method

$$\frac{dy}{dx} = xy \quad \text{with } y(1) = 5$$

in the interval [1, 1.5] with step-size $h = 0.1$ up to three decimal places.

Solution

Using Eqs. (7.6) and (7.7),

$$y_{i+1}^p = y_i + hf(x_i, y_i)$$

$$y_{i+1}^c = y_i + \frac{h}{2}[f(x_i, y_i) + f(x_{i+1}, y_{i+1}^p)]$$

For $i = 1$,

$$y_2^p = y_1 + hf(x_1, y_1)$$
$$= 5 + (0.1)(1)(5)$$
$$= 5.5$$

$$y_2^c = y_1 + \frac{h}{2}[f(x_1, y_1) + f(x_2, y_2^p)]$$
$$= 5 + \left(\frac{0.1}{2}\right)[(1)(5) + (1.1)(5.5)]$$
$$= 5.553$$

The second solution point is (1.1, 5.553).

For $i = 2$,

$$y_3^p = y_2 + hf(x_2, y_2)$$
$$= 5.553 + (0.1)(1.1)(5.553)$$
$$= 6.164$$

$$y_3^c = y_2 + \frac{h}{2}[f(x_2, y_2) + f(x_3, y_3^p)]$$

$$= 5.553 + \left(\frac{0.1}{2}\right)[(1.1)(5.553) + (1.2)(6.164)]$$

$$= 6.231$$

The third solution point is (1.2, 6.231).

For $i = 3$,
$$y_4^p = y_3 + hf(x_3, y_3)$$

$$= 6.231 + (0.1)(1.2)(6.231)$$

$$= 6.979$$

$$y_4^c = y_3 + \frac{h}{2}[f(x_3, y_3) + f(x_4, y_4^p)]$$

$$= 6.231 + \left(\frac{0.1}{2}\right)[(1.2)(6.231) + (1.3)(6.979)]$$

$$= 7.059$$

The fourth solution point is (1.3, 7.059).

For $i = 4$,
$$y_5^p = y_4 + hf(x_4, y_4)$$

$$= 7.059 + (0.1)(1.3)(7.059)$$

$$= 7.977$$

$$y_5^c = y_4 + \frac{h}{2}[f(x_4, y_4) + f(x_5, y_5^p)]$$

$$= 7.059 + \left(\frac{0.1}{2}\right)[(1.3)(7.059) + (1.4)(7.977)]$$

$$= 8.076$$

The fifth solution point is (1.4, 8.076).

For $i = 5$,
$$y_6^p = y_5 + hf(x_5, y_5)$$

$$= 8.076 + (0.1)(1.4)(8.076)$$

$$= 9.207$$

$$y_6^c = y_5 + \frac{h}{2}[f(x_5, y_5) + f(x_6, y_6^p)]$$

$$= 8.076 + \left(\frac{0.1}{2}\right)[(1.4)(8.076) + (1.5)(9.207)]$$

$$= 9.332$$

The sixth solution point is (1.5, 9.332).

7.16 Algorithm (AL74) for the Predictor-Corrector Method

This algorithm is transformed to a computer program written in C++ language and presented at the end of this chapter (see **p74.cpp**)

1. Declare/define the function/subprogram **func**.
2. Declare/define the function/subprogram **melrde** for R-K method.
3. Start the (main) function.
4. Define the main function which calls the appropriate subprogram/ function according to given choice.
5. Stop (main).

Details of function/subprogram **func()**:

1. Start
2. Define the inline function a*b
3. Return (value of the function)

Details of function/subprogram **melrde()**:

1. Start
2. Enter the interval points x1, xf
3. Enter the initial value y1 at x1
4. Enter the step-size, h, of x-values
5. Initialize i=1, x=x1, y=y1
6. Repeat

```
      y2=y+h*func(x,y)
      repeat
         y1=y2
         y2=y+(h/2)*(func(x,y)+func(x+h,y2))
      until |(y2–y1)/y2)|< 0.0001
         y=y2;
         x=x+h;
         i=i+1;
      output x,y
   until x>xf
```

7. Return

7.17 Solution of Second Order Differential Equation by Finite Difference Method

Let a second order differential equation be given by

$$y'' = \frac{d^2y}{d^2x} = f(x, y, y') \tag{7.8}$$

with boundary conditions: $y(a) = y_a$, $y(b) = y_b$.

The problem of finding the solution of this differential equation in the interval $a \le x \le b$ is called the boundary value problem. One of the most popular methods of solving such differential equations is by the finite difference method in which we make use of finite difference equivalents of the derivatives to form a set of simple algebraic equations. These algebraic equations can be then solved to obtain the solution of the differential equation at different values of x.

Let Eq. (7.8) be rewritten as

$$y''(x) + p(x)y'(x) + q(x)y(x) = r(x) \tag{7.9}$$

along with the boundary conditions: $y(a) = y_a$, $y(b) = y_b$.

Using Taylor's series expansion for $y(x)$, we have

$$y(x + h) = y(x) + hy'(x) + \frac{h^2}{2!}y''(x) + \cdots \tag{7.10}$$

Similarly, we can write

$$y(x - h) = y(x) - hy'(x) + \frac{h^2}{2!}y''(x) + \cdots \tag{7.11}$$

Subtracting Eq. (7.11) from Eq. (7.10) and neglecting the terms of order $O(h^2)$ or greater, we get

$$y'(x) = \frac{y(x+h) - y(x-h)}{2h} \tag{7.12}$$

Adding Eqs. (7.10) and (7.11) and neglecting the terms of order $O(h^3)$ or greater, we get

$$y''(x) = \frac{y(x-h) - 2y(x) + y(x+h)}{h^2} \tag{7.13}$$

In order to use Eqs. (7.12) and (7.13) for solving the boundary value problems we divide the interval $a \le x \le b$ into n sub-intervals of equal width size h. The value at $x = x_j$ is given by

$$x_j = a + jh \qquad \text{where } j = 1, 2, 3, \ldots, n.$$

Note that at $x = x_a = a$, $y = y_a$ and at $x = x_n = b$, $y = y_b$

The values $y(x_j) = y(a + jh) = y_j$ with $j = 1, 2, 3, \ldots, (n - 1)$ constitute the solution of the differential equation.

Using the subscript j in Eqs. (7.12) and (7.13), we get

$$y'_{j(x)} = \frac{y_{j+1} - y_{j-1}}{2h} \tag{7.14}$$

$$y''_{j(x)} = \frac{y_{j-1} - 2y_j + y_{j+1}}{h^2} \tag{7.15}$$

Equations (7.14) and (7.15) are called **finite differences** for the first and second order derivatives respectively.

Now putting Eqs. (7.14) and (7.15) back into the differential Eq. (7.9) for $x = x_j$, we get

$$\frac{y_{j-1} - 2y_j + y_{j+1}}{h^2} + p(x_j)\left[\frac{y_{j+1} - y_{j-1}}{2h}\right] + q(x_j)y_j = r(x_j) \quad (7.16)$$

where $j = 1, 2, 3, \ldots, (n - 1)$.

Simplifying Eq. (7.16), we finally obtain

$$\left[1 - \frac{h}{2}p_j\right]y_{j-1} + [q_j h^2 - 2]y_j + \left[1 + \frac{h}{2}p_j\right]y_{j+1} = r_j h^2 \quad (7.17)$$

where $p_j = p(x_j)$, $q_j = q(x_j)$, $r_j = r(x_j)$ and $j = 1, 2, 3, \ldots, (n - 1)$.

Equation (7.17) represents $(n - 1)$ algebraic equations in as many unknowns and thus can be solved by any of the methods used in solving simultaneous linear equations discussed in Chapter 3.

7.18 Numerical Examples (Finite Difference Method)

EXAMPLE 7.7 Solve the following differential equation using the finite difference method,

$$\frac{d^2y}{dx^2} = e^{x^2} \text{ with } y(0) = 0 \text{ and } y(1) = 0$$

in the interval [0, 1] with step-size $h = 0.25$ up to three decimal places.

Solution

We have to determine the value of y at $x = 0.25$, 0.5 and 0.75 using Eq. (7.17),

$$\left[1 - \frac{h}{2}p_j\right]y_{j-1} + [q_j h^2 - 2]y_j + \left[1 + \frac{h}{2}p_j\right]y_{j+1} = r_j h^2$$

in which substituting $h = 0.25$, $p_j = 0$, $q_j = 0$, $r_j = \exp(x_j)^2$ and $j = 1, 2, 3$ gives

for $j = 1$, $x = x_1 = 0.25$ $\quad y_0 - 2y_1 + y_2 = (\exp(0.25)^2)(0.25)^2 = 0.0665$

for $j = 2$, $x = x_2 = 0.5$ $\quad y_1 - 2y_2 + y_3 = (\exp(0.5)^2)(0.25)^2 = 0.0803$

for $j = 3$, $x = x_3 = 0.75$ $\quad y_2 - 2y_3 + y_4 = (\exp(0.75)^2)(0.25)^2 = 0.1097$

Using the boundary conditions $y_0 = y_4 = 0$, we get

$$-2y_1 + y_2 = 0.0665$$

$$y_1 - 2y_2 + y_3 = 0.0803$$

$$y_2 - 2y_3 = 0.1097$$

Solving these equations, we get $y_1 = -0.118$, $y_2 = -0.168$, $y_3 = -0.139$.

These values represent the solution of the given differential equation at the specified points.

Exercises

1. Using the Euler's method, solve the following equation to find $y(1)$,

$$\frac{dy}{dx} = -\frac{y}{1+x}$$

given: $h = 0.1$, $y(0) = 2$. [**Ans.** 0.948]

2. Using the Euler's method solve the following equation in the interval {0, 0.5},

$$\frac{dy}{dx} = x^2 + y^2$$

given: $h = 0.1$, $y(0) = 0$. [**Ans.** 0.001, 0.041, 0.05, 0.066]

3. Using the R-K second order method, solve the following equation to find the value of y at $x = 1.2$,

$$\frac{dy}{dx} = x^2 + y^2$$

given: $h = 0.1$, $y(1) = 1.5$. [**Ans.** 2.504]

4. Using the R-K fourth order method, solve the following equation to find the value of y at $x = 0.5$

$$\frac{dy}{dx} = \frac{1}{(x+y)}$$

given: $h = 0.5$, $y(0) = 1$. [**Ans.** 1.357]

5. Using the predictor-corrector method, solve the following equation to find the value of y at $x = 0.5$

$$\frac{dy}{dx} = x + y^2$$

given: $h = 0.1$, $y(0) = 0$. [**Ans.** 0.10046]

6. Solve the following second order differential equation in the interval {0, 1} with $h = 1/3$ and with boundary conditions $y(0) = 2$ and $y(1) = 0$,

$$\frac{d^2y}{dx^2} - \left(\frac{14}{x}\right)y'(x) + x^3y(x) = 2x^3$$

[**Ans.** $y(1/3) = 1.032$, $y(2/3) = 2.322$]

7. Solve the following second order differential equation in the interval {0, 2} with $h = 1/2$ and with boundary conditions $y(0) = 0$ and $y(2) = 3.267$

$$\frac{d^2y}{dx^2} - y(x) = 0$$

[**Ans.** $y(1/2) = 0.526$, $y(1) = 1.184$, $y(1.5) = 2.138$]

C++ Programs

The C++ programs can be implemented on any O/S, namely

1. Windows O/S using Turbo C++, Dev C++ and Visual C++ compilers.
2. Linux based Ubuntu/Knoppix/Redhat O/S using GNU C++ compiler.

These compilers have been discussed in Chapter 0. No change is required if Ubuntu is used.

While using Turbo C++, Dev C++ and Visual C++ compilers, note the following points for every program.

- Use header file #include <iostream.h> (for Turbo C++ only)
- Use header file #include <math.h>
- Use header file #include <conio.h>
- Use getch() function before the closing bracket '}' of the main() function.

Program: p71.cpp

```
//Euler's method to solve first order ordinary differential
equation
#include <iostream>
#include <cmath>
using namespace std;
inline float func(float a,float b )
{
   return (a*b);
   }
void elrde()
{
   int I;
   float x,y,x1,y1,h,xf;
cout<<"input the interval in which solution is required x1
xf\n";
   cin>>x1>>xf;
cout<<"input the value of y at initial point x1\n";
cin>>y1;
cout<<"input the step-size, h\n";
cin>>h;
i=1;x=x1;y=y1;
cout<<"I "<<" x "<<" y \n";
cout<<i<<" "<<x<<" "<<y<<endl;
   do
```

```
        {
          y=y+h*func(x,y);
          x=x+h;
          i=i+1;
        cout<<i<<" "<<x<<" "<<y<<endl;
        }
    while (x<xf);
}
    main()
{
    elrde();
}
```

Program: p72.cpp

```
//Runge-Kutta method of second order to solve first order
ordinary differential equation
#include <iostream>
#include <cmath>
using namespace std;
inline float func(float a,float b )
{
    return (a*b);
    }
void rk2de()
{
    int I;
    float x,y,x1,y1,h,xf,s,s1,s2;
cout<<"input the interval in which solution is required x1
xf\n";
    cin>>x1>>xf;
cout<<"input the value of y at initial point x1\n";
cin>>y1;
cout<<"input the step-size, h\n";
cin>>h;
i=1;x=x1;y=y1;
cout<<"I "<<" x "<<" y \n";
cout<<i<<" "<<x<<" "<<y<<endl;
    do
        {
          s1=func(x,y);
          s2=func(x+h,y+h*s1);
          s=(s1+s2)/2;
```

```
        y=y+h*s;
        x=x+h;
        i=i+1;
      cout<<i<<"  "<<x<<"  "<<y<<endl;
      }
    while (x<xf);
}
main()
{
    rk2de();
}
```

Program: p73.cpp

```
//Runge-Kutta method of fourth order to solve first order
ordinary differential equation
#include <iostream>
#include <cmath>
using namespace std;
inline float func(float a,float b )
{
   return (a*b);
   }
void rk4de()
{
   int I;
   float x,y,x1,y1,h,xf,s,s1,s2,s3,s4;
cout<<"input the interval in which solution is required x1
xf\n";
   cin>>x1>>xf;
cout<<"input the value of y at initial point x1\n";
cin>>y1;
cout<<"input the step-size, h\n";
cin>>h;
i=1;x=x1;y=y1;
cout<<"I "<<" x "<<" y \n";
cout<<i<<" "<<x<<" "<<y<<endl;
   do
     {
        s1=func(x,y);
        s2=func(x+h/2,y+(h/2)*s1);
        s3=func(x+h/2,y+(h/2)*s2);
```

```
        s4=func(x+h,y+h*s3);
        s=(s1+2*s2+2*s3+s4)/6;
        y=y+h*s;
        x=x+h;
        i=i+1;
      cout<<i<<"  "<<x<<"  "<<y<<endl;
      }
   while (x<xf);
}
main()
{
   rk4de();
}
```

Program: p74.cpp

```
//Predictor-corrector methods:Modified Euler's method to
solve first order ordinary differential equation
#include <iostream>
#include <cmath>
using namespace std;
inline float func(float a,float b )
{
   return (a*b);
   }
void melrde()
{
   int I;
   float x,y,x1,y1,y2,h,xf,eps=0.001;
cout<<"input the interval in which solution is required x1
xf\n";
   cin>>x1>>xf;
cout<<"input the value of y at initial point x1\n";
cin>>y1;
cout<<"input the step-size, h\n";
cin>>h;
i=1;x=x1;y=y1;
cout<<"I "<<" x "<<" y \n";
cout<<i<<"  "<<x<<"  "<<y<<endl;
   do
     {
       y2=y+h*func(x,y);
     do
```

```
        {
        y1=y2;
       y2=y+(h/2)*(func(x,y)+func(x+h,y2));
        } while (fabs((y2-y1)/y2)>eps);
        y=y2;
        x=x+h;
        i=i+1;
      cout<<i<<" "<<x<<" "<<y<<endl;
      }
        while (x<xf);
}
main()
{
   melrde();
}
```

8

Curve Fitting

8.1 Introduction

Consider a set of experimental data points (Table 8.1) x_i, y_i ($i = 1, 2, 3, \ldots, n$) plotted on a graph with dependent variable y representing a function of the independent variable x.

Table 8.1 Data points

x_i	x_1	x_2	x_3	$\cdots$	x_n
$y_i = f(x_i)$	y_1	y_2	y_3	$\cdots$	y_n

It is now possible to draw a smooth curve passing through these data points and compare with the desired or actual graph. The empirical relation can be written as

$$y = f(x) \tag{8.1}$$

For example, in an experiment involving simple harmonic motion of a pendulum, y represents the angular displacement θ of the body from the mean position and x represents the time t. The experimental graph can be compared with the actual graph which, we know, is a smooth sinusoidal function.

If the actual function is not known, the analysis can become difficult. For instance, it is possible to draw a number of smooth curves through the given data points and then we need to determine the best curve that correctly approximates the relationship between the independent and dependent variables. The function $f(x)$ in Eq. (8.1) should represent the best approximate curve of the actual function.

The method of finding a suitable function, which approximates the actual function, by plotting an approximating curve through data points is called **curve fitting**. The functional relationship (8.1) may be linear (straight-line), quadratic (parabola), power or an exponential function. Various methods of curve-fitting can be formulated depending upon the choice of the **error minimizing scheme**. An error is defined as the difference between the actual value y_a of the function and its approximate (experimental) value y at a given data point. Let the error between these values be defined by the parameter d given by

$$d = y - y_a$$

Let the co-ordinates (x_i, y_i) be plotted as experimental data points $p_1, p_2, p_3, \ldots$, etc. and the actual data points as $q_1, q_2, q_3, \ldots$, etc. as shown in Figure 8.1.

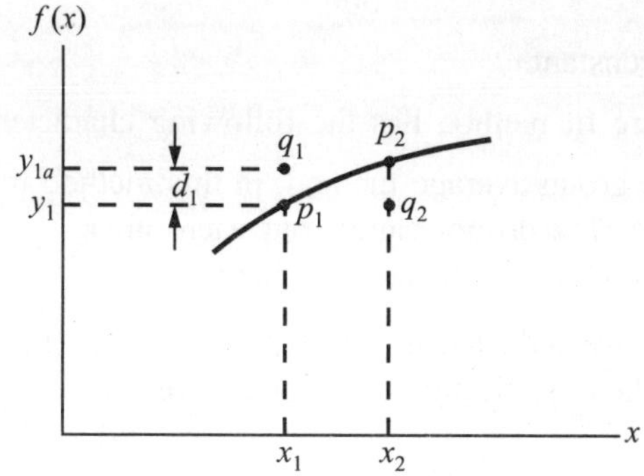

Figure 8.1 Curve-fit approximation.

At a point $x = x_i$ the error/deviation is given by

$$d_i = y_i - y_{ia}$$

For example at $x = x_1$, y_1 is the approximate value and y_{1a} is the actual value and d_1 is the error in approximation. Similarly, deviations at other data points can be calculated. For obtaining the best approximation to the actual function we must minimize the values of deviation/error at each data point. We can use the following schemes of minimization:

1. *Group of averages method:* min. Σd_i = min. $\Sigma y_i - y_{ia}$
2. *Least square fit method (LSF):* min. $\Sigma (d_i)^2$ = min. $\Sigma (y_i - y_{ia})^2$
3. *Chebyshev approximation method:* min. $\Sigma d_i < D$, where D is some constant.

The method of group averages is based upon taking the sum of deviations at all points to be zero, that is

$$\Sigma d_i = 0 \tag{8.2}$$

We can apply this method to obtain the best fit for the set of data points satisfying a given relationship between the dependent and the independent variables. This method can be used to fit a straight line, polynomial or a power function provided the deviations are not too large. However, if the deviations are large this method becomes inaccurate.

The second method is called the least square fit method, so called because its aim is to minimize the sum of the squares of the deviations. Defining the sum of the squares of deviations as

$$S = \Sigma(d_i)^2 = (d_1)^2 + (d_2)^2 + (d_3)^2 + \cdots = \Sigma(y_i - y_{ia})^2 \tag{8.3}$$

According to the principle of least square fitting, an approximated curve is a best fit if the sum S of the squares of the deviations of the data points is a minimum. For S to be a minimum,

$$\frac{\partial S}{\partial a} = 0 \tag{8.4}$$

where a is some constant.

The least square fit method has the following characteristics:

(a) Unlike the group average method, in this method the large deviations of opposite sign do not cancel out each other.
(b) It gives more weight to large deviations.

In this chapter we will discuss the least square fit (LSF) method as it is applied to obtain the best fitting curve for a given set of data points.

8.2 Straight Line Fit Using the LSF Method

Let a set of experimental data points be represented by coordinates (x_i, y_i) through which the best fitting curve needs to be determined by the LSF method. If we assume that the best fitting curve should be a straight line, then we need to find the best linear-fit to the given data points. Let the actual function be given by

$$y_{ia} = a + bx_i \tag{8.5}$$

From Eq. (8.3), we have

$$S = \Sigma(d_i)^2 = (d_1)^2 + (d_2)^2 + (d_3)^2 + \cdots = \Sigma(y_i - y_{ia})^2 = \Sigma(y_i - a - bx_i)^2$$

For S to be minimum,

$$\frac{\partial S}{\partial a} = (-2)(\Sigma(y_i - a - bx_i)) = 0$$

This gives

$$\Sigma y_i = na + b\Sigma x_i \tag{8.6}$$

Also minimizing with respect to b we get

$$\frac{\partial S}{\partial b} = (-2)(\Sigma(y_i - a - bx_i)x_i) = 0$$

This gives

$$\Sigma x_i y_i = a\Sigma x_i + b\Sigma(x_i)^2 \tag{8.7}$$

Equations (8.6) and (8.7) are called **normal equations for the linear fit**. These are used to find the values of a and b from the known values of the data points.

Solving Eqs. (8.6) and (8.7) by Cramer's rule, we get

$$b = \frac{n\Sigma x_i y_i - \Sigma x_i \Sigma y_i}{n\Sigma (x_i)^2 - (\Sigma x_i)^2} = \frac{n(XY) - XY}{nX^2 - X^2} \tag{8.8}$$

$$a = \frac{\Sigma y_i (\Sigma x_i)^2 - \Sigma x_i \Sigma x_i y_i}{n(\Sigma x_i)^2 - (\Sigma x_i^2)} = \frac{X^2 Y - (X)(XY)}{nX^2 - X^2} \tag{8.9}$$

where $X = \Sigma x_i$, $Y = \Sigma y_i$, $XY = \Sigma x_i y_i$, $X^2 = \Sigma (x_i)^2$ and $(X)^2 = (\Sigma x_i)^2$.

Equations (8.8) and (8.9) are used in Eq. (8.5) to obtain the best straight line fit for the given data points.

It is sufficient to find the value of b from the above expression since by using it in Eq. (8.6), we can find the value of a as

$$a = \frac{1}{n}\Sigma y_i - \frac{b}{n}\Sigma x_i = \frac{1}{n}Y - \frac{b}{n}X \tag{8.10}$$

It can be verified that we obtain a positive value of the second derivative of S with respect to a and b implying that the values of a and b indeed minimize S.

8.3 Reverse Straight Line Fit

Let the straight line be expressed as $x = k + my$.

The normal Eqs. (8.6) and (8.7) are now rewritten as

$$\Sigma x_i = nk + m\Sigma y_i \tag{8.11}$$

$$\Sigma x_i y_i = k\Sigma y_i + m\Sigma (y_i)^2 \tag{8.12}$$

Solving these equations gives

$$k = \frac{\Sigma x_i \Sigma (y_i)^2 - \Sigma y_i \Sigma x_i y_i}{n\Sigma (y_i)^2 - (\Sigma y_i)^2} \tag{8.13}$$

$$m = \frac{n\Sigma x_i y_i - \Sigma x_i \Sigma y_i}{n\Sigma (y_i)^2 - (\Sigma y_i)^2} \tag{8.14}$$

Also we can find k if m is known using the following relation

$$k = \frac{1}{n}\Sigma x_i - \frac{m}{n}\Sigma y_i \tag{8.15}$$

8.4 Numerical Examples (Straight Line Fit)

EXAMPLE 8.1 Determine the best linear fit to the following data points:

x	1	2	3	4	5
y	3	4	5	6	8

Solution

We have to determine the values of the slope b and the intercept a using Eqs. (8.8), (8.9) or (8.10). For this, we construct the following table of values (Table 8.2)

Table 8.2 Example 8.1

	x_i	y_i	x_i^2	$x_i y_i$
	1	3	1	3
	2	4	4	8
	3	5	9	15
	4	6	16	24
	5	8	25	40
$\Sigma =$	15	26	55	90

where $X = \Sigma x_i = 15$, $Y = \Sigma y_i = 26$, $XY = \Sigma x_i y_i = 90$, $X^2 = \Sigma(x_i)^2 = 55$ and $(X)^2 = (\Sigma x_i)^2 = 225$

$$b = \frac{n\Sigma x_i y_i - \Sigma x_i \Sigma y_i}{n\Sigma(x_i)^2 - (\Sigma x_i)^2} = \frac{n(XY) - (X)(Y)}{nX^2 - (X)^2}$$

$$= \frac{5(90) - 15(26)}{5(55) - 225} = 1.2$$

$$a = \frac{1}{n}\Sigma y_i - \frac{b}{n}\Sigma x_i = \frac{1}{n}Y - \frac{b}{n}X = \frac{26}{5} - (1.2)\frac{15}{5} = 1.6$$

Thus, $y = 1.6 + 1.2x$ is the best linear fit for the given data points.

8.5 Algorithm (AL81) for the Straight Line Fit by the LSF Method

This algorithm is transformed to a computer program written in C++ language and presented at the end of this chapter (see **p81.cpp**).

1. Declare/define the function/subprogram **slfit** by the LSF method.
2. Start the (main) function.
3. Define the main function which calls the subprogram/function.
4. Stop (main).

Details of function/subprogram **slfit()**:

1. Start
2. Input the number of data points, n
3. Initializing

   sumx=0

   sumy=0

```
   sumx2=0
   sumxy=0
4. For i=1 to n
   input the elements of arrays x_i and y_i
   sumx=sumx+x_i
   sumy=sumy+y_i
   sumx2=sumx2+x_i*x_i
   sumxy+=sumxy+x_i*y_i
   endfor
5. Denominator=n*sumx2–sumx*sumx
6. b=(n*sumxy–sumx*sumy)/denominator
7. a=(sumy–b*sumx)/n
8. Output a, b
9. Output 'a+bx' is the linear fit
10. Return
```

8.6 Polynomial Fit by the LSF Method

When the set of experimental data points do not appear to lie on a straight line but seem to satisfy a polynomial equation, we need to find the best polynomial fit to the set of data points. Thus the approximating function $f(x)$ will be a polynomial of degree n that passes through the given set of data points. We can use the least square fit method to find the best polynomial fit.

Consider the data points (x_i, y_i) that appear to lie on a curve represented by a polynomial of degree n given by

$$y = f(x) = b_1 + b_2x + b_3x^2 + \cdots + b_{n+1}x^n \tag{8.16}$$

The sum of squares of the deviations is given by

$$S = \Sigma(d_i)^2 = (d_1)^2 + (d_2)^2 + (d_3)^2 + \cdots = \Sigma(y_i - y_{ia})^2$$
$$= \Sigma(y_i - (b_1 + b_2x + b_3x^2 + \cdots + b_{n+1}x^n))^2$$

where $i = 1, 2, 3, \ldots, m$.

To minimize S, we differentiate S w.r.t. $b_1, b_2, \ldots, b_{n+1}$ respectively and equate each to zero. That is,

$$\frac{\partial S}{\partial b_1} = \Sigma y_i - b_1m - b_2\Sigma x_i - b_3\Sigma x_i^2 - \cdots -b_{n+1}\,\Sigma x_i^n = 0$$

$$\frac{\partial S}{\partial b_2} = \Sigma x_iy_i - b_1\Sigma x_i - b_2\Sigma x_i^2 - b_3\Sigma x_i^3 - \cdots -b_{n+1}\Sigma x_i^{n+1} = 0$$

$$\vdots$$

$$\frac{\partial S}{\partial b_n} = \Sigma x_i^ny_i - b_1\Sigma x_i^n - b_2\Sigma x_i^{n+1} - b_3\Sigma x_i^{n+2} - \cdots -b_{n+1}\Sigma x_i^{n+n} = 0$$

The above equations result in the following set of equations

$$\begin{aligned}
\Sigma y_i &= b_1 m + b_2 \Sigma x_i + b_3 \Sigma x_i^2 + \cdots + b_{n+1} \Sigma x_i^n \\
\Sigma x_i y_i &= b_1 \Sigma x_i + b_2 \Sigma x_i^2 + b_3 \Sigma x_i^3 + \cdots + b_{n+1} \Sigma x_i^{n+1} \\
&\vdots \\
\Sigma x_i^n y_i &= b_1 \Sigma x_i^n + b_2 \Sigma x_i^{n+1} + b_3 \Sigma x_i^{n+2} + \cdots + b_{n+1} \Sigma x_i^{n+n}
\end{aligned} \tag{8.17}$$

The set of Eqs. (8.17) are called normal equations for polynomial fit by the LSF method. These equations must be solved to find the coefficients b_1, b_2, b_3, ..., b_{n+1}.

A matrix equation can be formed of the equations as follows:

$$\begin{pmatrix} \Sigma y_i \\ \Sigma x_i y_i \\ \vdots \\ \Sigma x_i^n y_i \end{pmatrix} = \begin{pmatrix} m & \Sigma x_i & \Sigma x_i^2 & \dots & \Sigma x_i^n \\ \Sigma x_i & \Sigma x_i^2 & \Sigma x_i^3 & \dots & \Sigma x_i^{n+1} \\ \vdots & & \vdots & & \\ \Sigma x_i^n & \Sigma x_i^{n+1} & \Sigma x_i^{n+2} & \dots & \Sigma x_i^{n+n} \end{pmatrix} \begin{pmatrix} b_1 \\ b_2 \\ \vdots \\ b_{n+1} \end{pmatrix} \tag{8.18}$$

Rewriting the above

$$[A][B] = [C]$$

where the elements of $[A]$ are

$$a_{ij} = \sum_{k=1}^{m} x_k^{i+j-2} \tag{8.19}$$

where $i = 1, 2, 3, \ldots, (n + 1)$ and $j = 1, 2, 3, \ldots, (n + 1)$.
The elements of $[C]$ are

$$c_i = \sum_{k=1}^{m} x_k^{i-1} y_k \quad \text{where } i = 1, 2, 3, \ldots, (n+1) \tag{8.20}$$

and that of $[B]$ are b_i with $i = 1$ to $n + 1$.
For instance consider a polynomial of degree $n = 2$,

$$y = f(x) = b_1 + b_2 x + b_3 x^2$$

There will be $n + 1$ (= 3) normal equations resulting in a 3×3 coefficient matrix as follows:

$$\begin{pmatrix} a_{11} & a_{12} & a_{13} \\ a_{21} & a_{22} & a_{23} \\ a_{31} & a_{32} & a_{33} \end{pmatrix} \begin{pmatrix} b_1 \\ b_2 \\ b_3 \end{pmatrix} = \begin{pmatrix} \Sigma y_i \\ \Sigma x_i y_i \\ \Sigma x_i^2 y_i \end{pmatrix} \tag{8.21}$$

where the coefficients are defined as

$$\begin{array}{lll}
a_{11} = m & a_{12} = \Sigma x_i & a_{13} = \Sigma x_i^2 \\
a_{21} = \Sigma x_i & a_{22} = \Sigma x_i^2 & a_{23} = \Sigma x_i^3 \\
a_{31} = \Sigma x_i^2 & a_{32} = \Sigma x_i^3 & a_{33} = \Sigma x_i^4
\end{array}$$

If m data points (x_i, y_i) are given, we can determine the above coefficients and solve the matrix equation for b_1, b_2 and b_3 by Cramer's rule.

8.7 Numerical Examples (Polynomial Fit)

EXAMPLE 8.2 Determine the best polynomial fit to the following data points:

x	1	2	3	4
y	6	11	18	27

Solution

Here $m = 4$ and let $n = 2$ for a quadratic polynomial. There will be three normal equations resulting in a matrix Eq. (8.21). To determine the coefficients b_i, we construct Table 8.3.

Table 8.3 Example 8.2

x_i	y_i	x_i^2	x_i^3	x_i^4	x_iy_i	$x_i^2y_i$
1	6	1	1	1	6	6
2	11	4	8	16	22	44
3	18	9	27	81	54	162
4	27	16	64	256	108	432
Σ 10	62	30	100	354	190	644

Substituting into the matrix Eq. (8.21), we get

$$\begin{pmatrix} 4 & 10 & 30 \\ 10 & 30 & 100 \\ 30 & 100 & 354 \end{pmatrix} \begin{pmatrix} b_1 \\ b_2 \\ b_3 \end{pmatrix} = \begin{pmatrix} 62 \\ 190 \\ 640 \end{pmatrix}$$

Solving the above equations, we get $b_1 = 3$, $b_2 = 2$, $b_3 = 1$.

Thus the best polynomial for the given data points is given by

$$y = f(x) = x^2 + 2x + 3$$

8.8 Algorithm (AL82) for the Polynomial Fit by the LSF Method

This algorithm is transformed to a computer program written in C++ language and presented at the end of this chapter (see **p82.cpp**).

1. Declare/define function/subprogram **polfit** by LSF method.
2. Start the (main) function.
3. Define the main function which calls the subprogram/function.
4. Stop (main).

Details of function/subprogram **polfit()**:

```
1. Start
2. Input the degree of polynomial, n
3. Input the number of data points, m
4. For i=1 to n
      input the data elements of arrays x_i and y_i
5. Enter the elements of coefficient matrix, a_ij
   for i=1 to n+1
      for j=1 to n+1
         a_ij=0
            for k=1 to m
               a_ij=x_k^(i+j-2)
            endfor
            a_in+2=0
         for k=1 to m
            a_in+2=y_k* x_k^(i-1)
         endfor
   endfor
6. Solution of simultaneous equations by Gauss elimination method
   for k=1 to n
      for i=k+1 to n+1
         temp=a_ik/a_kk
      for j=k to n+2
         a_ij = a_ij_temp*a_kj
         endfor
      endfor
   endfor
   back substitution begins
      b_n+1=a_n+1 n+2/a_n+1 n+1
      for i=n to 1 in steps of -1
         sum=0;
            for (j=i+1; j<=n+1; j++)
               sum =sum+a_ij*b_j
            endfor
         b_i=(a_in+2–sum)/a_ii
   endfor
7. Values of coefficients b_ij's
   for i=1 to n+1
      output b_i
8. Return
```

8.9 Power Function Fit Using the LSF Method

Let a set of data points be represented by coordinates (x_i, y_i) through which the best fitting curve needs to be determined by the LSF method. If we assume that the best fitting curve should be represented by a power function we need to find the best curve fit to the given data points. Let the actual function be given by

$$y_{ia} = ax_i^p \tag{8.22}$$

where a is a constant and p is a real number.

We need to find the values of a and p to obtain the best curve fit. For this, we take the logarithm (base 10) of both sides of (8.22).

$$\log y = p \log x + \log a$$

Let $\quad Y = \log y,\ X = \log x,\ C = \log a$

The above equation can be rewritten as

$$Y = pX + C \tag{8.23}$$

This is the equation of a straight line in which we can find the coefficients p and C by using the normal Eqs. (8.8), (8.9) and (8.10) of linear fit with suitable modifications.

$$p = \frac{n\Sigma \log x_i \log y_i - \Sigma \log x_i\ \Sigma \log y_i}{n\Sigma(\log x_i)^2 - (\Sigma \log x_i)^2}$$

$$= \frac{n(\Sigma XY) - (\Sigma X)(\Sigma Y)}{n\Sigma X^2 - (\Sigma X)^2} \tag{8.24}$$

$$C = \frac{\Sigma \log y_i \Sigma(\log x_i)^2 - \Sigma \log x_i\ \Sigma \log x_i \log y_i}{n\Sigma(\log x_i)^2 - (\Sigma \log x_i)^2}$$

$$= \frac{(\Sigma X^2 Y) - (\Sigma X)(\Sigma XY)}{n\Sigma X^2 - (\Sigma X)^2} \tag{8.25}$$

where $X = \log x_i$, $Y = \log y_i$, $XY = \log x_i \log y_i$, $X^2 = (\log x_i)^2$, $(X)^2 = (\log x_i)^2$.

Equations (8.24) and (8.25) are used in Eq. (8.23) to obtain the best curve fit to the given data points.

It is sufficient to find the value of p from Eq. (8.24) as we can find the value of C from the following expression

$$C = \frac{1}{n}\Sigma \log y_i - \frac{p}{n}\Sigma \log x_i$$

$$= \frac{1}{n}\Sigma Y - \frac{b}{n}\Sigma X \tag{8.26}$$

As we know $C = \log a$.

Therefore $$a = 10^C \tag{8.27}$$

Using the value of C we can find a. Thus the power function (8.22) is completely determined.

8.10 Numerical Examples (Power Function Fit)

EXAMPLE 8.3 Determine the best power function fit to the following data points:

x	1	2	3	4	5	6
y	1200	900	600	200	110	50

Solution

We have to determine the values of the slope p and the intercept C using Eqs. (8.24), (8.25) or (8.26). For this, we construct the following table of values (Table 8.4).

Table 8.4 Example 8.3

x_i	y_i	$\log x_i$	$\log y_i$	$(\log x_i)^2$	$(\log x_i)(\log y_i)$
1	1200	0	3.0792	0	0
2	900	0.3010	2.9542	0.0906	0.8892
3	600	0.4771	2.7782	0.2276	1.3255
4	200	0.6021	2.3010	0.3625	1.3854
5	110	0.699	2.0414	0.4886	1.4269
6	50	0.7781	1.699	0.6054	1.322
$\Sigma =$ –	–	2.8573	14.853	1.7747	6.349

where $X = \Sigma \log x_i = 2.8573$, $Y = \Sigma \log y_i = 14.853$, $XY = \Sigma \log x_i \log y_i = 6.349$, $X^2 = \Sigma(\log x_i)^2 = 1.7747$.

$$p = \frac{n\Sigma \log x_i \log y_i - \Sigma \log x_i \ \Sigma \log y_i}{n\Sigma(\log x_i)^2 - (\Sigma \log x_i)^2} = \frac{n(XY) - (X)(Y)}{nX^2 - (X)^2}$$

$$= \frac{6(6.349) - (2.8573)(14.853)}{6(1.7747) - (2.8573)^2} = -1.7494$$

$$C = \frac{1}{n}\Sigma \log y_i - \frac{p}{n}\Sigma \log x_i = \frac{1}{n}Y - \frac{p}{n}X$$

$$= \frac{14.853}{6} - (-1.7494)\frac{2.8573}{6} = 3.3086$$

$$a = 10^C = 10^{3.3086} = 2035$$

Thus, $y = (2035)x^{-1.7494}$ is the best power fit for the given data points.

8.11 Algorithm (AL83) for the Power Function Fit by the LSF Method

This algorithm is transformed to a computer program written in C++ language and presented at the end of this chapter (see **p83.cpp**).

1. Declare/define the function/subprogram **powrfit** by the LSF method.
2. Start the (main) function.
3. Define the main function which calls the subprogram/function.
4. Stop (main).

Details of function/subprogram **powrfit()**:

1. Start
2. Input the number of data points, n
3. for i=1 to n
   input the elements of arrays x_i and y_i
4. initializing
   sumx=0
   sumy=0
   sumx2=0
   sumxy=0
5. For i=1 to n
   input the elements of arrays x_i and y_i
   sumx =sumx+log x_i
   sumy =sumy+log y_i
   sumx2 =sumx2+log x_i*log x_i
   sumxy =sumxy+log x_i*log y_i
   endfor
6. Denominator=n*sumx2–sumx*sumx
7. p=(n*sumxy–sumx*sumy)/denominator
8. c=(sumy–p*sumx)/n
9. a=10^c
10. Output a, p
11. Output 'y=ax^p' is the best power function fit
12. Return

8.12 Exponential Function Fit by the LSF Method

Let a set of data points be represented by coordinates (x_i, y_i) through which the best fitting curve needs to be determined by the LSF method. If we assume that the best fitting curve should be represented by an exponential function we need to find the best curve fit to the given data points. Let the actual function be given by

$$y_{ia} = ae^{Bx_i} \tag{8.28}$$

where a is a constant and B is a real number.

We need to find the values of a and B to obtain the best curve fit. For this, we take the logarithm (natural) of both sides of Eq. (8.28).

$$\ln y = \ln a + Bx \ln e$$

Rewriting the above as

$$Y = A + Bx \tag{8.29}$$

where $Y = \ln y$, $A = \ln a$.

Equation (8.29) is the equation of a straight line in which we can find the coefficients A and B by using the normal Eqs. (8.8), (8.9) and (8.10) of linear fit with suitable modifications.

$$B = \frac{n\Sigma x_i \ln y_i - \Sigma x_i \Sigma \ln y_i}{n\Sigma(x_i)^2 - (\Sigma x_i)^2}$$

$$= \frac{n(\Sigma x_i Y) - (\Sigma x_i)(\Sigma Y)}{n\Sigma x_i^2 - (\Sigma x_i)^2} \tag{8.30}$$

$$A = \frac{\Sigma \ln y_i \, \Sigma(x_i)^2 - \Sigma x_i \Sigma x_i \ln y_i}{n\Sigma(x_i)^2 - (\Sigma x_i)^2}$$

$$= \frac{(\Sigma x_i^2 Y) - (\Sigma x_i)(\Sigma x_i Y)}{n\Sigma x_i^2 - (\Sigma x_i)^2} \tag{8.31}$$

where $Y = \ln y_i$.

Also, we have

$$A = \frac{1}{n}\Sigma \ln y_i - \frac{B}{n}\Sigma x_i \tag{8.32}$$

Since

$$A = \ln a$$

Therefore,

$$a = e^A \tag{8.33}$$

Equations (8.30) and (8.33) are used in Eq. (8.29) to obtain the best exponential curve fit to the given data points.

8.13 Numerical Examples (Exponential Curve Fit)

EXAMPLE 8.4 Determine the best curve fit to the following data points:

x	2	4	6	8	10
y	4.08	11.08	30.13	81.9	222.62

Solution

We have to determine the values of the slope B and the intercept A using Eqs. (8.30), (8.31) and (8.32). For this, we construct the following table of values with $n = 5$ (Table 8.5).

Table 8.5 Example 8.4

	x_i	y_i	$\ln y_i$	x_i^2	$x_i \ln y_i$
	2	4.08	1.406	4	2.812
	4	11.08	2.405	16	9.62
	6	30.13	3.406	36	20.436
	8	81.9	4.406	64	35.248
	10	222.62	5.405	100	54.05
$\Sigma =$	30	–	17.028	220	122.166

where $X = \Sigma x_i = 30,\ \Sigma Y_i = \Sigma \ln y_i = 17.028,$

$XY = \Sigma x_i \ln y_i = 122.166,\ X^2 = \Sigma(x_i)^2 = 220$

$$B = \frac{n\Sigma x_i \ln y_i - \Sigma x_i \,\Sigma \ln y_i}{n\Sigma(x_i)^2 - (\Sigma x_i)^2}$$

$$= \frac{n(\Sigma x_i \ln y_i) - (\Sigma x_i)(\Sigma Y_i)}{n\Sigma x_i^2 - (\Sigma x_i)^2}$$

$$= \frac{5(122.166) - (30)(17.028)}{5(220) - 900}$$

$$= 0.5$$

$$A = \frac{1}{n}\Sigma \ln y_i - \frac{B}{n}\Sigma x_i = \frac{1}{n}Y - \frac{B}{n}X = \frac{1}{5}17.028 - \frac{0.5}{5}30$$

$$= 0.41$$

Using Eq. (8.33), we get

$$a = e^{0.41} = 1.51$$

The exponential function is given by $y = 1.51e^{0.5x}$.

8.14 Algorithm (AL84) for the Exponential Curve Fit by the LSF Method

This algorithm is transformed to a computer program written in C++ language and presented at the end of this chapter (see **p84.cpp**).

1. Declare/define the function/subprogram **expfit** by the LSF method.
2. Start the (main) function.
3. Define the main function which calls the subprogram/function.
4. Stop (main).

Details of function/subprogram **expfit()**:

1. Start
2. Input the number of data points, n

3. For i=1 to n
   input the elements of arrays x_i and y_i
4. Initializing
   sumx=0
   sumy=0
   sumx2=0
   sumxy=0
5. For i=1 to n
   input the elements of arrays x_i and y_i
   sumx =sumx+ x_i
   sumy =sumy+log y_i
   sumx2 =sumx2+ x_i*x_i
   sumxy =sumxy+ x_i*log y_i
   endfor
6. Denominator=n*sumx2-sumx*sumx
7. B=(n*sumxy–sumx*sumy)/denominator
8. A=(sumy–B*sumx)/n
9. a=e^A
10. Output a, B
11. Output '$y=ae^{Bx}$' is the best curve fit
12. Return

8.15 Error Estimation in LSF Method

The least square method is based on the principle that the best approximation for the function representing the data points is obtained by minimizing the sum of the errors involved in each data point. For the straight line fit, we write the sum of the errors as

$$\begin{aligned} S &= \Sigma(y_i - (a + bx_i))^2 \\ &= \Sigma(y_i - (a + bx_i))(y_i + (a + bx_i)) \\ &= \Sigma[y_i(y_i - (a + bx_i)) - a(y_i - (a + bx_i)) - bx(y_i - (a + bx_i))] \\ &= \Sigma[y_i(y_i - (a + bx_i))] - a\Sigma(y_i - (a + bx_i)) - b\Sigma x_i(y_i - (a + bx_i)) \end{aligned}$$

For S to be minimum,

$$\frac{\partial S}{\partial a} = \Sigma(y_i - a - bx_i) = 0$$

and

$$\frac{\partial S}{\partial b} = \Sigma(y_i - a - bx_i)x_i = 0$$

From the expression for S, we get

$$\begin{aligned} S_{\min} &= \Sigma(y_i - a - bx_i)y_i \\ &= \Sigma y_i^2 - a\Sigma y_i - b\Sigma x_i y_i \end{aligned} \tag{8.34}$$

Equation (8.34) gives the minimum value of error involved in the least square fit method for the straight line fit.

For a polynomial of degree 2, we can write the sum of errors as

$$S = \Sigma(y_i - (b_1 + b_2x + b_3x^2))^2$$

where $i = 1, 2, 3, \ldots, m$.

To minimize S, we differentiate S w.r.t. b_1, b_2, b_3 respectively and equate each to zero

$$\frac{\partial S}{\partial b_1} = \frac{\partial S}{\partial b_2} = \frac{\partial S}{\partial b_3} = 0$$

Thus, we get $S_{\min} = \Sigma(y_i - (b_1 + b_2x + b_3x^2))y_i$

$$= \Sigma y_i^2 - b_1\Sigma y_i - b_2\,\Sigma x_iy_i - b_3\,\Sigma x_i^2y_i \quad (8.35)$$

This gives the minimum value for the error when curve fitting is done by a polynomial function. For the calculation of error in the cases of power function and the exponential function we can use Eq. (8.34) for the linear fit with suitable changes.

8.16 Numerical Examples (Error Estimation in Curve Fitting)

EXAMPLE 8.5 Determine the minimum error in the best linear fit to the following data points:

x	0	1	2	3	4
y	1	1.8	1.3	2.5	6.3

Solution

First we have to determine the values of the slope b and the intercept a using Eqs. (8.8), (8.9) or (8.10). For this we construct the following table of values (Table 8.6).

Table 8.6 Example 8.5

x_i	y_i	y_i^2	x_iy_i	x_i^2
0	1	1	0	0
1	1.8	3.24	1.8	1
2	1.3	1.69	2.6	4
3	2.5	6.25	7.5	9
4	6.3	39.69	25.2	16
$\Sigma =$ 10	12.9	51.87	37.1	30

where $X = \Sigma x_i = 10$, $Y = \Sigma y_i = 12.9$, $XY = \Sigma x_iy_i = 37.1$,

$X^2 = \Sigma(x_i)^2 = 30$, $(X)^2 = (\Sigma x_i)^2 = 100$.

$$b = \frac{n\Sigma x_iy_i - \Sigma x_iy_i}{n\Sigma(x_i)^2 - (\Sigma x_i)^2} = \frac{n(XY) - (X)(Y)}{nX^2 - (X)^2}$$

$$= 1.33$$

$$a = \frac{1}{n}\Sigma y_i - \frac{b}{n}\Sigma x_i = \frac{1}{n}Y - \frac{b}{n}X = 0.32$$

Thus $y = 0.32 + 1.33x$ is the best linear fit for the given data points.

The error in the above calculation of slope and intercept is given by Eq. (8.34) as

$$\begin{aligned} S_{\min} &= \Sigma y_i^2 - a\Sigma y_i - b\Sigma x_i y_i \\ &= 51.87 - (0.32)12.9 - (1.33)37.1 \\ &= -1.6 \end{aligned}$$

8.17 Coefficient of Correlation (r^2)

The coefficient of correlation is defined as the measure of variation in the dependent variable y due to its assumed dependence on the independent variable x. For example, if a given set of data points seem to have straight line fit and we assume in our analysis that the dependent variable is a linear function too, then the value of the correlation coefficient will be unity or close to unity. But if we wrongly assume a quadratic dependence, then the value of the correlation coefficient will differ significantly from unity indicating sufficient amount of error. Mathematically, the correlation coefficient is defined as

$$r^2 = 1 - \frac{\sigma_{xy}^2}{\sigma_y^2} \tag{8.36}$$

where
$$\sigma_{xy}^2 = \frac{\Sigma(y_i - f(x_i))^2}{n}$$

$$\sigma_y^2 = \frac{\Sigma(y_i - \overline{y})^2}{n}$$

In the above formulas, $f(x_i)$ is the assumed function for the given data points and $\overline{y}$ is the average value of data points, y_i.

The value of correlation coefficient lies in the range $0 < r^2 \le 1$. The goodness of curve-fitting is determined by the value of r^2.

8.18 Weighted Least Square Fit Approximation (WLSF)

Consider a set of points given by

x_i	x_1	x_2	x_3	$\cdots$	x_n
y_i	y_1	y_2	y_3	$\cdots$	y_n

Let ε_i be the value of error, for approximating the function $f(x)$ by y. Let this be defined as

$$\varepsilon_i = y_i - f(x_i)$$

In contrast to the least square fitting approximation (LSF) method in which we minimize the sum of squares of the errors ε_i, in this WLSF method we minimize the **weighted** sum of the squares of the errors over all the given points.

Let w_i be the weights (positive numbers) associated with each of the data points (x_i, y_i) where $i = 1, 2, 3, \ldots, n$.

The weighted sum of the squares of the errors is given by

$$S_w = w_1[y_1 - f(x_1)]^2 + w_2[y_2 - f(x_2)]^2 + \cdots + w_n[y_n - f(x_n)]^2$$

or $$S_w = w_1\varepsilon_1^2 + w_2\varepsilon_2^2 + \cdots + w_n\varepsilon_n^2 \tag{8.37}$$

Note that in the LSF method the value of each weight equals unity.

8.19 Straight Line Fit Using the WLSF Method

Let a function $f(x) = a + bx$ represent the straight line to be fitted over the given data points (x_i, y_i). The weighted sum of the squares of the errors is given by

$$S_w = \Sigma w_i[y_i - f(x_i)]^2$$

where $i = 1$ to n are the number of data points.

$\therefore$ $$S_w = \Sigma w_i[y_i - (a + bx_i)]^2$$

For minimizing S_w w.r.t. a, we set

$$\frac{\partial S_w}{\partial a} = 0$$

or $$\frac{\partial S_w}{\partial a} = (-2)(\Sigma w_i(y_i - a - bx_i)) = 0$$

This gives $$\Sigma w_i y_i = a\Sigma w_i + b\Sigma w_i x_i \tag{8.38}$$

Also minimizing S_w with respect to b, we get

$$\frac{\partial S_w}{\partial b} = (-2)(\Sigma(y_i - a - bx_i)x_i) = 0$$

This gives $$\Sigma w_i x_i y_i = a\Sigma w_i x_i + b\Sigma w_i (x_i)^2 \tag{8.39}$$

Equations (8.38) and (8.39) are called **normal equations of the WLSF method**. These equations can be solved to obtain the unknown coefficients a and b.

8.20 Polynomial Curve Fit Using the WLSF Method

Let the approximating function $f(x)$ be a polynomial of degree m that passes through the given set of data points. We can use the WLSF method to find the best polynomial fit. Consider the data points (x_i, y_i) that appear to lie on a curve represented by a polynomial of degree m given by

$$y = f(x) = b_0 + b_1x + b_2x^2 + \cdots + b_mx^m \tag{8.40}$$

The weighted sum of squares of the deviations is given by

$$S_w = \Sigma w_i(y_i - f(x_i))^2$$

or

$$S_w = \Sigma w_i(y_i - (b_0 + b_1x_i + b_2x_i^2 + \cdots + b_mx_i^m))^2 \tag{8.41}$$

where $i = 1, 2, 3, \ldots, n$.

To minimize S_w, we differentiate S_w w.r.t. $b_0, b_1, \ldots, b_m$ respectively and equate each to zero. That is,

$$\frac{\partial S}{\partial b_0} = \Sigma w_i(y_i - b_0 - b_1x_i - b_2x_i^2 - \cdots - b_mx_i^m) = 0$$

$$\frac{\partial S}{\partial b_1} = \Sigma w_ix_iy_i - b_0\Sigma w_ix_i - b_1\Sigma w_ix_i^2 - b_2\Sigma w_ix_i^3 - \cdots - b_m\Sigma w_ix_i^m = 0$$

$$\vdots$$

$$\frac{\partial S}{\partial b_m} = \Sigma w_ix_i^m y_i - b_0\Sigma w_ix_i^m - b_1\Sigma w_ix_i^{m+1} - b_2\Sigma w_ix_i^{m+2} - \cdots - b_m\Sigma w_ix_i^{m+m} = 0$$

The above equations result in the following set of equations:

$$\Sigma w_iy_i = b_0\Sigma w_i + b_1\Sigma w_ix_i + b_2\Sigma w_ix_i^2 + \cdots + b_m\Sigma w_ix_i^m$$

$$\Sigma w_ix_iy_i = b_0\Sigma w_ix_i + b_1\Sigma w_ix_i^2 + b_2\Sigma w_ix_i^3 + \cdots + b_m\Sigma w_ix_i^{m+1}$$

$$\vdots$$

$$\Sigma w_ix_i^my_i = b_0\Sigma w_ix_i^m + b_1\Sigma w_ix_i^{m+1} + b_2\Sigma w_ix_i^{m+2} + \cdots + b_m\Sigma w_ix_i^{m+m} \tag{8.42}$$

The set of equations (8.42) are called **the normal equations for polynomial fit by WLSF method**. These equations must be solved to find the coefficients $b_0, b_1, b_2, \ldots, b_m$.

8.21 Numerical Examples (Curve Fitting by the WLSF Method)

EXAMPLE 8.6 Obtain the weighted least square fit for the following data points:

x_i	0	2	5	7
y_i	–1	5	12	20
w_i	1	10	1	1

Solution

First we have to determine the values of the slope b and the intercept a using Eqs. (8.38) and (8.39). For this, we construct the following table of values (Table 8.7).

Table 8.7 Example 8.6

x_i	y_i	w_i	w_ix_i	$w_ix_i^2$	w_iy_i	$w_ix_iy_i$
0	−1	1	0	0	−1	0
2	5	10	20	40	50	100
5	12	1	5	25	12	60
7	20	1	7	49	20	140
Σ = 14	36	13	32	114	81	300

Using normal Eqs. (8.38) and (8.39) with i = 1 to 4, from the above table, we get

$$\Sigma w_i y_i = a\Sigma w_i + b\Sigma w_i x_i$$

or

$$81 = 13a + 32b$$

and

$$\Sigma w_i x_i y_i = a\Sigma w_i x_i + b\Sigma w_i (x_i)^2$$

or

$$32a + 114b = 300$$

Solving the above two equations, we get $a = -0.799$ and $b = 2.856$.

Thus the best straight line is given by $y = -0.799 + 2.856x$.

For seeing the advantage of adding weight to a data point, we evaluate $y(2)$ where the weight is 10,

$$y(2) = -0.799 + 2.856(2) = 4.913$$

If we take $x = 5$, we get $y(5) = -0.799 + 2.856(5) = 13.48$.

We see that the value at $x = 2$ is a better approximation than that at $x = 5$, as seen from the given data points. This is the effect of adding more weight to the value at $x = 2$.

Exercises

1. Fit a straight line to the following data points:

x_i	5	10	15	20	25
y_i	15	19	23	26	30

[**Ans.** $0.7x + 11.5$]

2. Using the LSF method, obtain a suitable fit to the following data:

x_i	0	0.2	0.4	0.6	0.8	1.0
y_i	−1.85	−1.2	−0.55	0.15	0.8	1.35

[**Ans.** $y = 3.24x - 1.84$]

3. Fit a power function to the following data points:

x_i	$\pi/2$	π	$3\pi/2$	2π	$5\pi/2$
y_i	2.9	4.0	5.7	8.9	12.4

[**Ans.** $(1.9)x^{0.9}$]

4. Fit a parabola to the following data points:

x_i	1	2	3	4	5
y_i	2	3	5	8	10

[**Ans.** $y = 0.8 + 0.81x + 0.21x^2$]

5. Obtain an exponential fit to the following data:

x_i	5	6	7	8	9	10
y_i	133	55	23	7	2	2

[**Ans.** $y = 12624e^{-0.92}$]

6. A rubber band is stretched by a force f to increase its length x given by the following data:

x_i	2	3	4	5	6	7	8	9	10	11	12
$f(= y_i)$	10	17	21	28	36	43	51	60	70	83	93

Obtain a power fit for the force function. [**Ans.** $f = 4.077\ x^{1.232}$]

7. Obtain the weighted least square fit for the following data points:

x_i	0	3	7	10	16
y_i	3	5	10	17	20
w_i	2	3	1	4	5

[**Ans.** $y = 3 + 1.13x$]

C++ PROGRAMS

The C++ programs can be implemented on any O/S, namely

1. Windows O/S using Turbo C++, Dev C++ and Visual C++ compilers.
2. Linux based Ubuntu/Knoppix/Redhat O/S using GNU C++ compiler.

These compilers have been discussed in Chapter 0. No change is required if Ubuntu is used.

While using Turbo C++, Dev C++ and Visual C++ compilers, note the following points for every program.

- Use header file `#include <iostream.h>` (for Turbo C++ only)
- Use header file `#include <math.h>`
- Use header file `#include <conio.h>`
- Use `getch()` function before the closing bracket '}' of the `main()` function.

Program: p81.cpp

```
//Straight line fit using the least square fit method
#include <iostream>
using namespace std;
void slfit()
  {
  float x[20],y[20],den,a,b,smx,smx2,smy,smxy;
  int n,i;
  char choice;
  cout<<"For default values enter 'y' else 'n'\n";
  cin>>choice;
  if (choice=='y')
  {
  n=5;
  x[1]=1; y[1]=3;
  x[2]=2; y[2]=4;
  x[3]=3; y[3]=5;
  x[4]=4; y[4]=6;
  x[5]=5; y[5]=8;
  }
  else
  {
  cout<<"input the no. of data points, n\n";
  cin>>n;
  cout<<"input the data points, xi yi\n";
  for (i=1;i<=n;i++)
  {
    cout<<"x["<<i<<"]=";
    cin>>x[i];
```

```
    cout<<"y["<<i<<"]=";
    cin>>y[i];
  }
  }
  smx2=0;smx=0;smy=0;smxy=0;
  for (i=1;i<=n;i++)
  {
    smx  +=x[i];
    smy  +=y[i];
    smx2  +=x[i]*x[i];
    smxy  +=x[i]*y[i];
  }
  den=n*smx2-smx*smx;
  b=(n*smxy-smx*smy)/den;
  a=(smy-b*smx)/n;
  cout<<"values of coefficients a and b is \n";
  cout<<"a="<<a<<endl;
  cout<<"b="<<b<<endl;
  cout<<"y="<<a<<"+"<<b<<"x"<<"is the regression line"<<endl;
  }
main()
{
  slfit();
}
```

Program: p82.cpp

```
//Polynomial fit of order 'n' using the least square method
#include <iostream>
#include <cmath>
using namespace std;
void polfit()
  {
    float a[20][20],x[20],y[20],temp,b[20],sm;
    int n,i,k,j,m;
    char choice;
    cout<<"For default values enter 'y' else 'n'\n";
    cin>>choice;
    if (choice=='y')
    {
      n=2;
      m=4;
      x[1]=1; y[1]=6;
      x[2]=2; y[2]=11;
```

```
      x[3]=3;  y[3]=18;
      x[4]=4;  y[4]=27;
    }
  else
  {
  cout<<"input the order of polynomial, n\n";
  cin>>n;
  cout<<"input the no. of data points, m\n";
  cin>>m;
  cout<<"input the data points, xi yi\n";
    for (i=1;i<=m;i++)
      {
        cout<<"x["<<i<<"]=";
        cin>>x[i];
        cout<<"y["<<i<<"]=";
        cin>>y[i];
      }
  }
  for (i=1;i<=n+1;i++)
    {
      for (j=1;j<=n+1;j++)
      {
        a[i][j]=0;
          for (k=1;k<=m;k++)
            a[i][j] +=pow(x[k],i+j-2);
      }
    a[i][n+2]=0;
    for (k=1;k<=m;k++)
      a[i][n+2] +=y[k]*pow(x[k],i-1);
    }
  //solution of simultaneous equations by Gauss elimination
method.
    for (k=1;k<=n;k++)
      {
        for (i=k+1;i<=n+1;i++)
        {
          temp=a[i][k]/a[k][k];
          for (j=k;j<=n+2;j++)
            a[i][j] -=temp*a[k][j];
        }
      }
  b[n+1]=a[n+1][n+2]/a[n+1][n+1];
  for (i=n;i>=1;i–)
```

```
    {
      sm=0;
      for (j=i+1;j<=n+1;j++)
        sm +=a[i][j]*b[j];
      b[i]=(a[i][n+2]-sm)/a[i][i];
    }
  cout<<"values of coefficients b's are\n";
  for (i=1;i<=n+1;i++)
    cout<<"b["<<i<<"]="<<b[i]<<endl;
  cout<<"polynomial is y=[b1]+[b2]x+[b3]x2+...\n";
  }
  main()
{
  polfit();
}
```

Program: p83.cpp

```
//Power function using the least square fit method
#include <iostream>
#include <cmath>
using namespace std;
void powrfit()
  {
    float x[20],y[20],den,a,p,c,smx,smx2,smy,smxy;
    int n,i;
    char choice;
    cout<<"For default values enter 'y' else 'n'\n";
    cin>>choice;
    if (choice=='y')
    {
      n=6;
      x[1]=1; y[1]=1200;
      x[2]=2; y[2]=900;
      x[3]=3; y[3]=600;
      x[4]=4; y[4]=200;
      x[5]=5; y[5]=110;
      x[6]=6; y[6]=50;
      }
    else
    {
    cout<<"input the no. of data points, n\n";
    cin>>n;
    cout<<"input the data points, xi yi\n";
    for (i=1;i<=n;i++)
```

```
    {
      cout<<"x["<<i<<"]=";
      cin>>x[i];
      cout<<"y["<<i<<"]=";
      cin>>y[i];
    }
  }
  smx2=0;smx=0;smy=0;smxy=0;
  for (i=1;i<=n;i++)
  {
    smx  +=log10(x[i]);
    smy  +=log10(y[i]);
    smx2  +=log10(x[i])*log10(x[i]);
    smxy  +=log10(x[i])*log10(y[i]);
  }
 den=n*smx2-smx*smx;
 p=(n*smxy-smx*smy)/den;
 c=(smy-p*smx)/n;
 a=pow(10,c);
 cout<<"values of coefficients a and p is \n";
 cout<<"a="<<a<<endl;
 cout<<"p="<<p<<endl;
 cout<<"y=a*x (raised to the power) p"<<endl;
 }
main()
{
 powrfit();
}
```

Program: p84.cpp

```
//exponential function using the least square fit method
#include <iostream>
#include <cmath>
using namespace std;
void expfit()
 {
   float x[20],y[20],den,a,A,B,smx,smx2,smy,smxy;
   int n,i;
   char choice;
   cout<<"For default values enter 'y' else 'n'\n";
   cin>>choice;
   if (choice=='y')
```

```
    {
      n=5;
      x[1]=2;  y[1]=4.08;
      x[2]=4;  y[2]=11.08;
      x[3]=6;  y[3]=30.13;
      x[4]=8;  y[4]=81.9;
      x[5]=10;  y[5]=222.62;
      }
    else
    {
    cout<<"input the no. of data points, n\n";
    cin>>n;
    cout<<"input the data points, xi yi\n";
    for (i=1;i<=n;i++)
      {
        cout<<"x["<<i<<"]=";
        cin>>x[i];
        cout<<"y["<<i<<"]=";
        cin>>y[i];
      }
    }
    smx2=0;smx=0;smy=0;smxy=0;
    for (i=1;i<=n;i++)
    {
      smx  +=x[i];
      smy  +=log(y[i]);
      smx2  +=x[i]*x[i];
      smxy  +=x[i]*log(y[i]);
    }
   den=n*smx2-smx*smx;
   B=(n*smxy-smx*smy)/den;
   A=(smy-B*smx)/n;
   a=exp(A);
   cout<<"values of coefficients a and p is \n";
   cout<<"a="<<a<<endl;
   cout<<"B="<<B<<endl;
   cout<<"y=a*exp (raised to the power) B"<<endl;
   }
  main()
  {
   expfit();
  }
```

Index